Range Rover
The Anniversary Guide

Mike Gould

© Michael A Gould

All rights reserved. No part of this publication may be reproduced, stored in a retrieval system or transmitted, in any form or by any means, electronic, mechanical, photocopying, recording or otherwise, without prior permission in writing from the publisher.

First published in July 2010

ISBN 978-1-907085-05-5

Published by Porter Press International Ltd.

PO Box 2, Tenbury Wells,
WR15 8XX, UK.
Tel: +44 (0)1584 781588
Fax: +44 (0)1584 781630
sales@porterpress.co.uk
www.porterpress.co.uk

Designed by Grafx Resource
Printed by Butler Tanner & Dennis, UK

CARING FOR THE ENVIRONMENT

This book was printed in the UK by Butler Tanner and Dennis, saving the environmental cost of long distance transportation to major markets. The printing facility has all its operations under one roof and employs mainly local people, many cycling to work. It is certified to ISO 14001 and is aiming to soon achieve carbon neutrality. It was printed using 100% vegetable-based inks on Respecta Silk FSC paper. Respecta Silk FSC is produced from 100% Elemental Chlorine Free (EFC) pulp that is fully recyclable. It has a Forest Stewardship Council (FSC) accreditation and is produced by a mill which supports well-managed forestry schemes.

Range Rover
The Anniversary Guide

Mike Gould

Design by Andrew Garman

Porter Press International

CONTENTS

Introduction 1

Range Rover Generation One

Phase 1
Brief History 3
Range Rover Walkaround 8
Technical Description 14
Technical Data 18
Advertising and Brochures 28

Phase 2
Technical Description 30
Range Rover Walkaround 32
Technical Data 38
Advertising and Brochures 48

Phase 3
Technical Description 50
Technical Data 52
Advertising and Brochures 58

Phase 4
Technical Description 62
Technical Data 64
Advertising and Brochures 70

Range Rover Generation Two

Phase 1
Brief History 75
Styling Concepts 82
Range Rover Walkaround 84
Technical Description 90
Technical Data 98
Advertising and Brochures 108

Phase 2
Technical Description 112
Technical Data 114
Advertising and Brochures 124

CONTENTS

Range Rover Generation Three

Phase 1
Brief History 129
Technical Description 138
Styling Concepts 146
Technical Data 150
Advertising and Brochures 158

Phase 2
Technical Description 162
Technical Data 166
Advertising and Brochures 174

Phase 3
Technical Description 178
Range Rover Walkaround 180
Technical Data 186
Advertising and Brochures 194

Phase 4
Technical Description 198
Range Rover Walkaround 204
Technical Data 208
Advertising and Brochures 216

Phase 1
Technical Description 220
Technical Data 224

Limited Editions 232
Range Rover Concepts - Range Stormer 242
Range Rover Concepts - LRX 246

Range Rover Sport 250
Range Rover Specials 256
Timeline 274

COPYRIGHT AND FURTHER INFORMATION

The 'walk around' and detail photography of existing vehicles is by Mike Gould. We would like to thank the British Motor Industry Heritage Trust for access to the first production Range Rover which is normally on display at the Heritage Motor Centre at Gaydon. We are also grateful to Simon Phipps for the opportunity to photograph his restored Range Rover four door and to the Land Rover Experience Chilterns for the use of their facilities as a location. The Second Generation Range Rover belongs to the Land Rover Experience Solihull and we would like to thank Zoë Amarilli and Roger Crathorne for making it available and to Graham Silvers, former Range Rover Engineering Manager, for his help and information about the vehicle. Thanks also go to Lindsey Campton of Land Rover Public Relations for the use of the latest Range Rovers on their fleet. Photography of these vehicles took place at Culham, near Abingdon in Oxfordshire.

Geof Miller, Project Leader of the original Range Rover team, was kind enough to let us use some images of early vehicles, including the Velar prototype. Other early imagery, including that contained in brochures, is © the British Motor Industry Heritage Trust and we would like to thank Tim Bryan for his permission to use it in this book. Later images, including brochure material, are © Land Rover and we are grateful to Roger Crathorne and John Paul Mooney for permission to reproduce it here. Styling photographs and renderings came from the collections of Mike Sampson, George Thomson and Don Wyatt, and we are grateful for their permission to include it.

The cover image is © Land Rover with additional photography by Nick Dimbleby and digital re-work by Andy Garman of Grafx Resource. The image of the Queen in her review vehicle is from Getty Images.

Every effort has been made to trace and acknowledge copyright holders. Any omissions are unintentional and, should the need arise, the publishers would be pleased to insert the appropriate acknowledgement in subsequent editions.

For more information on where to see the first production Range Rover, some Land Rovers and other vehicles from the British motor industry visit www.heritage-motor-centre.co.uk

For more details on Land Rover Experience Centres around the world, including that at Solihull, see www.landroverexperience.com

To see details of current Range Rover and other Land Rover models visit www.landrover.com

ACKNOWLEDGEMENTS

In compiling a book of this type, information and help comes from many sources and everyone approached has responded with enormous enthusiasm, reflecting the pride in the Range Rover with current and former members of the Land Rover team and among the 'extended enterprise' surrounding it.

For archive material, I am indebted to Phil Bashall of the Dunsfold Land Rover Collection for access to, and use of, his unrivalled collection of Range Rover material including brochures, price lists, colour charts and photographs. I am also grateful to Jan Valentino, Photographic Archive Administrator for the British Motor Industry Heritage Trust, for her help in obtaining early images of Range Rover history and the people associated with developing the vehicle. Special thanks go to members of Land Rover's Communications and Public Affairs department for their help in providing images and information. Thanks also go to Land Rover's Global Marketing team for their support and kind permission to use their outstanding creative material.

Thanks also go to former members of the teams associated with the Range Rover over four decades. These include Kevin Beadle, Roger Crathorne, John Hall, John Holford, Helen Hughes, Geof Miller, Graham Silvers and David Sneath as well as designers Mike Sampson, George Thomson, Don Wyatt and Land Rover's Chief Designer, Gerry McGovern. All these and many others have been very generous with their time, information and support.

My thanks also go to Andrew McRobb for his support and enthusiasm for the project as well as to Phil Weeden of Kelsey Publishing who graciously deferred my start date as editor of *Land Rover World* while I completed the research for the book. Phil and sub-editor, Alan Turner, worked hard to produce the magazine for two months until I could start full-time.

Special personal thanks go to the team at Porter Press International, especially my publisher, Philip Porter, who was very patient in going through the text even though he was working on several other titles. Even more patient was designer, Andy Garman, who has produced some brilliant layouts from a mass of disparate material. Last, but not least, I am especially grateful to my wife, Jenny, for coping with a house full of 'research material' and me locking myself away for hours and days on end to finish the book.

As part of absorbing the full ethos of the vehicle, I became a member of the *Range Rover Register* and would like to thank its members, especially Chris Elliot, for their help. The UK-based *Range Rover Register* organises meetings, attends many shows and publishes a regular magazine, *Range Rover Owner and Enthusiast*.

Range Rover – The Anniversary Guide was compiled using original research but some other works have proved useful in checking details. These included *The Land Rover File* by Eric Dymock, *Range Rover – The Second Generation* by James Taylor and *Land Rover – The Unbeatable 4x4* by K & J Slavin with GN Mackie and D McDine. There is a lot of material to be found on the internet. Specialist sites include www.range-rover-classic.com, and www.rangeroverp38a.com as well as the Range Rover Register's own site: www.rrr.co.uk. For general information about the companies that formed the old British Leyland company, www.austin-rover.co.uk is an invaluable resource. The American website, www.rangerovers.net is also an impressive centre for Range Rover information.

DEDICATION

There have been many people involved with the Range Rover over the four decades of its production – far too many to recognise individually. But there is one person who, uniquely to our knowledge, has been involved with the product from its early development in the 1960s to the launch of the current 2011 model year vehicle.

Roger Crathorne began his working career as a Rover apprentice and was soon involved with the Range Rover development team, taking part in the 'Sahara South' expedition. His career progressed through Sales and Product Planning before he became involved with the Land Rover Experience. After many years demonstrating and training people on the company's products, he joined Communications and Public Affairs to provide a valuable technical resource for journalists on Land Rover's complex products.

On behalf of all those involved with Range Rover, this book is dedicated to Roger Crathorne.

Mike Gould

INTRODUCTION

Forty years on, it is difficult to appreciate just how much of an impact the Range Rover made on its début in 1970.

Here was a car that introduced, in a production vehicle, features that were previously the domain of the exotic. Permanent four-wheel drive was offered by the Jensen FF Interceptor but it was a hand-built, low volume car - not mass produced. All-round disc brakes were unusual, as was a dual line hydraulic system. Rover had a reputation as a leader in safety engineering in the UK and the Range Rover had a collapsible steering column as well as front safety belts anchored to the seats themselves. The exterior design, although described as 'business like', exhibited a purity of form that led to it being considered as a work of modern art and whose themes live on in current Land Rover models.

However, the Range Rover as a project was lucky to survive the acquisition of the Rover Company by Leyland Motors and the subsequent formation of British Leyland – a process that had seen sister vehicles like the Rover P8 cancelled. And, while the company revelled in the critical acclaim that the Range Rover received, it did little to develop the car for nearly 10 years.

It was the introduction of the four-door derivative that provided the launch pad for a series of dramatic and swift improvements that saw Range Rover sales rocket to overtake its utilitarian stablemate, despite the introduction of a Range Rover-inspired chassis and running gear for the Land Rover.

Time has shown that the 'Second Generation' Range Rover was a worthy successor to the original although, in the early days, it seemed that its technological advances were too much for the Solihull production lines. However, the eyes of Land Rover's new German owners were already looking to the future. After a short production run, a new Third Generation Range Rover emerged.

In the true tradition of the brand, it was another technological marvel, bearing the stamp of being engineered under BMW's wing. Even more imposing than before, it was a true driver's car as well as an accomplished off-roader. It was the epitome of the 'Car For All Reasons' promoted in the original Range Rover's publicity material.

Perhaps the greatest compliment to 'Spen' King and his original design team was that their concept virtually created a new company, the first fruit of which was the Range Rover Sport – an offspring that became Land Rover's most successful vehicle. This will soon be followed by a new Range Rover product based on the LRX concept, a vehicle truly suited to the 21st Century but whose lines recall those created by 'Spen' King in the 1960s - a lasting and worthy tribute.

Mike Gould
Abingdon, Oxfordshire, England
June 2010

Range Rover - The Anniversary Guide

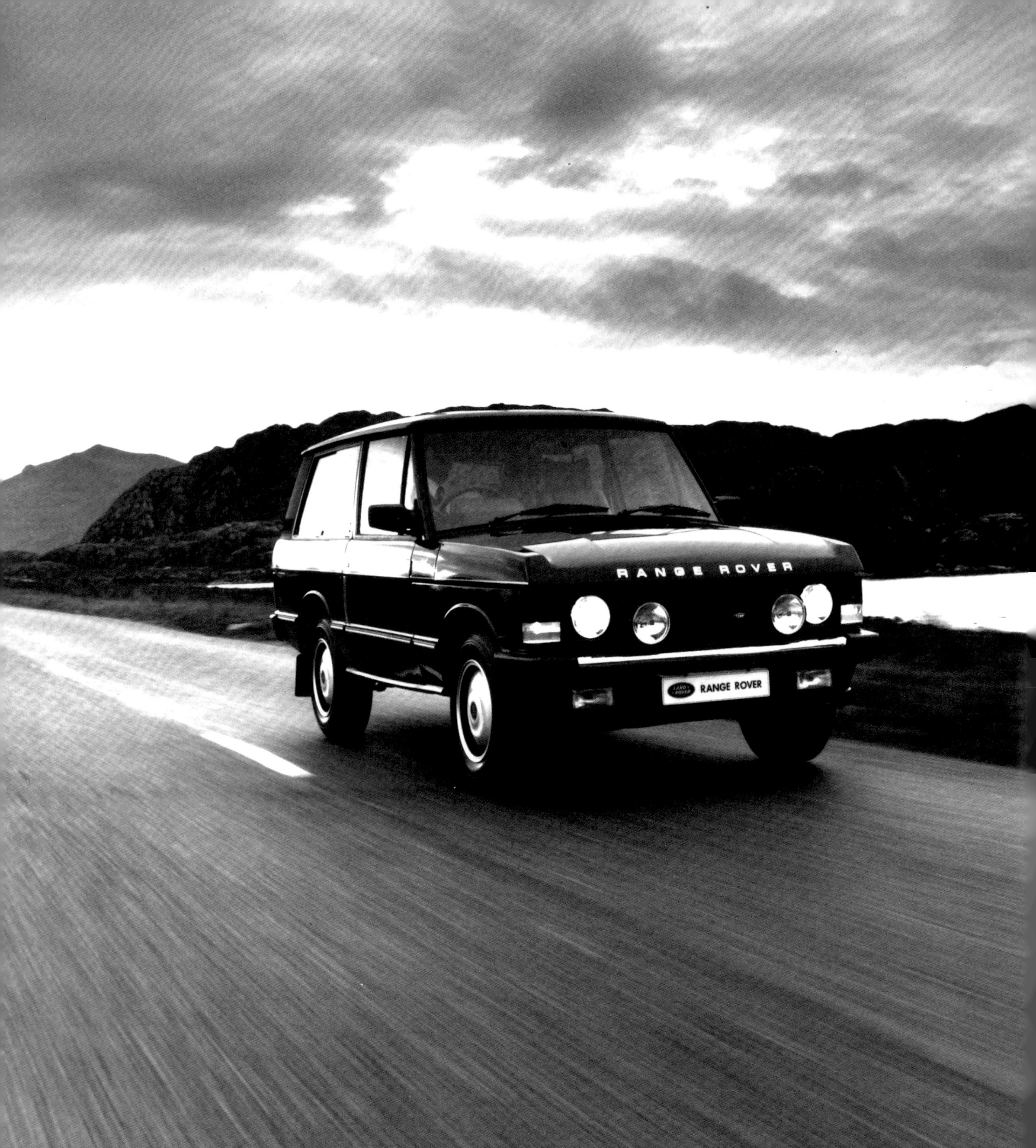
RANGE ROVER
LAND ROVER
RANGE ROVER

Range Rover - First Generation

A Brief History

In the mid-'60s the Rover Company was at a crossroads. It had a robust range of saloon cars including the P6, launched as the Rover 2000 to public and critical acclaim due to the quality of its engineering and concept. Equally, it had a highly successful utility vehicle in the shape of the Land-Rover, launched in 1948 and, by then, in its updated, Series II form.

The company was, however, facing a number of threats. Cars were becoming more complex to design, develop and build. With complexity came increased costs which were hard for small companies to bear. The British Government, under the new Labour Prime Minister, Harold Wilson, was urging British motor manufacturers to combine to benefit from the economies of scale that could make them major players on the world stage.

This Government was also reining back on Britain's overseas commitments which had a direct effect on Rover when the lucrative contracts it had been winning for military Land-Rovers began to dry up. They were also living with the effects of the boycott of Land-Rover products by Arab countries following the unrest in the Middle East.

The company was conscious of the growing 4 x 4 leisure market in the USA typified by vehicles such as the International Harvester Scout, Jeep Wagoneer and Ford Bronco. Indeed, the President of its American sales organisation had installed one of the new V8 engines, which the company had recently acquired the rights to manufacture from General Motors, into a Land-Rover 88-Inch Station Wagon, which earned the name 'Golden Rod' from

Range Rover First Generation

its yellow paintwork. It was, however, clear that this vehicle was too unrefined to be a credible offering in the sector.

Charles Spencer 'Spen' King was given a brief to develop a new leisure 4 x 4 vehicle by the Rover board and his designs soon crystallised around a vehicle with a 100-inch wheelbase – the project becoming known as the 'Interim Station Wagon' or '100-Inch Station Wagon'. With experience of coil spring suspension from the Rover P6 car, King settled on this system for his new vehicle. It would give the articulation for good off-road capability while retaining a competitive level of refinement on road. King also later opted for a Boge ride-levelling unit to ensure that, with its soft springs, the new vehicle would not 'squat' when fully laden.

Several power units were considered. These included the old, side exhaust valve six-cylinder petrol engine from the Long Wheelbase Land-Rover and a six-cylinder version of the Rover P6 engine. But the acquisition of General Motors' 3.5-litre all-alloy 'Fireball' engine gave them the power unit King was looking for. The V8 was light, compact and powerful – too powerful in fact for the Rover axles specified for the 100-Inch Station Wagon.

The only solution was permanent four-wheel drive to ensure that the torque of the V8 engine was shared equally between the axles. This required a new transmission and, after experimenting with some earlier permanent four-wheel drive gearbox prototypes originally built for Land-Rovers, a combined gear

(Top) The Velar brand name was devised to disguise the origin of the vehicle and enable prototypes to be driven around without camouflage. A company of the same name was even set up to enable the vehicles to be registered away from Solihull. In this case it nearly backfired for, although 'OY' is a Croydon plate, many Birmingham codes used O as a middle letter. (Bottom) 'Velar' prototypes were sent on a proving trip to the Sahara. The expedition was filmed as 'Sahara South' and the footage is available on the Heritage Motor Centre DVD, 'The Best of Range Rover'

A Brief History

and transfer box being developed for the military 101-Inch Forward Control was selected. While a handful of early vehicles were fitted with a GKN Powr-Lok limited slip centre differential which could also be fully engaged manually, a simple lockable system was quickly introduced with engagement by a vacuum device for simplicity and reliability.

With Rover now part of the Leyland Motor Corporation, all the design team were too busy on exciting new car projects to spare time for the 100-Inch Station Wagon so King's team designed the body themselves. It says something for their design that it was selected by the Louvre in Paris as a great example of modern art and became an icon that would last 40 years.

The 100-Inch Station Wagon was the first major project to be evaluated at what is now Land Rover's key test ground at Eastnor Castle near Ledbury in Herefordshire. To preserve secrecy, Rover formed a company, Velar, which would handle the registration of the development vehicles. Appropriately based on an Italian word meaning 'concealed', the subterfuge worked, with many who saw the vehicles assuming that it was some new exotic product of the Italian motor industry. The name 'Range Rover' was coined by designer, Tony Poole, at a meeting convened to christen the vehicle and it stuck.

At the time of its launch in June 1970, the vehicle was a sensation. Powerful V8 engines, permanent four-wheel drive and dual line disc braking systems were previously the domain of low-volume supercars, much less a vehicle that could match the famous Land-Rover in off-road capability.

The company, by now known as British Leyland and the result of several mergers, sold the Range Rover heavily on its dual purpose capability. It is doubtful, though, if anyone seriously took their pigs to market in the morning before donning a dinner jacket for an evening trip to the theatre in the same vehicle.

It is said that the vehicle was rushed into the market to preserve British Leyland chairman Donald Stokes's promise on the pace of new model launches. Certainly, cost-cutting had affected the quality of the interior trim which emerged in utilitarian, but not exactly hard-wearing, moulded PVC. Its target launch price was to be under £2000 and it achieved this by just £2, although the mandatory seat belts were priced as an option! Thus the on-the-

The Warwickshire countryside near to the Solihull plant was used for many early publicity shots. The first vehicles lacked the vinyl trim to the 'D' post, added later to disguise imperfections in the pressing. The 'floating roof' formed by this and the blacking out of the other pillars became an iconic feature of the Range Rover design

Range Rover - The Anniversary Guide

Range Rover First Generation

The Middle East was a vital market for the Range Rover – something reflected literally in this 1980s brochure cover shot

road price just broke the £2000 barrier.

Sales of the Range Rover were slow to get into their stride. At first, they were hampered by a lack of production capacity which led to the market being under supplied, customers often having to pay a premium to secure a vehicle. The shortcomings of the original design also became apparent once the honeymoon period was over. British Leyland soon introduced a more acceptable brushed nylon seat trim and put carpet on the gearbox tunnel which softened the utilitarian appearance of the interior although its main purpose was to attenuate noise from the transmission. Power assisted steering was also introduced to ease handling of this large vehicle and an attempt to reduce its massive fuel consumption was made by fitting a higher compression engine. Seizing the opportunity missed by the company, many specialist coachbuilders began offering luxury makeovers of the Range Rover.

One of these was Monteverdi, a Swiss-based automotive company who developed a four-door conversion, undertaken by the Italian firm, Fissore. While the original two-door design had been ingenious in allowing back seat passengers to open the doors from the rear, this cumbersome arrangement, coupled with the awkward nature of the front seat folding mechanism, was clearly a handicap to expanding the Range Rover's appeal.

The company, named Land Rover Limited in 1978 and set up as an independent operating division of British Leyland, had for some time been looking around for a suitable four-door conversion. The Monteverdi design was clearly the best in the market, not least for the pleasing arrangement of the door pillars which harmonised with the existing design. Land Rover approved and promoted the Monteverdi design while developing it so the four-door that could be produced at Solihull.

The beginning of the 1980s saw a number of factors coming together that would transform the Range Rover. Together with the four-door, the company launched its own up-market version in the shape of the 'In Vogue' limited edition. Following work done by Schuler Transmissions, an automatic version was offered with a Chrysler three-speed gearbox mated to the transfer box section of the clunky combined unit mounted in a new case. The final element of the mix was the arrival of a new charismatic Managing Director for Land Rover in the shape of Tony Gilroy.

Gilroy quickly saw that the salvation of the company lay with the Range Rover. Working with Business and Product Planning Director, Alan Edis, whom he had brought into the company, they instituted a programme of rapid development that would eventually see the vehicle being launched into the lucrative American market. Together with the introduction of a diesel engine version to conquer the European market, production was boosted to over 28,500 in the last year of the decade, overtaking that of the Land Rover itself and being nearly three times the volume enjoyed by the Range Rover 10 years earlier. Not only that, but the Range Rover platform had spawned the Discovery, enabling Land Rover to truly establish itself in the 4 x 4 leisure sector. This, combined with the fact that the Range Rover, now firmly positioned at the luxury end of the market, provided the financial basis to ensure the company's survival.

The pace of change continued in the 1990s with the introduction of an air suspension system to improve both the Range Rover's refinement and off-road capability. Along with an increase in wheelbase and earlier changes to the transmission to eliminate the final inheritance of its utility past, this made the Range Rover a real contender in the luxury car market, able to complete with brands such as Mercedes, BMW and Jaguar. With the added cachet of off-road ability for the country set, the Range Rover formed its own market niche. In a word coined by Land Rover marketing, the Range Rover was, indeed, 'Peerless'.

So strong was the appeal of the Range Rover that, with the 'New Range Rover' in the final stage of its development and close to launch, Land Rover gave a final reprieve to the original Range Rover. Re-naming it the 'Classic Range Rover' to distinguish it from the new model, the old model received a new fascia with driver and passenger airbags as well as other modifications. Codenamed 'Best Ever Range Rover', it was the climax of the development of the model launched 25 years earlier. In its life spanning a quarter of a century, over 326,000 vehicles had been produced.

The final 'soft dash' variant of the First Generation Range Rover was named as the 'Classic' to distinguish it from the Second Generation 'New Range Rover' when the new vehicle was launched in 1994. Despite the new arrival, the 25-year old vehicle still had its adherents, not least in Land Rover marketing. The final brochure featured some outstanding photography including this graceful ballerina (top). The apogee of the First Generation, the LSE, was almost as sleek (bottom)

A Brief History

Range Rover - The Anniversary Guide　　　7

| Range Rover First Generation | Phase One |

Range Rover Walkaround

Although there may have been more official design involvement in the style of the Range Rover than often supposed, Gerry McGovern, Land Rover's current design director, recognises the influence of its pure lines in his latest creations

The windscreen and glazed areas were extremely large in proportion to the rest of the body, something still echoed in Land Rover's 'Command Driving Position'

The seven-inch round headlamp also became an iconic feature, along with the massive indicator and side lamp cluster. Problems with bonnet fit persisted throughout the First Generation's production life

Door trim was utilitarian but the dual handles enabled the large door to be opened by the rear seat passengers

Range Rover - The Anniversary Guide

The metal slatted grille emerged from the Range Rover's time in David Bache's Solihull Styling Studio. The separate letters spelling out the vehicle's name required two holes each and were eventually replaced by a decal. The requirement for a starting handle dictated significant changes to the standard V8 engine

The 'castellations' on the front corners of the bonnet were designed to aid the driver in finding the extremities of this large vehicle. They also provided a convenient mounting point for the rear view mirrors

A massive door needed a massive door handle. The styling studio merged this into the Range Rover's distinctive swage line

The pressed steel wheel was produced in the 'Rostyle' pattern fashionable at the time. Tubeless tyres were regarded as difficult to repair in the field so it was not airtight, the Michelin XM+S tyres requiring an easily fixed (although more likely to puncture) inner tube

The Range Rover name was thought up by designer Tony Poole. The font used was typical of the period but a similar script is used 40 years later

Range Rover - The Anniversary Guide

9

Range Rover First Generation | Phase One

Range Rover Walkaround

The handbrake was attached to the transmission so moved with it, thus requiring a massive gaiter

The no-nonsense rear view is still readily discernable in the latest Range Rovers

A simple cover served to protect the contents of the loadspace area from the spare wheel

Early prototypes were disguised by 'Velar' badges and most observers considered them to be some exotic Italian newcomer. By the time of its launch, it was necessary to reveal its heritage in much the same way as the Discovery would nearly 20 years later

Typical of the period, the Range Rover required a massive ashtray. The floor covering, while designed to be capable of being hosed clean, was not very durable. Replacements are hard to find – even by the Heritage Motor Centre, who restored this vehicle

10   Range Rover - The Anniversary Guide

The fascia was a basic collection of plastic mouldings that didn't fit together very well. It was designed so that the same layout could be used for left- and right-hand drive by exchanging the position of the instrument binnacle and tray closing panel

The seats were trimmed in a moulded PVC cover which, like the floor, proved less durable than it looked. They are equally difficult for restorers to obtain. Mounting the seat belts directly to the seats was an innovative safety feature, but resulted in a complex design

The clutch and brake pedal rubbers were each marked by an 'R'. Twenty years later, the Discovery's origins were revealed by the same notation

The two piece tailgate arrangement became a requirement for subsequent generations

Range Rover - The Anniversary Guide

Range Rover First Generation — Phase One

Range Rover Walkaround

The Range Rover used Zenith Stromberg carburettors because their integral float chamber design prevented fuel starvation at the kind of angles encountered off road

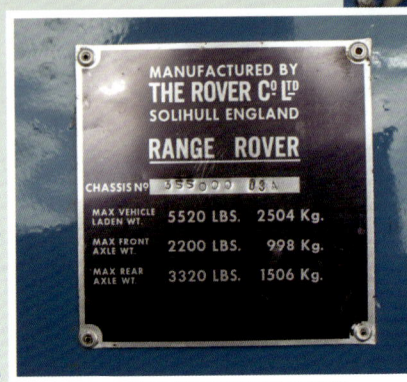

Although YVB153H bears chassis number 003, it was, in fact, the first production vehicle

The windscreen washer bottle was a proprietary Wipac unit with the pump motor built into the cap. The plate it is mounted to was interchangeable with the pedal box for a different hand of drive

Range Rover - The Anniversary Guide

The Rover 3.5-litre all-alloy V8 engine was a tight fit in the Range Rover's engine bay

The 'Otter' switch sensed the temperature of the coolant in the inlet manifold and illuminated the choke warning light on the fascia. An automatic choke was originally specified but deleted in favour of a conventional unit – hence the rather obvious afterthought of the mounting position of the choke control under the fascia

Although based on the engine used in Rover cars (and also the Morgan Plus 8 and MGB V8), the Range Rover's engine shared few common parts. Obvious here is the revised water pump designed to lift the fan clear of water when wading and to allow a starting handle to be engaged in the end of the crank. This arrangement caused problems with police users when running the engine with the vehicle at a standstill gave rise to cavitation in the water pump housing

Range Rover - The Anniversary Guide

Range Rover First Generation — Phase One

Technical Description

CHASSIS

The chassis was of steel, welded ladder-frame construction with longitudinal members made from interlocking C-sections to form a box. Mounting points for the front suspension towers and rear suspension 'A' frame, levelling unit and rear-mounted fuel tank were incorporated. The frame was treated with an electrophoretic paint process to resist corrosion.

ENGINE

The power unit was the Rover 3.5-litre (3528cc) V8 petrol engine. While this was also used in the Rover P6B and P5B cars, it was heavily modified to suit the Range Rover installation and its usage pattern. The modifications included:

- Compression ratio reduced to 8.5:1 to enable it to run on low octane petrol
- Twin Zenith-Stromberg CD2S constant-vacuum carburettors in lieu of SUs and designed to deliver fuel at extreme side and fore/aft angles. Manually-operated choke with warning light
- New, raised water pump to allow access for a crank handle for which a starting dog was provided at the front of the crankshaft
- New, five-blade cooling fan
- Starter motor solenoid re-positioned to top of starter

An alternator was fitted as standard.

TRANSMISSION

The clutch was of the hydraulically-operated, diaphragm spring type housed in an extended aluminium bell housing.

The four-speed main gearbox and two-speed transfer box were integrated in a common unit and offered permanent four-wheel drive with a centre differential. There was synchromesh on all four forward main gears. Early models, numbering only a few hundred, were fitted with a Salisbury Powr-Lok limited-slip device in the centre differential. The centre differential could also be locked by a vacuum-operated dog clutch engaged by a gearbox-mounted control with a built-in warning light. Main gear selection was by a directly-mounted cranked gear lever; transfer box selection was by a short lever via a remote linkage.

The front and rear prop shafts incorporated Hookes joints and sliding plunge joints. The front plunge joint was protected by a gaiter.

The front and rear axles were of Rover manufacture and of the pressed-steel banjo style with separate bolted differential pinion extensions. The open differentials were of the two-pin type with a unique final drive ratio. The half shafts were fully floating. The front hub arrangement incorporated constant-velocity joints.

SUSPENSION

The front axle longitudinal location was by tapering I-section forged leading arms attached to the axles by twin bonded rubber bushes and to their chassis mounting points by a rubber bush. Transverse location was by a Panhard rod with rubber bushes at both chassis and axle ends.

The rear axle was located by a two-part, forged I-section 'A' frame with a ball joint attachment to the axle and rubber bushes at the chassis end. The bottom links were tubular with rubber bushes at both ends.

Long travel coil springs were fitted front and rear and located in cups incorporated into the chassis frame. Damping was by hydraulic shock absorbers. Those at the front were coaxial with the front springs and housed in chassis-mounted towers. At the rear, they were mounted directly to the chassis frame, the right hand unit facing rearwards, the left hand forwards to provide an 'anti-tramp' capability.

A Boge self-levelling unit was mounted to the rear suspension 'A' frame ball joint assembly and to the chassis cross member.

The basic engine was the by then familiar 3.5-litre all-alloy V8, the production and design rights for which Rover had acquired from General Motors, who received a royalty for the privilege. As used in the Range Rover, it was a very different unit to that used in Rover's car range, with few common parts. Major changes included different carburettors, a modified water pump arrangement and a lower compression ratio

Range Rover - The Anniversary Guide

Technical Description

The chassis design differed from the Land-Rover in using side frames made from interlocking C-sections and incorporated the mountings for the coil spring suspension. The torque output of the 3.5-litre engine demanded permanent four wheel drive when used with the Rover axles, so the Range Rover shared the transmission with the military 101-Inch Forward Control. The Range Rover introduced many innovative safety features including a collapsible AC steering column

WHEELS AND TYRES

These were pressed steel 'Rostyle' styled wheels, of 16 x 6 inch size with JK rims and five-stud fixing. Tyres were either Michelin XM+S 205x16 tubed radials or Firestone Town and Country 205x16 tubed radials.

BRAKING SYSTEM

Disc brakes were fitted all round. The front brakes had twin calipers while single calipers were fitted on the rear. The hydraulic braking system incorporated a dual circuit: one operating one set of front brake calipers, the other one set of front brake calipers and the rear brakes. A leak was indicated by a warning light operated by a Pressure Differential Warning Actuator (PDWA) switch in the hydraulic system. Vacuum servo assistance was provided and fed from the engine inlet manifold.

The parking brake operated an internal-expanding drum brake on the transfer box rear output shaft with a mechanical linkage to a gearbox-mounted handbrake lever.

The quality of British cars in the 1970s was nothing to be proud of, but it wasn't through lack of trying. Range Rovers were regularly inspected on their way down the production line and every vehicle was put through a session on a special four wheel drive rolling road at the end of the track. Performance data was displayed on a special screen that was lowered from the roof during the test

Range Rover - The Anniversary Guide

Range Rover First Generation | Phase One

Technical Description

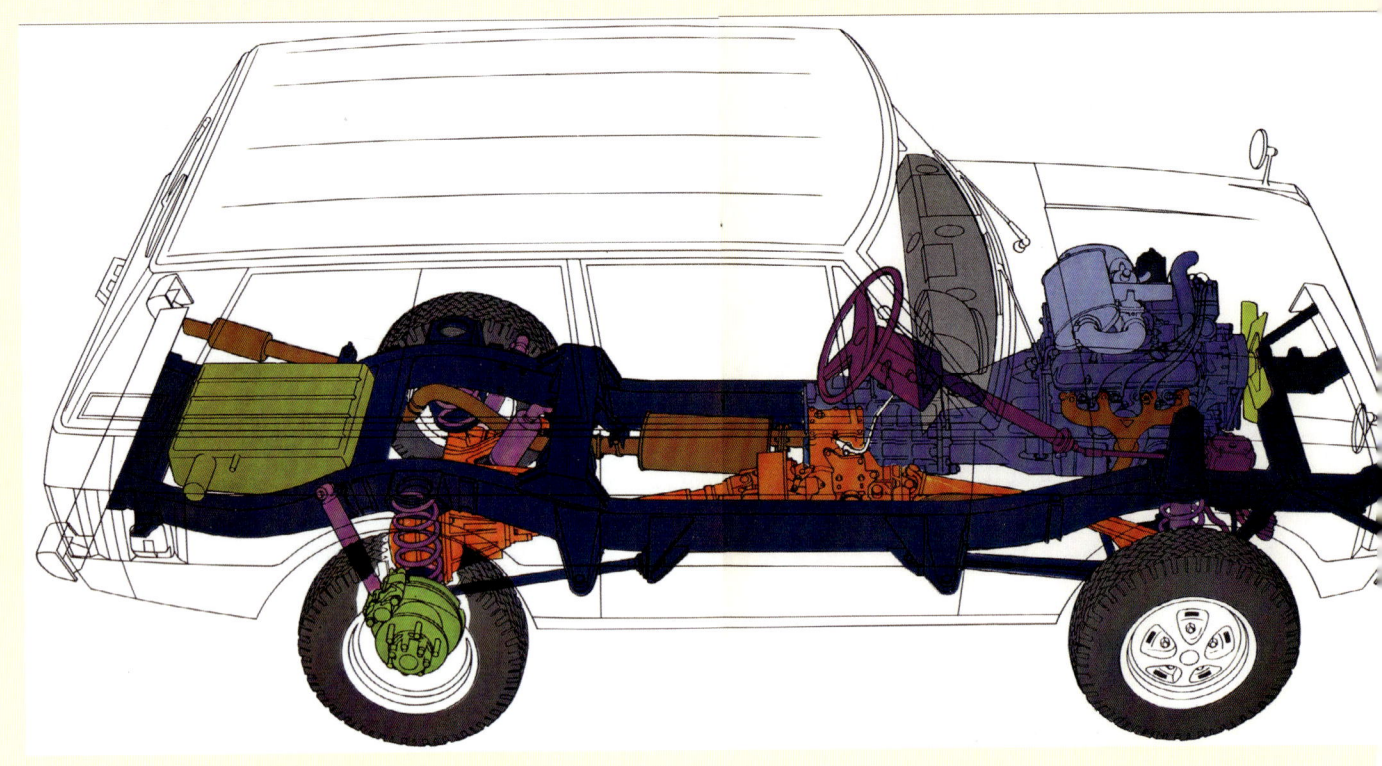

STEERING

Steering was of Burman manufacture and of the recirculating ball, worm-and-nut type. An AC collapsible safety steering column with steering column lock was employed. The large steering wheel was plastic and had three spokes.

BODY

The basic sub-structure was a steel frame incorporating the front inner wings. The front floor consisted of steel pressings with a separate gearbox tunnel and footwell plates bolted to the sub-structure. The intermediate floor was of ribbed steel, also bolted in place. The rear floor comprised corrugated aluminium panels for strength and rigidity, and these were pop-riveted to the sub-structure. The front seat bases were designed to take crash loads from the seat-mounted restraint belts.

Both the bonnet and tailgate were assembled from steel pressings while the front wings, rear wings, roof and 'E' post outer panel were aluminium pressings mechanically, fixed in place and separated by sealant from the steel sub-structure. Both front doors had steel door frames with aluminium outer skins. The front grille panel was of pressed steel. The rear tailgate was capable of carrying loads if required.

Steel body components were electro-primed and dipped in acrylic paint. Aluminium components were primed and painted using similar technology. All downward-facing surfaces were treated with underseal. Except for early production models, the 'E' post outer panel was covered in grained black vinyl.

All glass was rubber mounted and the front doors had wind up front windows while sliding windows were fitted in the rear. The front windscreen was of toughened glass with laminated glass available to meet some territorial requirements. Two-speed windscreen wipers were provided. The upper rear tailgate comprised a steel frame with a heated rear window and windscreen wiper. It was supported, when open, by pneumatic lift struts.

The front and rear bumper blades were of painted steel.

SEATING AND TRIM

The individual driver and front passenger seats were trimmed with 'Palamino' vacuum-formed PVC covers. There were integrally-mounted fixed lap and diagonal seat belts with lower mountings on the seat base and upper mountings incorporated into the seat frame. Both front seats were tipped forward using a lever, this action also moving the seat base forward to ease access and egress for rear seat passengers. Fore and aft adjustment was by a lever on the lower front of the seat. The passenger seat was fixed in one of two positions.

The rear bench seat was also trimmed in similar vacuum-formed PVC and had a jackknife folding action to increase load space area, operated by a lever on the reverse side of the squab. This area was a painted steel pressing.

Range Rover - The Anniversary Guide

Technical Description

The tunnel area over the bell housing and transmission soon received a carpet covering: not for any aesthetic reasons, but in an attempt to attenuate the noise generated by the massive gears within the combined gear and transfer box

There were two moulded PVC trim panels on each door, the upper incorporating twin grab handles and door lock remote controls, allowing the door to be opened from the rear seat if necessary. There was also a handle for the wind-up door glass and a sliding knob for door locking.

The interior rear quarter and 'E' post trim was also in 'Palamino'. A felt-backed PVC curtain in the rear compartment concealed the tool kit which was held in clips on the inner quarter panel structure. A felt-backed PVC cover protected the spare wheel.

The front, tunnel and intermediate floor trim was in 'Palamino' felt-backed moulded PVC with moulded rubber gaiters for the main gear lever, transfer box lever and brake lever. A large ashtray was fixed to the tunnel. A moulded ribbed rubber mat protected the load space compartment floor.

The roof lining comprised two fibreglass roof panels covered with 'Palamino' trim material. An interior light was provided that operated automatically by opening the front doors or by a separate switch. There were twin collapsible sun visors and an interior 'snap off' dipping mirror fitted above the windscreen.

FASCIA AND INSTRUMENTS

The fascia was in moulded plastic and designed to be suitable for right or left hand drive. The driver's side had a moulded plastic instrument binnacle, the passenger's side a soft moulded pad to form a stowage area. A perforated panel allowed for the mounting of a radio loud speaker in the top centre of the fascia. The radio itself could be fitted to a position alongside the steering column which acted as a storage pocket if a radio was not installed. There was provision to mount up to four auxiliary instruments in the heater cover panel. The steering column shroud was a plastic two-piece moulding and a separate moulded plastic box provided a mount for the choke control. The separate mounting was required as an automatic cold start system was originally specified and there was no provision on the fascia for a choke knob.

The instrument binnacle included the main speedometer and a multi-function instrument with fuel and water temperature gauges. There was also a warning light array which later included the centre diff lock engaged light as vibration was found to cause the original light on the control knob to fail. A clock was fitted in one of the auxiliary instrument positions. There was also a hazard warning light switch and terminals for 12 volt electrical power on the steering column shroud.

HEATING AND VENTILATION

A fascia-mounted fresh air heater with re-circulating provision was provided with a two-speed booster fan. Individual face-level nozzles for driver and front passenger with a centre vent provided fresh air while vents for windscreen de-misting were located in the fascia top panel. Extraction was by vents in the 'E' post.

PHASE 1 (LATE)

During the first few years of Range Rover production, various improvements were made. These included:

STEERING

Power assisted steering using a belt-driven, engine-mounted pump was introduced as an option.

BODY

A laminated windscreen and Sundym tinted glass were introduced as options.

SEATING AND TRIM

Brushed nylon fluted seat facings introduced as an option to replace the moulded PVC trim.
A brown carpet was fitted to tunnel area to reduce noise from the transmission reaching the interior.

FASCIA AND INSTRUMENTS

An ammeter, oil pressure gauge and oil temperature gauge were added to the clock installed on the heater cover panel.

The Range Rover gradually acquired more luxurious features with the original rather thin steering wheel rim gaining a leather cover. The radio positioning remained, rather inconveniently, to the outside of the driver

Range Rover - The Anniversary Guide

Range Rover First Generation — Phase One — Technical Data

Specification Sheets

GENERAL FEATURES

CONSTRUCTION
Two-door, five seat frame and panel body on separate steel chassis

POWER UNITS
3.5-litre V8 all-alloy petrol engine

TRANSMISSION
Permanent four wheel drive. Four-speed manual gearbox with integral two-speed transfer box with lockable centre differential. Single reduction beam axles

SUSPENSION
Long travel coil springs and hydraulic dampers. Ride levelling unit at rear. Cast radius arms with Panhard rod at front, radius arms with A-frame at rear

STEERING
Recirculating ball with hydraulic damper

BRAKING
Disc brakes all-round with dual-line hydraulic system. Transmission-mounted drum park brake

OTHER FEATURES
Collapsible safety steering column, front seat mounted safety belts

	UNITS	RANGE ROVER
Vehicle Type		Three-door Station Wagon
Construction		Separate chassis, panel-on-frame body
Number of Passengers		5
DIMENSIONS		
Overall Length	mm(in)	4470(176)
Overall Width (over mirrors)	mm(in)	1778(70)
Overall Height (nominal)	mm(in)	1778(70)
Wheelbase	mm(in)	2540(100)
Track Front/Rear	mm(in)	1485(58.5)
Luggage Capacity (Seat Up)	l(cu in)	1050(37.08)
Luggage Capacity (Seat Folded)	l(cu in)	2075(73.28)
WEIGHTS		
Kerb Weight (EEC)	kg(lb)	1758(3880)
Gross Vehicle Weight	kg(lb)	2504(5520)
Front Axle Maximum Weight	kg(lb)	998(2200)
Rear Axle Maximum Weight	kg(lb)	1506(3320)
Maximum Payload	kg(lb)	746(1640)
Maximum On Road Trailer Weight	kg(lb)	2000(4408) with over-run brakes, 4000(8816) four-wheel trailer with power brakes
Maximum Off Road Trailer Weight	kg(lb)	1000(2204)
CAPABILITIES		
Drag Coefficient	Cd	0.45
Approach Angle (Maximum)	Deg	45
Under Body (Ramp) Angle (Maximum)	Deg	160
Departure Angle (Maximum)	Deg	33
Turning Circle (Kerb to kerb)	m(ft)	11.74(38.5)
PERFORMANCE		
Maximum Speed	kp/h(mph)	148(92)
Acceleration 0 - 100 kp/h (tested)	secs	17.7
Acceleration 0 - 60 mph (tested)	secs	13.9

Specification Sheets

	UNITS	RANGE ROVER
FUEL CONSUMPTION		
Typical (as tested)	l/100km (mpg)	17.7(16.0)
Overall (as tested)	l/100km (mpg)	19.6(14.4)
DIN Standard (calculated)	l/100km (mpg)	18.8(15.0)
ENGINE		
Type		V8
Position in Vehicle		Front, in-line
Fuel		Petrol (gasoline)
Number of Cylinders		8
Number of Camshafts		1
Valves per Cylinder		2
Valve System		Overhead rockers, hydraulic tappets
Bore	mm(in)	88.90(3.5)
Stroke	mm(in)	71.12(2.8)
Capacity	cc(cu in)	3528(215)
Compression Ratio	:1	8.5
Cylinder Head Material		Aluminium alloy
Cylinder Block Material		Aluminium alloy
Crankshaft Bearings		5
Lubrication System		Gear-driven oil pump with full-flow filter
Fuelling		Twin Zenith/Stromberg CD2 carburetters
Fuel System		Bendix electric lift pump
Distributor		Lucas 35DM8
Boost System		None
Cold Start System		Manual choke with warning light
Air Cleaning System		Paper element
Cooling System		Pressurised with expansion tank and crossflow radiator
Battery Capacity	Amp/hr	60
Max Power	kW(bhp)	95.6(128)
At	rpm	5000
Max Torque	Nm(lb/ft)	251(185)
At	rpm	2500
CAPACITIES		
Engine Oil Sump	l(Imp Gall) [US Gall]	5.68(1.25)[1.50]
Cooling Circuit	l(Imp Gall) [US Gall]	11(2.42)[2.91]
Fuel Tank (Maximum Usable)	l(Imp Gall) [US Gall]	86(19)[22.5]
TRANSMISSION		
Type		Permanent four-wheel drive
Flywheel		Cast iron, toothed
Clutch Type		Diaphragm spring, single dry plate
Clutch Diameter	mm(in)	267(10.5)
Gearbox Type		Manual
Number of Forward Gears		4
Selection Mechanism		Lever

Range Rover - The Anniversary Guide

Range Rover First Generation — Phase One — Technical Data

Specification Sheets

	UNITS	RANGE ROVER
Transfer Box Type		Gear driven, integral with gearbox
Number of Ratios		2
Selection Mechanism		Lever
Slip Control System		Vacuum-operated lockable centre differential
Front Prop Shaft Type		Open with universal joints and sliding joint with gaiter
Rear Prop Shaft Type		Open with universal joints
Front Axle Type		Rover beam axle with swivel pins and 2-pinion differential
Rear Axle Type		Rover beam axle with 2-pinion differential
Wheel Type		Styled pressed steel, J-type rim
Wheel Size - Standard	mm(in)	406(16)
Wheel Size - Options	mm(in)	N/A
Tyre Size - Standard		Michelin XM+S radial 205x16
Tyre Size - Options		Firestone Town and Country radial 205X16
RATIOS		
1st Gear Ratio	:1	4.069
2nd Gear Ratio	:1	2.448
3rd Gear Ratio	:1	1.505
4th Gear Ratio	:1	1.000
Reverse Gear	:1	3.664
High Range Ratio	:1	1.174
Low Range Ratio	:1	3.321
Front Axle Ratio	:1	3.540
Rear Axle Ratio	:1	3.540
1st Gear Ratio Overall High Range	:1	16.910
2nd Gear Ratio Overall High Range	:1	10.174
3rd Gear Ratio Overall High Range	:1	6.255
4th Gear Ratio Overall High Range	:1	4.156
Reverse Gear Overall High Range	:1	15.227
1st Gear Ratio Overall Low Range	:1	47.837
2nd Gear Ratio Overall Low Range	:1	28.780
3rd Gear Ratio Overall Low Range	:1	17.693
4th Gear Ratio Overall Low Range	:1	11.756
Reverse Gear Overall Low Range	:1	43.075
SUSPENSION		
Front Suspension Type		Beam axle located by radius arms and Panhard rod
Rear Suspension Type		Beam axle located by radius arms, support rods and centre wishbone
Front Springs		Coil
Rear Springs		Coil
Front Dampers		Long-stroke hydraulic telescopic dampers
Rear Dampers		Long-stroke hydraulic telescopic dampers
Ride Levelling		Boge Hydromat self-energising located on rear centre wishbone
Anti Roll Bar Diameter Front	mm(in)	N/A
Anti Roll Bar Diameter Rear	mm(in)	N/A
STEERING		
Type		Recirculating ball, worm and nut with AC safety column
Assistance		Hydraulic power (option)

Range Rover - The Anniversary Guide

Specification Sheets

	UNITS	RANGE ROVER
Number of Turns Lock to Lock		4.75
BRAKES		
Type		Dual-line, servo assisted
Front Disc Type		Solid
Front Disc Diameter	mm(in)	298.5(11.75)
Rear Disc Type		Solid
Rear Disc Diameter	mm(in)	290.0(11.42)
Park Brake Type		Internal expanding drum mounted on transmission
TECHNOLOGIES		
Dual Line Braking System		Yes
Anti Lock Braking System (ABS)		No
Electronic Traction Control (ETC)		No
Electronic Brakeforce Distribution (EBD)		No
Emergency Brake Assist (EBA)		No
Dynamic Stability Control (DSC)		No
Hill Descent Control (HDC)		No
Terrain Response™		No
NOTES		

Data acquired from the best available sources but the publisher is not liable for any mistakes or omissions. Readers are advised to consult other sources e.g. manufacturer's workshop manuals before working on vehicles. The publication of performance and capability figures does not imply that this will be achieved in practice. Caution must be exercised in all driving activities especially off-road.
Units are expressed in the relevant international standard (SI). Where appropriate recognised conversion factors have been applied.

Range Rover - The Anniversary Guide

CHASSIS and ENGINE NUMBERS

RANGE ROVER AND RANGE ROVER CLASSIC

VEHICLE	ENGINE	PERIOD	TRANSMISSION	CHASSIS NUMBER PREFIX	ENGINE NUMBER PREFIX	COMMENTS
Range Rover 2-Door	3.5-litre V8 petrol carburetter	1970 - 1979	4-speed manual	355, 356 or 358	341, 355, 359 or 398	
		1979 - 1986		SALLHABV1AA		From introduction of Vehicle Identification Number (VIN) system
Range Rover 4-Door	3.5-litre V8 petrol carburetter	1981 - 1986	4-speed manual 3-speed automatic	SALLHAMV	11D, 13D, 15D, 17D	Engine number suffix B denotes electronic ignition
			4-speed automatic		26D, 27D, 28D, 29D, 30D	Engine number suffix C denotes SU carburetters (replacing Stromberg)
Range Rover 4-Door	3.5-litre V8 petrol fuel injection	1985 - 1989	5-speed manual 4-speed automatic	SALLHAML	22D, 23D, 24D, 25D, 31D	
Range Rover 4-Door	2.4-litre turbo diesel	1986 - 1989	5-speed manual	SALLHAME	11A	
Range Rover 4-Door	3.9-litre petrol fuel injection	1989 - 1996	5-speed manual 4-speed automatic	SALLHAMM	35D, 36D, 37D, 38D	Engine number suffix B denotes crank driven oil pump
Range Rover 4-Door	2.5-litre turbo diesel	1989 - 1992	5-speed manual	SALLHAMN	95A	
Range Rover 4-Door LSE	4.2-litre petrol fuel injection	1992 - 1996	4-speed automatic	SALLHBM3	40D	
Range Rover 4-Door	2.5-litre Tdi diesel	1992 - 1996	5-speed manual	SALLHAMF	12L, 17L, 18L, 19L, 20L	
			4-speed automatic		21L, 22L	Automatic only with 300 Tdi engine

PRICE LIST (UK)

RANGE ROVER FIRST GENERATION, PHASE ONE EARLY

DATE	MODEL	PRICE	NOTES
		£sd Inc Purchase Tax	
1970	Range Rover	1998.00.00	
OPTIONS			
	Static Seat Belts	7.16.08	Mandatory fit in UK

22

Range Rover - The Anniversary Guide

Lounge Chair & Ottoman
Design: Charles & Ray Eames, 1956

Designed to last for generations.
Since 1956 the Eames Lounge Chair has been
the modern icon of luxury and comfort.

vitra.
The Authorised Original

Experience the Lounge Chair at the following Vitra retailers: **Belfast** Living Space 02890 244 333 **Brighton** The Lollipop Shoppe 01273 699119 **Epping** Geoffrey Drayton 01992 573 929 **Glasgow** The Lighthouse 0141 221 6362 **Liverpool** Utility 0151 708 4192 **London** Aram Store 020 7557 7557 Chaplins 020 8421 1779 Couch Potato Company 020 8894 1333 Skandium 020 7584 2066 TwentyTwentyone 020 7837 1900 **Manchester** Urban Suite 0161 831 9966 **Sheffield** Electric Works 0114 286 6200 **Wakefield** Yorkshire Sculpture Park 01924 832 631   www.vitra.com/loungechair

Vitra is the only authorised manufacturer of all Eames furniture designs for Europe and the Middle East. Historic Eames Family photos © Eames Office LLC.
Lounge Chair & Ottoman: © Vitra ®

COLOUR & TRIM

RANGE ROVER FIRST GENERATION PHASE 1 EARLY

YEAR	PAINTWORK		LRC NUMBER	NOTES
	COLOUR	TYPE		
1970	Amazon Green	Solid	238	Used on pre-production only
	Bahama Gold	Solid	235	
	Davos White	Solid	354	
	Lincoln Green	Solid	233	
	Masai Red	Solid	234	
	Sahara Dust	Solid	239	
	Tuscan Blue	Solid	236	

INTERIOR TRIM

	COLOUR	MATERIAL		
	Palamino	PVC		

Wheels could be painted in Sahara Dust or Silver. The vast majority were Silver

24

Range Rover - The Anniversary Guide

COLOUR & TRIM

RANGE ROVER FIRST GENERATION PHASE 1 LATE

YEAR	PAINTWORK		LRC NUMBER	NOTES
	COLOUR	TYPE		
1982	Nevada Gold	Metallic	321	
	Sierra Silver	Metallic	305	
	Vogue Blue	Metallic	303	
	Arctic White	Solid	273	
	Lincoln Green	Solid	233	
	Masai Red	Solid	234	
	Russet Brown	Solid	318	
	Sahara Dust	Solid	239	
	Shetland Beige	Solid	302	
	Venetian Red	Solid	301	

INTERIOR TRIM

	COLOUR	MATERIAL		
	Bronze Velvet	Cloth		Vogue only
	Palamino	Vinyl		Vogue or with Interior Pack

Range Rover - The Anniversary Guide

Range Rover First Generation | Phase One | Technical Data

J.D Classics®

Office: (01621) 879579 **Facsimile:** (01621) 850370 **Mobile:** (07850) 966005

THE FINEST SELECTION OF
XK JAGUARS

WE ARE THE PREMIER DEALER FOR CLASSIC JAGUARS. WE HAVE FULL SERVICING AND RESTORATION FACILITIES TO THE HIGHEST STANDARDS,

We urgently require for stock, more Classic Jaguars of the highest quality, particularly 'Genuine Competiton Cars' and XKs. If you own a superb Jaguar, and are thinking about selling, please contact us with an accurate description of your vehicle.

IF THE CAR YOU ARE LOOKING FOR IS NOT LISTED ABOVE, PLEASE TALK TO US ABOUT IT. WE ARE HAPPY TO DISCUSS EVERY ASPECT OF CLASSIC CAR OWNERSHIP INCLUDING CLASSIC CAR FINANCE, AND TO GIVE YOU OUR BEST ADVICE.

WEB SITE: www.jdclassics.co.uk
Email: jd@jdclassics.net
OFFICE: (01621) 879579 FACSIMILE: (01621) 850370
MOBILE NUMBER: (07850) 966005

J.D Classics®

WYCKE HILL BUSINESS PARK, WYCKE HILL, MALDON, ESSEX CM9 6UZ, U.K.

Range Rover First Generation | Phase One | Advertising

Advertising & Brochures

The Darien Breakthrough

The British Trans America Expedition of 1971 – 72 used Range Rovers to drive from Alaska to Cape Horn conquering the jungles of the infamous Darien Gap on the way. Despite the problems encountered with the vehicles, this was a tremendous publicity boost to the company and they produced their own brochure to commemorate the event. One of the vehicles is exhibited at the Heritage Motor Centre

Very few pre- and early production vehicles were available for publicity purposes, most of them in the YVB...H number plate range like YVB 153H, the first production vehicle featured in our 'walkaround' gallery. The first brochure featured the now familiar font for the Range Rover name but, like the vehicle, included the 'By Land Rover' oval in case anyone was doubtful of the newcomer's heritage

Advertising & Brochures

In the British Leyland era, brochure photography became more stylish. This example was actually produced in the days of Land-Rover Ltd which was formed as a separate operating unit within BL Cars in 1978

This brochure from 1974 stressed the multi-purpose nature of the Range Rover, echoing the 'Car For All Reasons' marketing strapline used at the vehicle's launch. The brochure included sections on 'Leisure and Pleasure', 'Town and County' and 'The Professionals' Choice' which showed police vehicles as well as an ambulance conversion and the Carmichael 6-wheel fire appliance

While not exactly having the most engaging cover, this brochure revealed that Land-Rover Ltd was now part of BL's Jaguar Rover Triumph group. The quality of British Leyland vehicles reached its nadir during the 1970s, something the company tried to remedy by introducing the 'Supercover' warranty package which applied to the Range Rover as well as the Allegro. If the dealer failed to provide satisfaction, the customer was provided with a card to contact the factory direct in the hope of resolving the issue

Range Rover - The Anniversary Guide

Range Rover First Generation — Phase Two

Technical Description

Although the basic structure of the Range Rover remained unchanged, significant improvements were made to the vehicle with the introduction of the four-door derivative.

ENGINE

A high compression (9.35:1) version was introduced although the low compression version remained as an alternative.

TRANSMISSION

A three-speed automatic version was introduced as an option – on the introduction of the four-door, this option was confined to that model only. The standard Chrysler 727 gearbox was modified to improve oil sealing and venting. A new transfer box was fitted to automatic vehicles, based on the rotating parts from the manual unit in a new case. The automatic gearbox control was mounted on the gearbox tunnel. The transfer box control lever included a high/low shift and mechanically-operated centre differential lock engagement.

WHEELS AND TYRES

Three-spoke styled alloy wheels were introduced as an option.

BODY

Four-door version introduced alongside the original two-door. This involved revisions to the steel sub-structure to include a 'B/C' post, a 'D' post, and a rear wheel arch. The new doors were of similar construction to the original but all incorporated wind-up windows with fixed quarter lights. Exterior door handles were modified from Triumph TR7 units with a separate key entry on both front doors. Door-mounted exterior rear view mirrors. Revised seat bases for front seats as seat belt loads were no longer carried by the seat.

Metallic paint was offered as an option.

While the two-door had always been popular in overseas markets, the four-door Range Rover was even more so. The Middle East was a vital area for Land Rover who had a regional office in Dubai to concentrate on the market

SEATING AND TRIM

All seats now trimmed in brushed nylon with a ribbed stitch pattern. Front seat belts on the four-door model were now of the inertia reel type with the upper anchorage on the 'B/C' post. Both front seats incorporated a map pocket on their rear face. Armrests were offered as an option for both front and rear seats and head restraints were available as an option for the rear seat, being standard on the front seats. Both front seats on the four-door were able to recline.

Lap and diagonal rear seat belts were standard, the upper anchorage being fixed to the 'E' post. The centre rear seat position had a lap belt.

Four-door interior door trim was vinyl-covered board with window handles and interior door remote controls which were standard British Leyland corporate parts. Wooden door cappings were available as an option on four-door models only.

All floor coverings were now in carpet material. The spare wheel cover and tool curtain were also in matching carpet.

A cubby box was added to the tunnel area between the front seats.

HEATING AND VENTILATION

In-dash air conditioning was offered as an option with a separate, fascia-mounted control.

Technical Description

The launch of the Range Rover into the US market transformed Land Rover's fortunes but was a bit of a gamble. Senior managers knew that quality wasn't really up to the standards of the market, but put in place a special parts distribution system as well as offering an extended warranty. Its British connotations were ruthlessly exploited by Land Rover, even to the extent of portraying typical English rain in this brochure shot

Range Rover - The Anniversary Guide

Range Rover First Generation | Phase Two

Range Rover Walkaround

This Range Rover 4-door, owned and restored by Simon Phipps, is typical of a mid-1980s vehicle as the model was undergoing a rapid programme of improvements. Some older features, such as the exposed front door hinges remain but it has the new fuel filler cover and an upgraded interior

A head-on shot reveals iconic Range Rover styling but the vehicle now has a plastic grille with horizontal slats – in this case missing the Land Rover 'Jewel Badge'. The bib spoiler was another new addition and could be removed when going off road

Headlamp washers were now fitted to the Range Rover, but there was no disguising the poor fit of the bonnet

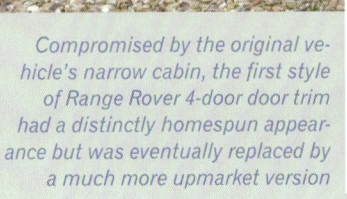

Compromised by the original vehicle's narrow cabin, the first style of Range Rover 4-door door trim had a distinctly homespun appearance but was eventually replaced by a much more upmarket version

32   Range Rover - The Anniversary Guide

New British Leyland corporate style 'flap' door handles were fitted to the 4-door. The Range Rover used the version employed by the TR7 which were of higher quality than those used on the Marina and Allegro and had the correct profile for the Range Rover

The hatch for the fuel filler aperture was a new addition and vastly improved the appearance of the Range Rover

The exposed front door hinges were a legacy of the original Range Rover. Considerable engineering effort was expended into concealing them, something eventually achieved as part of the development of the Discovery which shared a common body sub-structure

Colour keyed three-spoke alloy wheels were fitted to Range Rover Vogue models. The original tyres were Michelin XM+S 244 205 R16s

The Land Rover 'Jewel Badge' was introduced as part of a branding exercise leading up the launch of the Discovery

Range Rover - The Anniversary Guide

33

Range Rover First Generation — Phase Two

Range Rover Walkaround

The two-piece tailgate was an iconic Range Rover feature. Problems with corrosion on the lower tailgate were solved by adopting a decal for the vehicle's name, but the upper tailgate was always difficult to latch. Lamp guards were a popular accessory. The flag sticker is not original

Several designs were studied before Land Rover settled on the Monteverdi conversion as being the most pleasing – something mostly due to the rake of the door pillars. The 'floating roof' was one of many features to become iconic and reflected in later Range Rovers designs

The fascia was also in the process of being steadily improved during the 1980s. It would be only for the 1995 model year, in the last few months of the Range Rover's life, that it would get a fully moulded version worthy of its luxury status

A cluster of switches covered operation of the rear fog lights, spoiler mounted driving lamps, interior light and heated rear screen

34

Range Rover - The Anniversary Guide

e heater controls were much improved
er the original and improvements had also
en made to the fit and finish of the fascia
mponents. The radio is a replacement – the
ginal was made by Clarion and was a tight
 between the fascia and the gearbox tunnel.
e large red warning light was illuminated
en the centre differential lock was engaged

A revised instrument panel was housed in a new moulded binnacle. The design of the graphics reflected the fashion of the time, being similar to those employed on the contemporary Maestro and Montego

Increasingly upmarket trim materials were being employed to raise the profile of the Range Rover in the luxury car market although leather was not yet an option. The condition of the trim in Simon Phipps's vehicle is remarkable

The instrument column stalks were
another dip into the British Leyland
's bin, being modified from Maestro
and Montego items. The master
light switch was separate but also
mounted on the steering column

The introduction of the new seat design, upgraded materials and the new centre console was a great improvement to the interior ambiance of the Range Rover. The positioning of the window lift switches on the front face of the cubby box was an awkward, if long lasting, feature of the vehicle

Range Rover - The Anniversary Guide

Range Rover First Generation — Phase Two

Range Rover Walkaround

The Vehicle Identification Number (VIN) plate bears the name of Land Rover UK Ltd, then a separate operating company within British Leyland. The number itself is, however, flanked by the 'Flying Orifice' BL symbol to deter fraudulent alteration of the number. Other names for the symbol, not suitable for publication, were often used within the company. Body colour information – in this case, Alaskan Blue, was offered on a separate label also mounted on the bonnet latching platform

The operation of the two-piece tailgate was modified to allow for the lower half to be opened from the inside once the upper tailgate was open and the old external lever was deleted. A sturdy, chrome-plated handle was employed and was recessed to lower heavy loads to be slid over the tailgate

The new loadspace cover had shallow trays moulded into it for umbrellas and the like and also had a recess to allow access to the lower tailgate's interior catch. The prominent lifting 'ears' were provided to assist in raising the heavy steel tailgate

Simon Phipps has kept the engine bay in a satisfyingly original condition. Some of the complex structure of the vehicle is evident in the number of fixings used to assemble the components. The bonnet was a massive structure and its proper alignment both in manufacture and service was a constant struggle

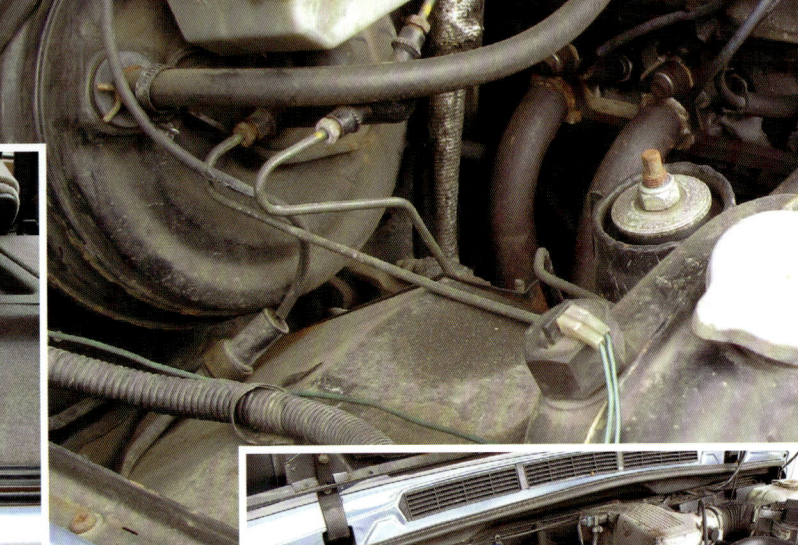

Range Rover - The Anniversary Guide

The plenum chamber for the fuel injection system was a massive aluminium casting and prominent in the engine bay. Simon Phipps has thankfully resisted the temptation to convert his Range Rover to run on LPG

The right hand side of the engine bay was dominated by the integrated brake servo and master cylinder in this pre-ABS vehicle. The blue knob to its right is the top of the oil dipper rod for the automatic gearbox – modern units are filled at the factory and sealed for life.

The label warned of the presence of asbestos in the vehicle's components. At the time, the dangerous substance was a common element of friction materials such as clutch plates and brake linings

Air was fed through the air filter in the foreground through the air flow meter, a crude, but key component in the fuel injection system. The alternator is mounted high to allow for a sensible wading depth but the engine now had more in common with that once fitted to cars than the original Range Rover unit. One feature unchanged from the earliest days was the bright orange oil filler cap

Range Rover - The Anniversary Guide

37

Specification Sheets

GENERAL FEATURES

CONSTRUCTION
Two-door, five seat frame and panel body on separate steel chassis

POWER UNITS
3.5-litre V8 all-alloy petrol engine

TRANSMISSION
Permanent four-wheel drive. Five-speed manual gearbox or three-speed automatic transmission. Separate two-speed transfer box with lockable centre differential. Single reduction beam axles

SUSPENSION
Long travel coil springs and hydraulic dampers. Ride levelling unit at rear. Cast radius arms with Panhard rod at front, radius arms with A-frame at rear

STEERING
Recirculating ball with hydraulic damper

BRAKING
Disc brakes all-round with dual-line hydraulic system. Transmission-mounted drum park brake

OTHER FEATURES
Collapsible safety steering column, front seat mounted safety belts

	UNITS	RANGE ROVER FIVE-SPEED MANUAL	RANGE ROVER THREE-SPEED AUTOMATIC
Vehicle Type		Three-door Station Wagon	Three-door Station Wagon
Construction		Separate chassis, panel-on-frame body	Separate chassis, panel-on-frame body
Number of Passengers		5	5
DIMENSIONS			
Overall Length	mm(in)	4470(176)	4470(176)
Overall Width (over mirrors)	mm(in)	1778(70)	1778(70)
Overall Height (nominal)	mm(in)	1778(70)	1778(70)
Wheelbase	mm(in)	2540(100)	2540(100)
Track Front/Rear	mm(in)	1485(58.5)	1485(58.5)
Luggage Capacity (Seat Up)	l(cu in)	1050(37.08)	1050(37.08)
Luggage Capacity (Seat Folded)	l(cu in)	2075(73.28)	2075(73.28)
WEIGHTS			
Unladen Weight	kg(lb)	1762(3883)	1762(3883)
Kerb Weight	kg(lb)	1895(4177)	1895(4177)
Gross Vehicle Weight	kg(lb)	2510(5532)	2510(5532)
Front Axle Maximum Weight	kg(lb)	1000(2204)	1000(2204)
Rear Axle Maximum Weight	kg(lb)	1510(3328)	1510(3328)
Maximum Payload	kg(lb)	615(1649)	615(1649)
Maximum On Road Trailer Weight	kg(lb)	2000(4408) with over-run brakes, 4000(8816) four-wheel trailer with power brakes	2000(4408) with over-run brakes, 4000(8816) four-wheel trailer with power brakes
Maximum Off Road Trailer Weight	kg(lb)	1000(2204)	1000(2204)
CAPABILITIES			
Drag Coefficient	Cd	0.45	0.45
Approach Angle (Maximum)	Deg	45	45
Under Body (Ramp) Angle (Maximum)	Deg	160	160
Departure Angle (Maximum)	Deg	33	33
Turning Circle (Kerb to kerb)	m(ft)	11.74(38.5)	11.74(38.5)

Range Rover - The Anniversary Guide

Specification Sheets

	UNITS	RANGE ROVER FIVE-SPEED MANUAL	RANGE ROVER THREE-SPEED AUTOMATIC
PERFORMANCE			
Maximum Speed	kp/h(mph)	148(92)	149(93)
Acceleration 0 - 100 kp/h (tested)	secs	17.7	N/K
Acceleration 0 - 60 mph (tested)	secs	13.9	16.3
FUEL CONSUMPTION			
Simulated Urban	l/100km (mpg)	19.7(14.3)	19.5(14.5)
Constant 56mph(90kph)	l/100km (mpg)	10.7(26.4)	12.2(23.2)
Constant 75mph(120kph)	l/100km (mpg)	13.9(20.2)	15.2(18.6)
ENGINE			
Type		V8	V8
Position in Vehicle		Front, in-line	Front, in-line
Fuel		Petrol (gasoline)	Petrol (gasoline)
Number of Cylinders		8	8
Number of Camshafts		1	1
Valves per Cylinder		2	2
Valve System		Overhead rockers, hydraulic tappets	Overhead rockers, hydraulic tappets
Bore	mm(in)	88.90(3.5)	88.90(3.5)
Stroke	mm(in)	71.12(2.8)	71.12(2.8)
Capacity	cc(cu in)	3528(215)	3528(215)
Compression Ratio	:1	8.5	8.5
Cylinder Head Material		Aluminium alloy	Aluminium alloy
Cylinder Block Material		Aluminium alloy	Aluminium alloy
Crankshaft Bearings		5	5
Lubrication System		Gear-driven oil pump with full-flow filter	Gear-driven oil pump with full-flow filter
Fuelling		Twin Zenith/Stromberg CD2 carburetters	Twin Zenith/Stromberg CD2 carburetters
Fuel System		Mechanical lift pump	Mechanical lift pump
Distributor		Lucas 35DM8	Lucas 35DM8
Boost System		None	None
Cold Start System		Manual choke with warning light	Manual choke with warning light
Air Cleaning System		Paper element	Paper element
Cooling System		Pressurised with expansion tank and crossflow radiator	Pressurised with expansion tank and crossflow radiator
Battery Capacity	Amp/hr	60	60
Max Power	kW(bhp)	95.6(128)	95.6(128)
At	rpm	5000	5000
Max Torque	Nm(lb/ft)	251(185)	251(185)
At	rpm	2500	2500

Range Rover - The Anniversary Guide

Range Rover First Generation — Phase Two — Technical Data

Specification Sheets

	UNITS	RANGE ROVER FIVE-SPEED MANUAL	RANGE ROVER THREE-SPEED AUTOMATIC
CAPACITIES			
Engine Oil Sump	l(Imp Gall) [US Gall]	5.68(1.25)[1.50]	5.68(1.25)[1.50]
Cooling Circuit	l(Imp Gall) [US Gall]	11(2.42)[2.91]	11(2.42)[2.91]
Fuel Tank (Maximum Usable)	l(Imp Gall) [US Gall]	86(19)[22.5]	86(19)[22.5]
TRANSMISSION			
Type		Permanent four-wheel drive	Permanent four-wheel drive
Flywheel		Cast iron, toothed	Cast iron, toothed
Clutch Type		Diaphragm spring, single dry plate	Diaphragm spring, single dry plate
Clutch Diameter	mm(in)	267(10.5)	267(10.5)
Gearbox Type		Manual	Manual
Number of Forward Gears		4	4
Selection Mechanism		Lever	Lever
Transfer Box Type		Gear driven, integral with gearbox	Gear driven, integral with gearbox
Number of Ratios		2	2
Selection Mechanism		Lever	Lever
Slip Control System		Vacuum-operated lockable centre differential	Vacuum-operated lockable centre differential
Front Prop Shaft Type		Open with universal joints and sliding joint with gaiter	Open with universal joints and sliding joint with gaiter
Rear Prop Shaft Type		Open with universal joints	Open with universal joints
Front Axle Type		Rover beam axle with swivel pins and 2-pinion differential	Rover beam axle with swivel pins and 2-pinion differential
Rear Axle Type		Rover beam axle with 2-pinion differential	Rover beam axle with 2-pinion differential
Wheel Type		Styled pressed steel, J-type rim	Styled pressed steel, J-type rim
Wheel Size - Standard	mm(in)	16(406)	16(406)
Wheel Size - Options	mm(in)	NA	NA
Tyre Size - Standard		Michelin XM+S radial 205x16	Michelin XM+S radial 205x16
Tyre Size - Options		Firestone Town and Country radial 205X16	Firestone Town and Country radial 205X16
RATIOS			
1st Gear Ratio	:1	4.069	2.450
2nd Gear Ratio	:1	2.448	1.450
3rd Gear Ratio	:1	1.505	1.000
4th Gear Ratio	:1	1.000	
5th Gear Ratio	:1		
Reverse Gear	:1	3.664	2.200
High Range Ratio	:1	1.174	1.003
Low Range Ratio	:1	3.321	3.321
Front Axle Ratio	:1	3.540	3.540

Range Rover - The Anniversary Guide

Specification Sheets

	UNITS	RANGE ROVER FIVE-SPEED MANUAL	RANGE ROVER THREE-SPEED AUTOMATIC
Rear Axle Ratio	:1	3.540	3.540
1st Gear Ratio Overall High Range	:1	16.910	8.699
2nd Gear Ratio Overall High Range	:1	10.174	5.148
3rd Gear Ratio Overall High Range	:1	6.255	3.550
4th Gear Ratio Overall High Range	:1	4.156	
Reverse Gear Overall High Range	:1	15.227	7.811
1st Gear Ratio Overall Low Range	:1	47.837	28.803
2nd Gear Ratio Overall Low Range	:1	28.780	17.047
3rd Gear Ratio Overall Low Range	:1	17.693	11.756
4th Gear Ratio Overall Low Range	:1	11.756	
Reverse Gear Overall Low Range	:1	43.075	25.863
SUSPENSION			
Front Suspension Type		Beam axle located by radius arms and Panhard rod	Beam axle located by radius arms and Panhard rod
Rear Suspension Type		Beam axle located by radius arms, support rods and centre wishbone	Beam axle located by radius arms, support rods and centre wishbone
Front Springs		Coil	Coil
Rear Springs		Coil	Coil
Front Dampers		Long-stroke hydraulic telescopic dampers	Long-stroke hydraulic telescopic dampers
Rear Dampers		Long-stroke hydraulic telescopic dampers	Long-stroke hydraulic telescopic dampers
Ride Levelling		Boge Hydromat self-energising located on rear centre wishbone	Boge Hydromat self-energising located on rear centre wishbone
Anti Roll Bar Diameter Front	mm(in)	N/A	N/A
Anti Roll Bar Diameter Rear	mm(in)	N/A	N/A
STEERING			
Type		Recirculating ball, worm and nut with AC safety column	Recirculating ball, worm and nut with AC safety column
Assistance		Hydraulic power (option)	Hydraulic power (option)
Number of Turns Lock to Lock		4.75	4.75
BRAKES			
Type		Dual-line, servo assisted	Dual-line, servo assisted
Front Disc Type		Solid	Solid
Front Disc Diameter	mm(in)	298.5(11.75)	298.5(11.75)
Rear Disc Type		Solid	Solid
Rear Disc Diameter	mm(in)	290.0(11.42)	290.0(11.42)
Park Brake Type		Internal expanding drum mounted on transmission	Internal expanding drum mounted on transmission
TECHNOLOGIES			
Dual Line Braking System		Yes	Yes
Anti Lock Braking System (ABS)		No	No

Price List

	UNITS	RANGE ROVER FIVE-SPEED MANUAL	RANGE ROVER THREE-SPEED AUTOMATIC
Electronic Traction Control (ETC)		No	No
Electronic Brakeforce Distribution (EBD)		No	No
Emergency Brake Assist (EBA)		No	No
Dynamic Stability Control (DSC)		No	No
Hill Descent Control (HDC)		No	No
Terrain Response™		No	No
NOTES			

Data acquired from the best available sources but the publisher is not liable for any mistakes or omissions. Readers are advised to consult other sources e.g. manufacturer's workshop manuals before working on vehicles. The publication of performance and capability figures does not imply that this will be achieved in practice. Caution must be exercised in all driving activities especially off-road.
Units are expressed in the relevant international standard (SI). Where appropriate recognised conversion factors have been applied.

PRICE LIST (UK)

RANGE ROVER PHASE 2 1983 - 1988

DATE	MODEL	PRICE	NOTES
		£ Inc Car Tax and VAT	
1989 (1990 Model Year)	4 Door Turbo D	23,784	
	Vogue Turbo D	25,905	
	Vogue EFI	25,506	
	Vogue SE EFI	31,949	
	OPTIONS		
	Air Conditioning	1585	Standard on Vogue SE
	Alloy Wheels	795	Turbo D only - standard on other models
	ABS	1250	Standard on Vogue SE
	Automatic Transmission	1324	Petrol models only, standard on Vogue SE
	Catalyst Exhaust System	450	Petrol models only
	Heated windscreen	150	Turbo D only - standard on other models
	Metallic Paint	430	Turbo D only - standard on other models
	Front Mudflaps	32	
	Radio Cassette	397	Turbo D only - standard on other models
	Electric Sun Roof	1003	Standard on Vogue SE
	Towing Pack	126	

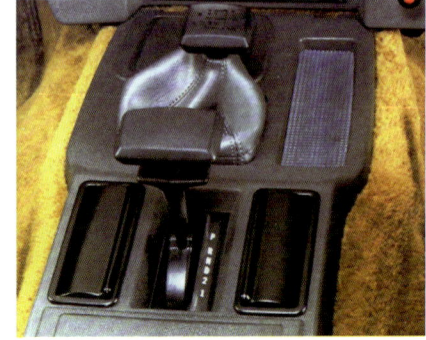

Range Rover - The Anniversary Guide

ENJOY VENTURING OFF-ROAD?

LAND ROVER *monthly* SPECIAL OFFER

CLAIM 3 ISSUES OF LAND ROVER *monthly* FOR JUST £1

Discover Land Rover Monthly, the world's biggest Land Rover Magazine, with 3 issues for just £1. Month after month you'll be kept up-to-date with the latest news from the world of Land Rovers, Discovery and Range Rovers. Each issue is packed with news and stories from around the world, technical tips, history, adventure, modified vehicles and hundreds of Land Rovers for sale every month.

CLAIM 3 ISSUES OF LAND ROVER MONTHLY FOR £1 NOW

If you enjoy reading it after the introductory period your subscription will automatically continue by Direct Debit at the low rate of just **£19.99 every 6 issues** – saving you 15% on the shop price. Claim your 3 issues for £1 with no obligation today!

CALL NOW
0844 499 1762

Or order online at: **www.dennismags.co.uk/lrm**
quoting offer code G1006ANN

COLOUR & TRIM

RANGE ROVER FIRST GENERATION PHASE 2

YEAR	PAINTWORK		LRC NUMBER	NOTES
	COLOUR	TYPE		
1983	Arctic White	Solid	273	
	Arizona Tan	Solid	341	
	Balmoral Green	Solid	340	
	Russet Brown	Solid	318	
	Sahara Dust	Solid	239	
	Venetian Red	Solid	301	
	Derwent Blue	Metallic	303	
	Nevada Gold	Metallic	321	
	Sierra Silver	Metallic	305	

INTERIOR TRIM

COLOUR	MATERIAL		
Silver Grey	Cloth		
Bronze Check	Cloth		

RANGE ROVER FIRST GENERATION PHASE 2

YEAR	PAINTWORK		LRC NUMBER	NOTES
	COLOUR	TYPE		
1987	Astral Silver	Metallic	364	Vogue with Silver Grey trim
	Caspian Blue	Metallic	366	Vogue with Silver Grey trim
	Cassis Red	Metallic	382	Vogue with Silver Grey trim
	Cypress Green	Metallic	367	Vogue with Silver Grey trim
	Savannah Beige	Metallic	365	Vogue with Bracken trim
	Ascot Green	Solid	001	Vogue with Bracken trim
	Cambrian Grey	Solid	348	Vogue with Silver Grey trim
	Chamonix White	Solid	354	Vogue with Silver Grey trim
	Tasman Blue	Solid	327	Vogue with Silver Grey trim
	Venetian Red	Solid	301	Vogue with Bracken trim

INTERIOR TRIM

COLOUR	MATERIAL		NOTES
Silver Grey	Cloth		Vogue only
Bracken	Cloth		Vogue or with Interior Pack
Bronze Check	Cloth		

Colour & Trim

Range Rover - The Anniversary Guide

Range Rover First Generation | Phase Two | Technical Data

SIERRA SILVER METALLIC

NEVADA GOLD METALLIC

DERWENT BLUE METALLIC

ARCTIC WHITE

ARIZONA TAN

SAHARA DUST

VENETIAN RED

RUSSET BROWN

BALMORAL GREEN

The colours reproduced here are subject to the limitations of the printing process and may therefore vary from the actual finish.

RANGE ROVER VOGUE

RANGE ROVER 4 DOOR

SILVER GREY TRIM

BRONZE CHECK TRIM

RANGE ROVER 2 DOOR

Range Rover - The Anniversary Guide

RANGE ROVER REGISTER
25 YEARS
1985 - 2010

RRR
RANGE ROVER
REGISTER

Multi Award Winning Club for all Range Rover Marques

Keeping a legend alive
Celebrating 40 years of RANGE ROVER
1970 - 2010

Tel: 08707 297 406   www.rrr.co.uk

| Range Rover First Generation | Phase Two | Advertising |

Advertising & Brochures

Early attempts at air conditioning for the Range Rover were clumsy affairs using a roof-mounted system originally designed for American motor homes. The arrival of a factory-fitted in-dash system was significant enough to warrant this special brochure of 1980.

Range Rover~Air Conditioning

The new air conditioning system used an engine-driven compressor with a condenser cooled by twin electric fans in front of the main radiator. The evaporator was hidden in the fascia with cooled air being supplied through vents

48

Range Rover - The Anniversary Guide

Advertising & Brochures

When the Range Rover was introduced in America, it was backed up by brochure and advertising photography intended to reinforce its position in the luxury market sector. Special, fully-trimmed 'bucks' with the doors, pillars and other panels removed to aid photography were supplied to studios for interior shots. Backgrounds were added later

The cover of the 1983 brochure had a flysheet which opened to reveal the two-door variant. By this time, the four-door was well established and the Range Rover's re-positioning had begun. The brochure featured the three-speed automatic gearbox, central locking and in-dash air conditioning

Range Rover - The Anniversary Guide

Technical Description

The 1980s saw a massive investment in the Range Rover. This led to new engine specifications, revisions to the transmission and significant upgrading of the trim and equipment. The two-door model was eventually dropped.

ENGINE

The V8 engine was fitted with a fuel injection system and subsequently its capacity was increased to 3.9 litres. A diesel-powered variant was introduced using a 4-cylinder engine from Italian manufacturers, VM.

TRANSMISSION

A five-speed manual gearbox was introduced along with the option of a ZF four-speed automatic gearbox. Both gearboxes were mated to a separate two-speed transfer box with locking centre differential. Later, this gear-driven unit was replaced with a chain-driven transfer box by Borg Warner which incorporated an automatic viscous coupling for differential control. The transfer box operating lever was re-styled and re-positioned and lost the differential lock function with the advent of the viscous coupled differential. The automatic gearbox torque converter had a lock-up feature and a higher gear ratio to improve fuel economy.

SUSPENSION

Anti-roll bars were added front and rear. These were optional or standard, depending on trim level.

WHEELS AND TYRES

Body-coloured alloy wheels were standard on the Vogue SE model.

BRAKING SYSTEM

The front discs were replaced by vented units. ABS was incorporated as standard.

Parking brake actuation was now by cable and the lever was also revised.

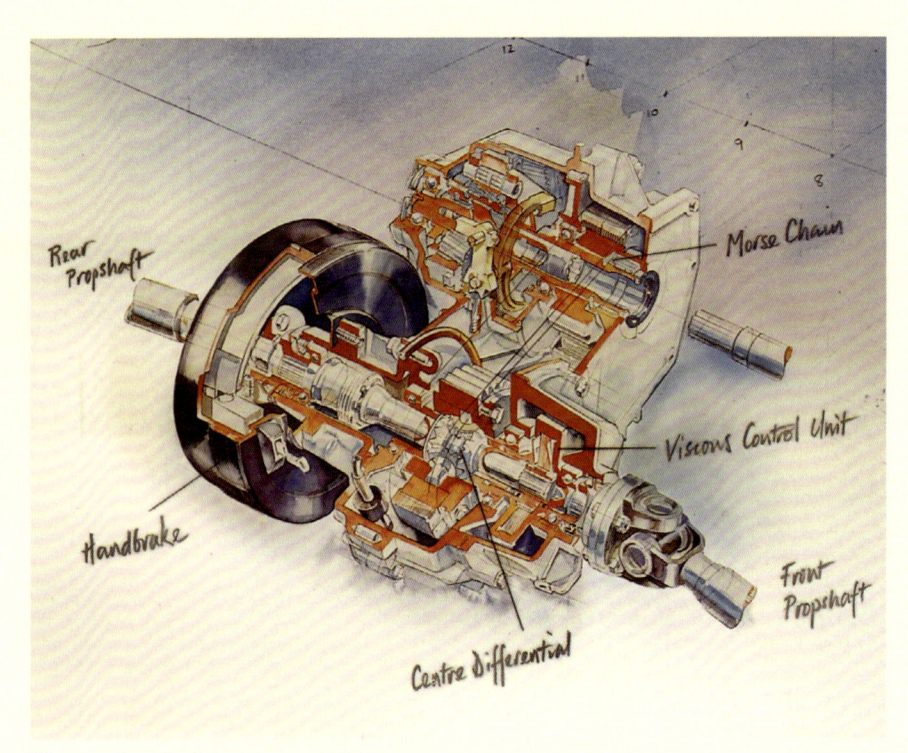

The new transfer box was sourced from Borg Warner and built in their factory in Margam, Wales. With its chain drive and viscous coupled centre differential, it was a step change from earlier transmissions and played a big part in establishing the Range Rover as a true luxury vehicle

STEERING

The steering wheel was re-designed with two spokes and a large centre pad. It was also of smaller diameter. The covering was now soft feel and the rim was leather trimmed, except on the basic model.

BODY

The body structure was revised to incorporate changes such as a one-piece pressed floor that was concurrently developed for the Project Jay (Discovery) programme and designed to improve the structural integrity of the sub-structure which the two vehicles shared. There were also modifications to the fuel system including a door for the fuel filler cap.

An electrically-operated retractable sun roof with sliding blind was now available as an option. This was standard on the Vogue SE model but there was a delete option as the cassette arrangement for the sunroof required a modified roof trim that reduced headroom.

A heated front windscreen was available as an option although it was standard on the Vogue SE. Variable-speed windscreen wipers were fitted.

Central door-locking, operated by the lock on the front doors was introduced. This locked all the doors and the tailgate. The door locks and windscreen washer jets were heated.

Electric windows became standard with a one-touch down facility on the driver's door only.

A front spoiler with two driving lamps was fitted to Vogue and Vogue SE models. All but the basic model had a side rubbing strip while the Vogue SE was distinguished by a pin stripe.

SEATING AND TRIM

All seats were trimmed in cloth as

Technical Description

standard with Connolly leather as an option. The rear seat was re-styled with a high back incorporating head restraints and an asymmetric seat split. Armrests were provided for both front seats with centre and wing armrests for the rear. The front seats had adjustable head restraints. Electric adjustment of the seats, including height and a memory function which included the exterior mirrors, was fitted to the Vogue SE model. The front seats were also heated.

The door trims were re-designed to incorporate armrests with integral door pulls, carpeted panels and radio speakers. Wood veneer inserts were included on all but the basic model. The veneer itself depended on trim level.

A new tunnel-mounted trim section included an ashtray and oddment trays while the cubby box incorporated illuminated window lift switches on its front panel.

The interior light now had a delay function and an interior mirror with integral map lamps was available on all but the basic model. On the Vogue SE, the mirror incorporated an auto dip feature.

FASCIA, INSTRUMENTS AND EQUIPMENT

A revised plastic instrument binnacle was fitted incorporating the speedometer, a rev. counter (which also included the fuel and water temperature gauges) and a revised warning light cluster. An oddments tray was positioned in the centre of the fascia top. A grab handle was added to the passenger side closing panel – this was leather-trimmed on the Vogue SE model.

The lower fascia rail and heater cover panel were revised to include face-level vents for the heating and air conditioning system, and to provide a central mounting position for the radio. Heating, ventilation and air conditioning controls were now integrated on an illuminated central panel which also housed a cigar lighter and switches for the heated front seats. The panel included an array of auxiliary switches.

The steering column shroud was also revised and new column stalks, based on those used on the Austin Rover Maestro/Montego range, were fitted.

A security-coded radio cassette player was fitted as standard with a six-CD autochanger available as an option. A six-speaker system, including a special bass speaker in the front doors, was fitted when the CD player was specified.

Headlamp power wash was fitted to all but the basic model.

HEATING AND VENTILATION

Ducting was incorporated to channel air to the rear compartment.

The revised interior was a massive leap forward over earlier designs. While retaining the essential structure of the original, the fit and finish were much improved and the quality of the materials far superior. The Range Rover's position in the luxury car market was now assured, a far cry from its utilitarian beginnings

Range Rover - The Anniversary Guide

Specification Sheets

GENERAL FEATURES

CONSTRUCTION
Two-door, five seat frame and panel body on separate steel chassis

POWER UNITS
3.9-litre V8 fuel injected, 2.5-litre turbocharged VM diesel

TRANSMISSION
Permanent four wheel drive. Five-speed manual gearbox or four-speed ZF automatic. Two-speed chain drive transfer box with automatic viscous coupling. Single reduction beam axles

SUSPENSION
Long travel coil springs and hydraulic dampers. Ride levelling unit at rear

Cast radius arms with Panhard rod at front, radius arms with A-frame at rear

STEERING
Recirculating ball with power steering

BRAKING
Disc brakes all-round with dual-line hydraulic system. Transmission-mounted drum park brake

OTHER FEATURES
Optional ABS braking system (standard on Vogue SE). Upgraded 'Vogue' interior.

	UNITS	RANGE ROVER 3.9-LITRE FIVE-SPEED MANUAL	RANGE ROVER 3.9-LITRE FOUR-SPEED AUTOMATIC	RANGE ROVER 2.5-LITRE DIESEL MANUAL
Vehicle Type		Four-door Station Wagon	Four-door Station Wagon	Four-door Station Wagon
Construction		Separate chassis, panel-on-frame body	Separate chassis, panel-on-frame body	Separate chassis, panel-on-frame body
Number of Passengers		5	5	5
DIMENSIONS				
Overall Length	mm(in)	4470(176)	4470(176)	4470(176)
Overall Width (over mirrors)	mm(in)	1778(70)	1778(70)	1778(70)
Overall Height (nominal)	mm(in)	1778(70)	1778(70)	1778(70)
Wheelbase	mm(in)	2540(100)	2540(100)	2540(100)
Track Front/Rear	mm(in)	1485(58.5)	1485(58.5)	1485(58.5)
Luggage Capacity (Seat Up)	l(cu in)	1050(37.08)	1050(37.08)	1050(37.08)
Luggage Capacity (Seat Folded)	l(cu in)	2075(73.28)	2075(73.28)	2075(73.28)
WEIGHTS				
Kerb Weight (EEC)	kg(lb)	1920(4233)	1951(4301)	2031(4478)
Gross Vehicle Weight	kg(lb)	2510(5534)	2510(5534)	2510(5534)
Front Axle Maximum Weight	kg(lb)	1200(2646)	1200(2646)	1200(2646)
Rear Axle Maximum Weight	kg(lb)	1510(3329)	1510(3329)	1510(3329)
Maximum Payload	kg(lb)	590(1301)	559(1233)	479(1056)
Maximum On Road Trailer Weight	kg(lb)	2000(4408) with over-run brakes, 4000(8816) four-wheel trailer with power brakes		
Maximum Off Road Trailer Weight	kg(lb)	1000(2204)	1000(2204)	1000(2204)
CAPABILITIES				
Drag Coefficient	Cd	0.45	0.45	0.45
Approach Angle (Maximum)	Deg	30	30	30
Under Body (Ramp) Angle (Maximum)	Deg	151	151	151
Departure Angle (Maximum)	Deg	30	30	30
Turning Circle (Kerb to kerb)	mm(in)	11,735(38.5)	11,735(38.5)	11,735(38.5)
PERFORMANCE				
Maximum Speed	kp/h(mph)	183(114)	177(110)	149(93)
Acceleration 0 - 100 kp/h (tested)	secs	N/A	N/A	17.7
Acceleration 0 - 60 mph (tested)	secs	9.9	11.3	16.3

Specification Sheets

	UNITS	RANGE ROVER 3.9-LITRE FIVE-SPEED MANUAL	RANGE ROVER 3.9-LITRE FOUR-SPEED AUTOMATIC	RANGE ROVER 2.5-LITRE DIESEL MANUAL
FUEL CONSUMPTION				
Urban	l/100km (mpg)	18.1(15.6)	19.6(14.4)	11.1(25.4)
Constant 90kph (56mph)	l/100km (mpg)	10.5(26.9)	10.5(26.9)	8.6(32.9)
Constant 120kph (75mph)	l/100km (mpg)	13.4(21.0)	13.4(21.0)	11.7(24.1)
ENGINE				
Type		V8	V8	Four-Cylinder
Position in Vehicle		Front, in-line	Front, in-line	Front, in-line
Fuel		Petrol (gasoline)	Petrol (gasoline)	Diesel
Number of Cylinders		8	8	4
Number of Camshafts		1	1	1
Valves per Cylinder		2	2	2
Valve System		Overhead rockers, hydraulic tappets	Overhead rockers, hydraulic tappets	Pushrod operated overhead valves
Bore	mm(in)	94.0(3.70)	94.0(3.70)	92.0(3.62)
Stroke	mm(in)	71.1(2.80)	71.1(2.80)	94(3.70)
Capacity	cc(cu in)	3947(241)	3947(241)	2500(152)
Compression Ratio	:1	9.35	9.35	22
Cylinder Head Material		Aluminium alloy	Aluminium alloy	Aluminium alloy (separate heads)
Cylinder Block Material		Aluminium alloy	Aluminium alloy	Cast iron
Crankshaft Bearings		5	5	5
Lubrication System		Gear-driven oil pump with full-flow filter	Gear-driven oil pump with full-flow filter	Gear-driven oil pump with full-flow filter
Fuelling		Lucas L-Jetronic fuel injection	Lucas L-Jetronic fuel injection	Indirect fuel injection
Fuel System		Electric lift pump	Electric lift pump	Rotary fuel pump
Distributor		Lucas electronic distributor with amplifier	Lucas electronic distributor with amplifier	N/A
Boost System		None	None	KKK turbocharger integral wastegate and intercooler
Cold Start System		Manual choke with warning light	Manual choke with warning light	Automatic heater plugs
Air Cleaning System		Paper element	Paper element	Paper element
Cooling System		Pressurised with expansion tank and crossflow radiator	Pressurised with expansion tank and crossflow radiator	Pressurised with expansion tank and crossflow radiator
Battery Capacity	Amp/hr	60	60	60
Max Power	kW(bhp)	95.6(128)	95.6(128)	84(112)
At	rpm	5000	5000	4200
Max Torque	Nm(lb/ft)	251(185)	251(185)	248(183)
At	rpm	2500	2500	2400
CAPACITIES				
Engine Oil Sump	l(Imp Gall)[US Gall]	5.68(1.25)[1.50]	5.68(1.25)[1.50]	5.68(1.25)[1.50]
Cooling Circuit	l(Imp Gall)[US Gall]	11(2.42)[2.91]	11(2.42)[2.91]	11(2.42)[2.91]
Fuel Tank (Maximum Usable)	l(Imp Gall)[US Gall]	86(19)[22.5]	86(19)[22.5]	86(19)[22.5]

Range Rover - The Anniversary Guide

Range Rover First Generation — Phase Three — Technical Data

Specification Sheets

	UNITS	RANGE ROVER 3.9-LITRE FIVE-SPEED MANUAL	RANGE ROVER 3.9-LITRE FOUR-SPEED AUTOMATIC	RANGE ROVER 2.5-LITRE DIESEL MANUAL
TRANSMISSION				
Type		Permanent four-wheel drive	Permanent four-wheel drive	Permanent four-wheel drive
Flywheel		Cast iron, toothed	Drive plate with torque converter	Cast iron, toothed
Clutch Type		Diaphragm spring, single dry plate	N/A	Diaphragm spring, single dry plate
Clutch Diameter	mm(in)	267(10.5)	N/A	267(10.5)
Gearbox Type		Manual	Automatic, ZF4HP22	Manual
Number of Forward Gears		4	4	5
Selection Mechanism		Lever	Console mounted selector lever	Lever
Transfer Box Type		Chain driven	Chain driven	Chain driven
Number of Ratios		2	2	2
Selection Mechanism		Lever	Lever	Lever
Slip Control System		Viscous coupled automatic centre differential	Viscous coupled automatic centre differential	Viscous coupled automatic centre differential
Front Prop Shaft Type		Open with universal joints and sliding joint with gaiter	Open with universal joints and sliding joint with gaiter	Open with universal joints and sliding joint with gaiter
Rear Prop Shaft Type		Open with universal joints	Open with universal joints	Open with universal joints
Front Axle Type		Rover beam axle with swivel pins and 2-pinion differential	Rover beam axle with swivel pins and 2-pinion differential	Rover beam axle with swivel pins and 2-pinion differential
Rear Axle Type		Rover beam axle with 2-pinion differential	Rover beam axle with 2-pinion differential	Rover beam axle with 2-pinion differential
Wheel Type		Styled cast alloy, J-type rim	Styled cast alloy, J-type rim	Styled pressed steel JK-type rim
Wheel Size - Standard	mm(in)	16(406)	16(406)	16(406)
Wheel Size - Options	mm(in)	Styled pressed steel JK-type rim	Styled pressed steel JK-type rim	N/A
Tyre Size - Standard		Michelin XM+S 244 radial 205x16	Michelin XM+S 244 radial 205x16	Michelin XM+S 244 radial 205x16
Tyre Size - Options		Goodyear Wrangler radial 205 x 16	Goodyear Wrangler radial 205 x 16	N/A
RATIOS				
1st Gear Ratio	:1	3.321	2.480	3.692
2nd Gear Ratio	:1	2.312	1.480	2.132
3rd Gear Ratio	:1	1.397	1.000	1.397
4th Gear Ratio	:1	1.000	0.728	1.000
5th Gear Ratio	:1	0.728	N/A	0.770
Reverse Gear	:1	3.429	2.086	3.429
High Range Ratio	:1	1.206	1.206	1.206
Low Range Ratio	:1	3.243	3.243	3.243
Front Axle Ratio	:1	3.540	3.540	3.540
Rear Axle Ratio	:1	3.540	3.540	3.540
1st Gear Ratio Overall High Range	:1	14.178	10.588	15.762
2nd Gear Ratio Overall High Range	:1	9.878	6.319	9.102
3rd Gear Ratio Overall High Range	:1	5.964	4.269	5.964
4th Gear Ratio Overall High Range	:1	4.269	3.108	4.269
5th Gear Ratio Overall High Range	:1	3.108	N/A	3.287
Reverse Gear Overall High Range	:1	14.639	8.906	14.639
1st Gear Ratio Overall Low Range	:1	38.126	28.471	42.385
2nd Gear Ratio Overall Low Range	:1	26.542	16.991	24.475
3rd Gear Ratio Overall Low Range	:1	16.038	11.480	16.038
4th Gear Ratio Overall Low Range	:1	12.117	8.358	11.480
5th Gear Ratio Overall Low Range	:1	8.358	N/A	8.840

Range Rover - The Anniversary Guide

Specification Sheets

	UNITS	RANGE ROVER 3.9-LITRE FIVE-SPEED MANUAL	RANGE ROVER 3.9-LITRE FOUR-SPEED AUTOMATIC	RANGE ROVER 2.5-LITRE DIESEL MANUAL
Reverse Gear Overall Low Range	:1	39.365	23.948	39.366
SUSPENSION				
Front Suspension Type		Beam axle located by radius arms and Panhard rod	Beam axle located by radius arms and Panhard rod	Beam axle located by radius arms and Panhard rod
Rear Suspension Type		Beam axle located by radius arms, support rods and centre wishbone		
Front Springs		Coil	Coil	Coil
Rear Springs		Coil	Coil	Coil
Front Dampers		Long-stroke hydraulic telescopic dampers	Long-stroke hydraulic telescopic dampers	Long-stroke hydraulic telescopic dampers
Rear Dampers		Long-stroke hydraulic telescopic dampers	Long-stroke hydraulic telescopic dampers	Long-stroke hydraulic telescopic dampers
Ride Levelling		Boge Hydromat self-energising located on rear centre wishbone		
Anti Roll Bar Diameter Front	mm(in)	N/A	N/A	N/A
Anti Roll Bar Diameter Rear	mm(in)	N/A	N/A	N/A
STEERING				
Type		Recirculating ball, worm and nut with collapsible column		
Assistance		Hydraulic power (option)	Hydraulic power (option)	Hydraulic power (option)
Number of Turns Lock to Lock		3.375	3.375	3.375
BRAKES				
Type		Dual-line, servo assisted, ABS optional	Dual-line, servo assisted, ABS optional	Dual-line, servo assisted, aABS optional
Front Disc Type		Ventilated	Ventilated	Ventilated
Front Disc Diameter	mm(in)	298.5(11.75)	298.5(11.75)	298.5(11.75)
Rear Disc Type		Solid	Solid	Solid
Rear Disc Diameter	mm(in)	290.0(11.42)	290.0(11.42)	290.0(11.42)
Park Brake Type		Internal expanding drum mounted on transmission	Internal expanding drum mounted on transmission	Internal expanding drum mounted on transmission
TECHNOLOGIES				
Dual Line Braking System		Yes	Yes	Yes
Anti Lock Braking System (ABS)		Option	Option	Option
Electronic Traction Control (ETC)		No	No	No
Electronic Brakeforce Distribution (EBD)		No	No	No
Emergency Brake Assist (EBA)		No	No	No
Dynamic Stability Control (DSC)		No	No	No
Hill Descent Control (HDC)		No	No	No
Terrain Response™		No	No	No
NOTES				

Data acquired from the best available sources but the publisher is not liable for any mistakes or omissions. Readers are advised to consult other sources e.g. manufacturer's workshop manuals before working on vehicles. The publication of performance and capability figures does not imply that this will be achieved in practice. Caution must be exercised in all driving activities especially off-road.
Units are expressed in the relevant international standard (SI). Where appropriate recognised conversion factors have been applied.

Range Rover - The Anniversary Guide

COLOUR & TRIM

RANGE ROVER PHASE 3 1989 - 1993

YEAR	PAINTWORK		LRC NUMBER	NOTES
	COLOUR	TYPE		
1992	Roman Bronze	Metallic		
	Aegean Blue	Micatallic		
	Ardennes Green	Micatallic		
	Aspen Silver	Micatallic		
	Mosswood	Micatallic		Vogue LSE only
	Plymouth Blue	Micatallic		
	Sonoran Brown	Micatallic		
	Trocadero Red	Micatallic		
	Westminster Grey	Micatallic		Vogue SE only
	Beluga Black	COB Solid		Vogue LSE and SE only
	Alpine White	Solid		
	Arles Blue	Solid		
	Eastnor Green	Solid		
	Pembroke Grey	Solid		
	Portofino Red	Solid		

INTERIOR TRIM

	COLOUR	MATERIAL		
	Winchester	Cloth		
	Brogue	Cloth		
	Dark Sable	Leather		Standard Vogue SE only
	Winchester	Leather		Standard Vogue SE, optional Vogue
	Saddle	Leather		Vogue LSE only
	Sorrell	Leather		Standard Vogue SE, optional Vogue

PINKSTER & PARTNERS

CLASSIC & EXCLUSIVE CAR CONSULTANTS & BROKERS

With over 20 years of experience, Pinkster & Partners Ltd is specialised in classic and exclusive car consultancy and brokerage services.

What sets us apart from other reputable brokers is that we work exclusively for the buyer. We do not accept any seller's commission and are therefore completely unbiased and independent.

Whether you are a first time buyer looking for a dream car or an experienced car collector searching for a rare addition to your collection, we can assist you with objective, expert advice.

PINKSTER & PARTNERS LTD:

INDEPENDENT CONSULTANTS & BROKERS

100 Pall Mall
St James
London SW1Y 5NQ
United Kingdom

t   +44 (0)20 7321 3767
e   info@pinksterandpartners.com
w   www.pinksterandpartners.com

I'm as passionate about Range Rovers as you are, which is why I think you'll love our insurance deals.

Adrian Flux Insurance Services has been built around the enthusiast markets and understands that people who are passionate about their cars take good care of them. Call us today to obtain a no obligation quote for your Range Rover based on your own personal requirements and driving history.

FREEPHONE
0800 081 8989

Quoteline hours:
Mon to Fri 9am-7pm | Sat 9am-4pm

adrianflux.co.uk

Authorised and regulated by the Financial Services Authority

ADRIAN FLUX
Passionate about insurance

Clive. Adrian Flux Maintenance Manager.

Home | Luxury | Classic | Van | 4x4 | Bike | Campers | Performance | Specialist

Range Rover First Generation | Phase Three | Advertising

Advertising & Brochures

Where do you suppose they keep the Range Rover?

A Range Rover is quite at home in weather that would keep other luxury cars, well, at home.

After all, with its permanent 4-wheel drive and powerful V-8 engine, you can plow through unplowed roads.

Tool along slushy streets.

Make it up sleet-covered hills.

And easily cope with conditions that would discourage a sled dog.

In fact, the Range Rover County even comes with an anti-lock braking system considered by many to be the most sophisticated one on four wheels.

Which not only means you can drive with a reassuring amount of control.

You can stop with it too.

So why not call 1-800-FINE 4WD for one of our select Canadian dealers?

And plan to come in for a test drive next time it snows.

Provided, of course, you can get out of your garage.

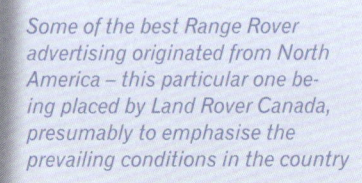

RANGE ROVER

Brochure photography was lit to emphasise the sumptuous ambiance of the Range Rover's luxury interior

Some of the best Range Rover advertising originated from North America – this particular one being placed by Land Rover Canada, presumably to emphasise the prevailing conditions in the country

Range Rover advertising also concentrated on the huntin', shootin' and fishin' set. Research showed that, in fact, a large proportion of Range Rovers were used off-road on country estates

58　　　　　　　　　　　　　　　　　　Range Rover - The Anniversary Guide

Advertising & Brochures

Range Rover of North America was often bold in their advertising approach. This startling shot was accompanied by the admonition to 'Drive responsibly off road'

It was easy for Americans to imagine that the Range Rover's natural habitat was Rodeo Drive and Malibu. Advertising like this, backed by some spectacular off-road PR events, proved that it had a rougher side

Surprisingly no-one bothered to remove the obviously British number plate even though this is a left-hand drive, US-spec vehicle. A Welsh quarry often stood in for the wilds of America on Land Rover photoshoots

Range Rover - The Anniversary Guide   59

Range Rover First Generation | Phase Three | Advertising

Advertising & Brochures

The 1989 brochure featured a full range of vehicles from the 2 Door Standard, through the Vogue Turbo D to the fuel-injected Vogue SE

The arrival of the extended wheelbase LSE model not only addressed some of the issues of rear seat legroom and access but introduced the multiple-height, electronically-controlled air suspension system. Offering benefits in ride and off-road ability, it was adopted following assessment of similar systems on American vehicles, although the Range Rover one was produced in conjunction with Dunlop and based on a truck suspension. Development of the system was protracted and problems led to a full 12-month postponement, with the system being launched on the LSE and standard wheelbase models in 1992. Air suspension was made standard on Second Generation and all subsequent Range Rovers

Range Rover - The Anniversary Guide

Advertising & Brochures

The Vogue SE was so special that, in 1988, it demanded an equally impressive brochure all of its own

Just some of the places the new Range Rover outperforms the old one.

How's this for an opening? Introducing the 1993 Range Rover County LWB, the strongest, quietest, most luxurious and technologically-advanced Range Rover ever built.

It has a unique electronic air suspension system that automatically adjusts its height to suit road conditions, and can rise above rough terrain, or kneel down to curb height at the press of a button.

It also has the longest wheelbase of any Range Rover, so passengers in back can stretch their legs nearly twice as far.

What's more, with our new electronic traction control, along with ABS, the County LWB can take you down roads lost in snow, or through pond-size puddles with better traction than ever.

And powered by a 4.2 liter, V-8 engine, it even turns in a more impressive performance on a smoothly paved highway.

Why not call 1-800-FINE 4WD for a dealer near you? Granted, it may not be the most inexpensive Range Rover we've ever built. It is, however, the best.

Reason enough for looking into it.

In a another bold move, given the Range Rover's service history in the US, Land Rover of North America (the name changed from Range Rover of North America in 1992) showed the new 'County LWB' in an embarrassing state. Like other scenarios in US advertising, this is something you should not try yourself!

The interior of the Range Rover was by now a far cry from the utilitarian version of the original with leather, carpet, and wood veneers replacing PVC. Shots like this were achieved using special trimmed 'bucks' with the middle post removed. Once in the studio, setting up the lighting to show the interior to its best advantage might take many days before the final image was taken

Range Rover - The Anniversary Guide

Range Rover First Generation — Phase Four

Technical Description

The position of the Range Rover at the forefront of automotive development continued in the early 1990s with the introduction of the Electronic Air Suspension (EAS) system. This also heralded the début of the extended wheelbase LSE (known as the County LWB in America) additional model and Electronic Traction Control as well as some engine changes. In an unusual move, Land Rover elected to keep the model in production after the launch of the Second Generation P38A, renaming it the 'Range Rover Classic'. The pace of change continued in the last few months of its life with the introduction of a new fascia.

CHASSIS

While retaining the same basic construction, the chassis was modified to allow for a 203mm (8-inch) extension in the wheelbase. The frame was also modified to accept the new air suspension arrangement including mounting points for the air reservoir.

ENGINE

The V8 engine was increased in capacity to offer a 4.2-litre variant. The 300 Tdi 2.5-litre direct injection, turbocharged, intercooled diesel engine replaced the bought-out VM unit.

SUSPENSION

An electronically-controlled air suspension system was offered as an option and was standard on the Vogue SE and Vogue LSE. In this system, air springs replaced the coils. They were fed by a compressor which pressurised the system via an air reservoir mounted to the chassis. The springs were then supplied with air through an electronically-controlled manifold. The system provided three automatic modes – standard ride height, low profile (20mm [0.78in] less than standard) adopted at over 80 kph (50 mph) to reduce drag, and extended profile adopted to prevent grounding out when off road. The driver could select high profile (40mm [1.58in] greater than standard) to increase ground clearance travelling off road or access mode (60mm [2.36in] less than standard) to ease entering and leaving the vehicle. He or she could also override the low profile setting.

WHEELS AND TYRES

New styles of alloy wheels were introduced.

BRAKING AND TRACTION CONTROL SYSTEM

The WABCO ABS system was enhanced to provide Electronic Traction Control (ETC) on the rear wheels only.

STEERING

For the Range Rover Classic, the steering wheel was re-designed with four spokes and incorporated a driver's air bag. The steering column was also revised to allow rake adjustment. These changes

The biggest change for the new model was a new fascia incorporating a passenger airbag and new instrument cluster. The new fascia shared its sub-structure with the 1995 model year Discovery and the cancelled 'Challenger' project for a new Defender. The steering wheel, now adjustable, also came from Discovery

Range Rover - The Anniversary Guide

Technical Description

were common with the Discovery and based on the Rover 800 (R17) design.

BODY

The body was modified to incorporate the changes necessary to accommodate the increase in wheelbase. These were chiefly confined to a revised, larger rear door. Side impact door beams were also added.

SEATING AND TRIM

The rear door trim panel was revised to fit the new rear side door on the LSE model.

FASCIA, INSTRUMENTS AND EQUIPMENT

A new one-piece fascia was installed on the Range Rover Classic. Using a common armature with the 1995 model year Discovery and the later-to-be-cancelled 'Defender II' (Challenger) programme, the Range Rover had a unique UEV covering to distinguish it. The fascia was designed to accommodate a passenger airbag to supplement the steering wheel-mounted driver's air bag and also included protective knee bolsters on the glove box lid and on the driver's lower panel. It featured a new integral instrument binnacle with revised instruments, again common with 1995 model year Discovery. The centre panel included mountings for the radio, rotary heater controls, clock and auxiliary switch panel. There was also a 'pop-out' cup holder and a pull out ashtray.

The centre console was modified to suit the new fascia with revised gearbox and transfer box controls, handbrake and centre cubby box.

HEATING AND VENTILATION

A new heater and air conditioning unit was installed using CFC-free refrigerant in the air-conditioning system.

The shape of the Range Rover was now iconic to the extent that Land Rover was reluctant to part with it, keeping the vehicle in production alongside the New Range Rover

Range Rover First Generation — Phase Four — Technical Data

Specification Sheets

GENERAL FEATURES

CONSTRUCTION
Four-door, five seat frame and panel body on separate steel chassis. Extended wheelbase (LSE)

POWER UNITS
4.2-litre all-alloy V8 petrol, 2.5-litre direct injection diesel

TRANSMISSION
Permanent four wheel drive. Four-speed automatic (petrol) or five-speed manual (diesel) gearbox. Two-speed transfer box with lockable centre differential. Single reduction beam axles

SUSPENSION
Electronically-controlled variable height air suspension (std on LSE). Long travel coil springs and hydraulic dampers. Ride levelling unit at rear (diesel) Cast radius arms with Panhard rod at front, radius arms with A-frame at rear

STEERING
Recirculating ball with hydraulic damper

BRAKING
Disc brakes all-round with dual-line hydraulic system. Transmission-mounted drum park brake

OTHER FEATURES
Electonic Traction Control (ETC) on rear wheels. New fascia with twin airbags from 1994 (1995 model year)

	UNITS	RANGE ROVER LSE 4.2-LITRE FOUR-SPEED AUTOMATIC	RANGE ROVER 2.5-LITRE TDI DIESEL MANUAL
Vehicle Type		Four-door Station Wagon	Four-door Station Wagon
Construction		Separate chassis, panel-on-frame body	Separate chassis, panel-on-frame body
Number of Passengers		5	5
DIMENSIONS			
Overall Length	mm(in)	4648(183.00)	4470(176)
Overall Width (over mirrors)	mm(in)	1778(70.00)	1778(70)
Overall Height (nominal)	mm(in)	1835(72.24)	1778(70)
Wheelbase	mm(in)	2743(108.00)	2540(100)
Track Front/Rear	mm(in)	1486(58.50)	1485(58.5)
Luggage Capacity (Seat Up)	l(cu in)	1050(37.08)	1050(37.08)
Luggage Capacity (Seat Folded)	l(cu in)	2075(73.28)	2075(73.28)
WEIGHTS			
Kerb Weight (EEC)	kg(lb)	2195(4839)	2110(4652)
Gross Vehicle Weight	kg(lb)	2620(5776)	2620(5776)
Front Axle Maximum Weight	kg(lb)	1200(2646)	1200(2646)
Rear Axle Maximum Weight	kg(lb)	1620(3572)	1620(3572)
Maximum Payload	kg(lb)	425(937)	510(1124)
Maximum On Road Trailer Weight	kg(lb)	2000(4408) with over-run brakes, 4000(8816) four-wheel trailer with power brakes	
Maximum Off Road Trailer Weight	kg(lb)	1000(2204)	1000(2204)
CAPABILITIES			
Drag Coefficient	Cd	0.45	0.45
Approach Angle (Maximum)	Deg	43 (high profile, bib spoiler removed)	40 (bib spoiler removed)
Under Body (Ramp) Angle (Maximum)	Deg	150 (high profile)	151
Departure Angle (Maximum)	Deg	33 (high profile)	30
Turning Circle (Kerb to kerb)	m(ft)	13.64(44.75)	11.89(39.00)
PERFORMANCE			
Maximum Speed	kp/h(mph)	177(110)	149(93)
Acceleration 0 - 100 kp/h (tested)	secs	10.8	17.7
Acceleration 0 - 60 mph (tested)	secs	13.9	16.6

Specification Sheets

	UNITS	RANGE ROVER LSE 4.2-LITRE FOUR-SPEED AUTOMATIC	RANGE ROVER 2.5-LITRE TDI DIESEL MANUAL
FUEL CONSUMPTION			
Urban	l/100km (mpg)	21.6(13.1)	8.57(32.9)
Constant 56 mph	l/100km (mpg)	11.7(24.2)	6.88(41.0)
Constant 75 mph	l/100km (mpg)	18.7(15.1)	6.69(29.1)
ENGINE			
Type		V8	Four-Cylinder
Position in Vehicle		Front, in-line	Front, in-line
Fuel		Petrol (gasoline)	Diesel
Number of Cylinders		8	4
Number of Camshafts		1	1
Valves per Cylinder		2	2
Valve System		Overhead rockers, hydraulic tappets	Pushrod operated overhead valves
Bore	mm(in)	94.0(3.70)	90.5(3.56)
Stroke	mm(in)	77.0(3.03)	97.0(3.82)
Capacity	cc(cu in)	4278(261)	2495(152)
Compression Ratio	:1	8.9	19.5
Cylinder Head Material		Aluminium alloy	Aluminium alloy
Cylinder Block Material		Aluminium alloy	Cast iron
Crankshaft Bearings		5	5
Lubrication System		Crankshaft driven oil pump with full-flow filter	Gear-driven oil pump with full-flow filter
Fuelling		Lucas L-Jetronic fuel injection	Direct injection, Bosch VE4/11F pump
Fuel System		Electic lift pump	Mechanical fuel pump
Ignition System		Lucas electronic distributor with amplifier	N/A
Boost System		None	Garrett turbocharger integral wastegate and intercooler
Cold Start System		Automatic via ECU	Automatic heater plugs
Air Cleaning System		Paper element	Paper element
Cooling System		Pressurised with expansion tank and crossflow radiator	Pressurised with expansion tank and crossflow radiator
Battery Capacity	Amp/hr	60	60
Max Power	kW(bhp)	149(200)	83(111)
At	rpm	4850	4000
Max Torque	Nm(lb/ft)	339(250)	265(195)
At	rpm	3250	1800
CAPACITIES			
Engine Oil Sump inc filter	l(Imp Gall) [US Gall]	6.6(1.45)[1.74]	7.0(1.54)[1.85]
Cooling Circuit	l(Imp Gall) [US Gall]	11.4(2.51)[3.01]	11.4(2.51)[3.01]
Fuel Tank (Maximum Usable)	l(Imp Gall) [US Gall]	89(19.5)[23.0]	89(19.5)[23.0]
TRANSMISSION			
Type		Permanent four-wheel drive	Permanent four-wheel drive
Flywheel		Torque converter	Cast iron, toothed
Clutch Type		N/A	Diaphragm spring, single dry plate
Clutch Diameter	mm(in)	N/A	267(10.5)
Gearbox Type		Automatic ZF4HP22	Manual
Number of Forward Gears		4	5

Range Rover - The Anniversary Guide

Range Rover First Generation — Phase Four — Technical Data

Specification Sheets

	UNITS	RANGE ROVER LSE 4.2-LITRE FOUR-SPEED AUTOMATIC	RANGE ROVER 2.5-LITRE TDI DIESEL MANUAL
Selection Mechanism		Console mounted selector	Lever
Transfer Box Type		Chain driven	Chain driven
Number of Ratios		2	2
Selection Mechanism		Lever	Lever
Slip Control System		Viscous coupled automatic centre differential	Viscous coupled automatic centre differential
Front Prop Shaft Type		Open with universal joints and sliding joint with gaiter	Open with universal joints and sliding joint with gaiter
Rear Prop Shaft Type		Open with universal joints. Rear rubber coupling on late models	Open with universal joints. Rear rubber coupling on late models
Front Axle Type		Rover beam axle with swivel pins and 2-pinion differential	Rover beam axle with swivel pins and 2-pinion differential
Rear Axle Type		Rover beam axle with 2-pinion differential	Rover beam axle with 2-pinion differential
Wheel Type		Styled cast alloy	Styled cast alloy, J-type rim
Wheel Size - Standard	mm(in)	16(406)	16(406)
Tyre Size - Standard		Michelin XM+S radial 205x16	Michelin XM+S radial 205x16
RATIOS			
1st Gear Ratio	:1	2.480	3.692
2nd Gear Ratio	:1	1.480	2.132
3rd Gear Ratio	:1	1.000	1.397
4th Gear Ratio	:1	0.728	1.000
5th Gear Ratio	:1	N/A	0.770
Reverse Gear	:1	2.086	3.429
High Range Ratio	:1	1.206	1.206
Low Range Ratio	:1	3.244	3.244
Front Axle Ratio	:1	3.540	3.540
Rear Axle Ratio	:1	3.540	3.540
1st Gear Ratio Overall High Range	:1	10.588	15.762
2nd Gear Ratio Overall High Range	:1	6.318	9.102
3rd Gear Ratio Overall High Range	:1	4.269	5.964
4th Gear Ratio Overall High Range	:1	3.108	4.269
5th Gear Ratio Overall High Range	:1	N/A	3.287
Reverse Gear Overall High Range	:1	8.980	14.639
1st Gear Ratio Overall Low Range	:1	28.480	42.398
2nd Gear Ratio Overall Low Range	:1	16.996	24.483
3rd Gear Ratio Overall Low Range	:1	11.483	16.043
4th Gear Ratio Overall Low Range	:1	8.360	11.484
5th Gear Ratio Overall Low Range	:1	N/A	8.842
Reverse Gear Overall Low Range	:1	23.955	39.378
SUSPENSION			
Front Suspension Type		Beam axle, radius arms, Panhard rod and anti-roll bar	Beam axle, radius arms, Panhard rod and anti-roll bar
Rear Suspension Type		Beam axle, radius arms, support rods and anti-roll bar	Beam axle, radius arms, support rods, centre wishbone and anti-roll bar
Front Springs		Air	Coil
Rear Springs		Air	Coil
Front Dampers		Long-stroke hydraulic telescopic dampers	Long-stroke hydraulic telescopic dampers
Rear Dampers		Long-stroke hydraulic telescopic dampers	Long-stroke hydraulic telescopic dampers
Ride Levelling		Automatic via electonically-controlled air springs	Boge Hydromat self-energising located on rear centre wishbone

Range Rover - The Anniversary Guide

Specification Sheets

	UNITS	RANGE ROVER LSE 4.2-LITRE FOUR-SPEED AUTOMATIC	RANGE ROVER 2.5-LITRE TDI DIESEL MANUAL
Anti Roll Bar Diameter Front	mm(in)	24(0.95)	24(0.95)
Anti Roll Bar Diameter Rear	mm(in)	18.5(0.73)	18.5(0.73)
STEERING			
Type		Recirculating ball, worm and nut with collapsible column	Recirculating ball, worm and nut with collapsible column
Assistance		Hydraulic power from engine driven pump	Hydraulic power from engine driven pump
Number of Turns Lock to Lock		3.8	3.8
BRAKES			
Type		Dual-line, servo assisted with ABS	Dual-line, servo assisted
Front Disc Type		Ventilated	Ventilated
Front Disc Diameter	mm(in)	298.5(11.75)	298.5(11.75)
Rear Disc Type		Solid	Solid
Rear Disc Diameter	mm(in)	290.0(11.42)	290.0(11.42)
Park Brake Type		Internal expanding drum mounted on transmission	Internal expanding drum mounted on transmission
TECHNOLOGIES			
Dual Line Braking System		Yes	Yes
Anti Lock Braking System (ABS)		Yes	Optional
Electronic Traction Control (ETC)		Yes (rear only)	No
Electronic Brakeforce Distribution (EBD)		No	No
Emergency Brake Assist (EBA)		No	No
Dynamic Stability Control (DSC)		No	No
Hill Descent Control (HDC)		No	No
Terrain Response™		No	No

NOTES

Data acquired from the best available sources but the publisher is not liable for any mistakes or omissions. Readers are advised to consult other sources e.g. manufacturer's workshop manuals before working on vehicles. The publication of performance and capability figures does not imply that this will be achieved in practice. Caution must be exercised in all driving activities especially off-road.
Units are expressed in the relevant international standard (SI). Where appropriate recognised conversion factors have been applied.

Range Rover - The Anniversary Guide

Range Rover First Generation — Phase Four — Technical Data

Price List

PRICE LIST (UK)

DATE	MODEL	PRICE	NOTES
		£ Inc Car Tax and VAT	
1992	Range Rover Vogue Manual	26,783	
	Range Rover Vogue Auto	27,839	
	Range Rover Vogue SE	35,419	
	Range Rover Vogue LSE	38,393	
OPTIONS			
	Air Conditioning	1567	Standard on Vogue SE and Vogue LSE
	Electronic Air Suspension	1344	Standard on Vogue SE and Vogue LSE
	Anti-lock braking system	1238	Standard on Vogue SE and Vogue LSE
	CD Autochanger	1008	Vogue only. Included additional door speakers
	CD Autochanger	671	Vogue SE and Vogue LSE only
	Cruise Control	312	Standard Vogue SE and Vogue LSE
	Electronic Traction Control	480	Available only with Anti-Lock braking. Standard Vogue SE and Vogue LSE
	Heated windscreen	152	Standard on Vogue SE and Vogue LSE
	Heated Front Seats	322	Standard on Vogue SE and Vogue LSE
	Connolly Leather Upholstery	1291	Standard on Vogue SE and Vogue LSE
	Front Mudflaps	35	
	Electric Sun Roof	990	Standard on Vogue SE and Vogue LSE
	Towing Pack	128	

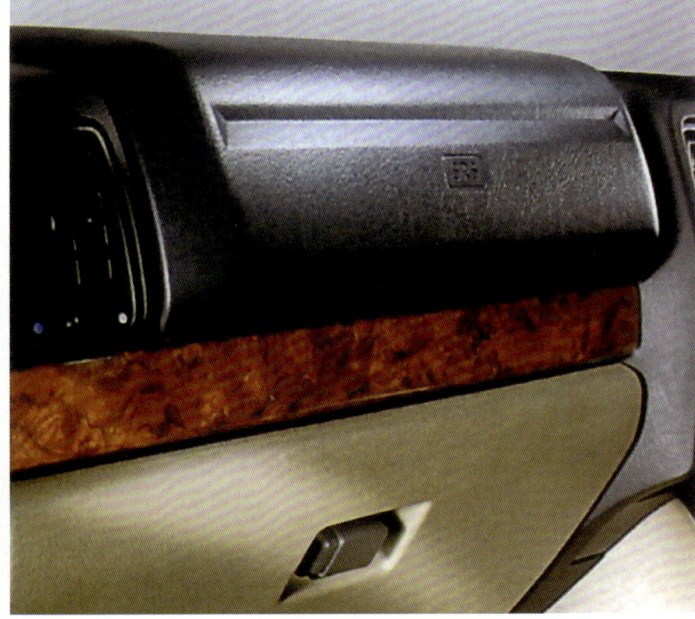

Range Rover - The Anniversary Guide

Range Rover - The Anniversary Guide

Range Rover First Generation — Phase Four — Advertising

The British really know how to live.

What accessories could possibly further the lifestyle of those already draped in impeccably distinguished everything?

Dual airbags.

Granted, they don't come with a guarantee, but they do come within the polished armor of Land Rover's new Range Rover.

The first 4x4 ever to have them. With permanent four-wheel drive, ABS, plus side door beams, an immense chassis, and steel inner body cage, every passenger, aristocrat or not, is truly well-off.

Especially sitting in its posh and genteel interior, now even more resplendidly appointed than ever.

And whether going from the muddy grounds of a polo match to tea at the Ritz, or jaunting up to the Cotswalds, via mettled roads that wind, curl, and bump over the English countryside, a Range Rover's electronic air suspension always provides a smooth and secure ride.

Even when it's not pouring rain.

Why not call 1-800-FINE 4WD for the nearest dealer? Of course, at just under $53,000,* it's a significant investment. But what can we say?

Long live the Queen.

LAND ROVER — RANGE ROVER

American advertising made much of the twin air bag installation on the 1995 model year Classic Range Rover, pointing out that it was the first such system employed on a 4x4. The system had undergone brutal 'abuse testing' on the Discovery to ensure that violent off-road manoeuvres didn't cause accidental deployment

Advertising & Brochures

With Electronic Air Suspension, Electronic Traction Control and viscous centre differential, the off-road performance of the Classic Range Rover was impressive

The new traction systems and ABS brakes helped in snow too – especially valuable as many Range Rover customers were fond of skiing. With only two seven-inch round headlamps, auxiliary driving lamps were a popular accessory

Range Rover - The Anniversary Guide

| Range Rover First Generation | Phase Four | Advertising |

Advertising & Brochures

The First Generation Range Rover survived the launch of the New Range Rover, becoming the 'Classic Range Rover'. Late model US vehicles featured chrome bumpers and bright finish 'Cyclone' wheels

Land Rover of North America publicised the 'Tread Lightly' programme extensively in the USA, although Range Rover imagery heavily promoted the joys of hunting, shooting and fishing

The last phase of the First Generation of Range Rovers featured twin front air bags sharing the basic fascia structure of the Discovery. In a 'first' for an SUV, extreme 'abuse' testing was done to negate the possibility of accidental deployment off-road

Despite being a highly-specified luxury vehicle, the late model Range Rover was a fully capable off-roader with Electronic Traction Control and a viscous-coupling centre differential

Range Rover - The Anniversary Guide

Geoffrey Parker
The ultimate in luxury gaming

Play the high-life with our *Billionaire* edition Monopoly®

Makers of the World's finest games and gifts

GEOFFREY PARKER GAMES LTD • WIMBISH VILLAGE
SAFFRON WALDEN • ESSEX • CB10 2XJ • UK
Tel +44 (0) 1799 599 100 • Fax: +44 (0) 1799 599 733
e-mail: bespoke@geoffreyparker.com • www.geoffreyparker.com

www.geoffreyparker.com
UNIQUE PIECES Since 1958

1958 - 2008 Geoffrey Parker CELEBRATING 50 YEARS OF EXCELLENCE

For life in the fast-lane, our *Super-car* leather *Tournament* Backgammon is a must!

LAND ROVER SCRAPBOOK

Written to coincide with the 60th anniversary of Land Rover, this most British of all icons is put under the microscope. Company insider, Mike Gould, leads the reader on a fascinating journey through the highs, the lows, the designs and the decisions that put the Solihull firm on the map! Over 500 fabulous illustrations help set the scene.

- The great Land Rover story in a very different style
- A history in which the vehicles take centre stage, including
    Land Rover, Defender, Range Rover, Discovery,
    Freelander, Range Rover Sport
- Foreword by Bob Dover, first CEO under Ford
- Presenting rare and unseen images and documents
- Secret projects and their code names revealed
- Stylists' own sketches, plus rarely glimpsed mock-ups and models
- 'Dip-in, dip-out' or read from cover to cover
- Restored vehicles section
- Packed with intriguing detail, stunning
    images and fascinating revelations

The Land Rover Scrapbook:
Standard Edition, 161 pages,
300x350mm (12"x14"), hardback.
The Land Rover Scrapbook:
De-Luxe Limited Edition - individually numbered, leather-bound book & slipcase.
Signed by Mike Gould and Bob Dover.

info & order direct from: www.porterpress.co.uk
+44 (0)1584 781 588   info@porterpress.co.uk

Range Rover - The Anniversary Guide

Range Rover - Second Generation

A Brief History

The story of the vehicles that make up the history of the British motor industry has been inextricably linked with politics and the relationship of successive British governments with manufacturing in general and the motor industry in particular. The history of the Second Generation Range Rover is no exception and may even have been one of those vehicles most affected.

The arrival of Tony Gilroy as Land Rover Limited's Managing Director led to a strategy of concentrating on new markets and sectors focussed on the Range Rover platform. During the latter half of the 1980s the main thrust of Land Rover's engineering effort was on improving the basic platform to enable it to compete in demanding markets such as North America, but also as a foundation for Project Jay (the Discovery) and, later, for a Defender replacement – the stillborn Project Challenger.

When the major development work on Project Jay was completed and the vehicle entered the production engineering phase, Land Rover management attention turned to a replacement for the Range Rover itself – a project initially codenamed Discovery, then Pegasus, as the original name was applied to Project Jay at its public launch.

This was a fraught period for Land Rover. The Conservative Government under Margaret Thatcher was desperate to rid itself of British Leyland, so long the epitome of poor management, inefficiency and waste – although most of this applied to Austin Rover rather than the Land Rover operation. Ford was being encouraged to take over Austin Rover but the General Motors bid for Land Rover was a much more

Range Rover Second Generation

likely deal. This move was skilfully fought off by Tony Gilroy who, with a consortium of senior managers and financiers, aimed to take over the company himself. Reeling from the fallout caused by the sale of Westland Helicopters, Thatcher was, for political reasons, opposed to the sale of another high-profile British company to the Americans, but there was also the fear that the sale of Land Rover separately would leave the Government saddled with Austin Rover. So, in 1988, in a sudden and surprising move, it sold BL – as the company was now known - to British Aerospace (BAe). This led to Gilroy's departure, his place being taken by George Simpson.

Against this turbulent background, plans for the new Range Rover went ahead. The vehicle was intended to be a genuine competitor for luxury cars such as the Mercedes S-Type as well as being a fully capable off-road machine worthy of the Land Rover badge it would bear. It would incorporate the new Electronic Air Suspension (EAS), a system developed on the last First Generation models. It would also have the 108-inch wheelbase of the LSE variant of the Range Rover. Although planned for launch in 1991, problems with developing the air suspension system led to a full 12-month postponement of this feature's launch. It eventually appeared early in 1992.

The new vehicle, now known as P38A at the project team's location at Solihull (following fears that the

(Top) While some of the themes for the Second Generation Range Rover – known at various stages of its life as project Discovery, Pegasus and P38A – were very futuristic, the design soon settled down to a more recognisable Range Rover complete with clamshell bonnet and 'floating' roof. An advanced styling property is shown ready for a viewing by Land Rover Managing Director, John Towers, in the 'Styling Garden' at the design studio, then located at the Triumph plant at Coventry. (Right) The rendering shows the familiar design of the eventual production vehicle

A Brief History

Project Pegasus name had been compromised) would have a separate chassis – albeit of advanced design - but the body would be an integrated design rather than the frame and panel construction of its predecessor. Use of Land Rover's trademark aluminium would be maximised. Power would come from up-rated versions of the venerable V8 alloy engine with a six-cylinder diesel supplied by BMW.

Designs were commissioned from a number of in-house teams and, when none of these appealed, from Italian designers, Bertone. Some of the themes were advanced, monobox styles, but eventually one of the more conventional Solihull designs by George Thomson won through. The interior was much more akin to that of a luxury saloon rather than a 4 x 4 with the design team coming up with the innovative 'H-Gate' automatic gearbox shift to eliminate the clutter of an additional transfer box control. With the H-Gate, the gear lever was moved across to select low range, the actual gear selector fork being moved by an electric motor. On the manual version, a simple fascia-mounted switch effected the change. The need for a differential lock was eliminated by specifying the same, chain-driven, transfer box with a viscous-coupled differential as on later versions of the previous model.

P38A had a complex electrical system intended to provide the driver with a mass of information and incorporating a central computer, dubbed the Body Electronic Control Module (BeCM). In an age where TV programmes were nightly filled with scenes of stolen cars being 'displayed' by miscreants, the security system was also extremely sophisticated, using a multi-function remote control and requiring a special 'Emergency Key Access' (EKA) to be employed in case of problems with the remote.

The development period of the P38A took place over the same timescale as BAe's ownership of Rover Group, as the now fully-integrated company was known. As the launch date of the vehicle approached, the company was acquired by BMW – the German company having been especially impressed by Land Rover's forward model programme during negotiations for the use of its diesel engine in the P38A.

As the launch approached, Land Rover decided to keep the old model in production concurrently with the new vehicle. This move was motivated by the fact that, after nearly a quarter of a century of production, the Range Rover had a considerable loyal following. It was not unusual for some customers to have bought a succession of vehicles, sometimes

The New Range Rover was launched at Cliveden, once the seat of the Astor family and famous for its role in the Profumo Affair. By 1994, it was a luxury hotel. The model was launched in 4.6 HSE, 4.0 SE, 2.5DT and 2.5DSE variants

Range Rover - The Anniversary Guide

Range Rover Second Generation

headed up Ford's Premier Automotive Group (PAG) since being ousted from BMW in an earlier boardroom shake-up, he was now re-united with his project for a completely new vehicle, now coded L322 under the Ford naming system.

With the new vehicle slated for a 2002 launch, it was nearly the end of the road for the New Range Rover. However, there was nearly a last minute reprieve. The new vehicle was considerably larger and consequently much more expensive than its predecessor so the possibility of continuing with the New Range Rover was examined. It would be re-engineered to a lower specification, including a coil spring suspension, and offered in a restricted model range. However, in America, it was feared that this would undermine the residual values of the new model which would affect lease rates, a vital factor in the US car market. So the project was abandoned. However, the study did reveal the potential of the Range Rover brand that the L322's move upmarket opened up. This eventually led to the Range Rover Sport which shared the T5 platform with the Discovery 3 – the

Although known everywhere by its project code name, P38A, Ford policy dictated that the last production example would drive off the line under a 'Second Generation' banner. John Hall is in the driving seat with Spen King, 'father' of the Range Rover alongside him

Range Rover - The Anniversary Guide

A Brief History

Range Rover Sport became the most successful Land Rover model ever.

By December 2001 it was literally the end of the line for the New Range Rover. Under the Ford policy of not revealing model code names, it was called 'The Second Generation Range Rover' in the press release announcing the build of the last vehicle at Solihull – the sign announcing its arrival at the end of the track having to be quickly repainted from reading, "The Last P38A Range Rover". The final example was handed over to the Heritage Motor Centre but was not there long – it was not sufficiently highly regarded to survive a clearing out exercise and was sold off the following year.

While its time in production had been exceptionally short in Land Rover terms, the Second Generation Range Rover was far from being a failure. In eight years of production, over 167,000 vehicles had been built, peaking at over 30,000 units per year – something never approached by its predecessor.

While it never gained the accolades showered on its predecessor, the Second Generation Range Rover redefined the luxury 4 x 4 sector

Range Rover - The Anniversary Guide

Range Rover Second Generation

Styling Concepts

(Top) In the 1980s, Land Rover acquired a Renault Espace for evaluation and this influenced several projects at the time. While the Espace's construction method was used for the cab of the ill-fated Llama forward control, the smooth, monobox lines inspired some early themes for a new Range Rover, then code-named Project Discovery. (Above) George Thompson's design of early 1988 had an unusually low waistline, even for a Land Rover, while Mike Sampson's rendering (right) has more familiar Range Rover lines

Range Rover - The Anniversary Guide

Styling Concepts

A new perspective of an early theme for Project Discovery (top) shows the innovative arrangement of the side opening windows together with a full-length glass roof – a feature that would appear much later on the Range Stormer concept car and on the Discovery 3 and Freelander 2 in production vehicles. Land Rover commissioned Bertone to prepare a design for the new Range Rover shown here as 'Theme A' photographed in the garden adjacent to Block P38A at Solihull which later gave the project its name. 'Theme B' was by Solihull designer, George Thompson, and was eventually chosen for development into the final vehicle. A further design by Mike Sampson, featuring a stepped waistline, also made it to theme selection. Both Sampson's and the Bertone design were felt to be too delicate for a vehicle like the Range Rover

Range Rover - The Anniversary Guide

83

Range Rover Second Generation | Phase One

Range Rover Walkaround

This late model Second Generation Range Rover, owned by the Home of The Legend centre at the Solihull factory is a rare example of a limited edition originally produced for the Japanese market

Seen from head on, the Second Generation Range Rover reveals some of the design cues of the original vehicle such as the clamshell bonnet and deep windscreen

As part of the minor facelift of 1999, the headlamp units received a black-out treatment to replicate the round lights of the first Range Rover

84

Range Rover - The Anniversary Guide

The bars of the radiator grille were part of the bold horizontal style lines that continued around the vehicle. The Rover oval 'Jewel' badge had been fitted to the company's vehicles since the launch of the Discovery in 1989

Interior door handles were finished in high-quality chrome plating. A red reflector warned other drivers that the rear door was open

'Comet' six-spoke 18-inch wheels were standard on Vogue and Vogue SE models

 door trims remained effectively unchanged for the short pro tion life of the vehicle. Contrasting leather armrests and special veneers were originally part of the Autobiography programme the features were used extensively on limited editions

Range Rover - The Anniversary Guide

Range Rover Second Generation | Phase One

Range Rover Walkaround

A leather covered handbrake grip and gear lever knob raised the luxury feel of the vehicle compared with the moulded plastic of early vehicles

Often unfairly compared to the rear profile of a London taxi, the Second Generation Range Rover was a distinctive vehicle from behind. Most later models had body coloured bumpers, again originally an Autobiography feature

Light walnut veneer adds a distinctive touch to the complex 'centre stack' of the Solihull vehicle

The centre console lid flipped over to convert it into a multiple cup holder

86   Range Rover - The Anniversary Guide

Paired ventilator outlets in the centre fascia provided ample fresh air. The oddment tray was strangely offset from the centre line

The two tone leather steering wheel was part of this limited edition and also available under the Autobiography scheme

e Second Generation nge Rover echoed e 'floating roof' of the ginal model with blacked t door pillars and a black yl-covered 'E' post

The spare wheel cover in the boot was supported by a strut while the wheel rested on a harness to ease its extraction from the well

The loadspace area was massive and versatile thanks to the split folding rear seats

Range Rover - The Anniversary Guide

Range Rover Second Generation | Phase One

Range Rover Walkaround

The glove box was quite shallow and prone to rattles thanks to a complicated method of adjustment

The seats went through several variations of stitch patterns during the model's life but were always comfortable and supportive

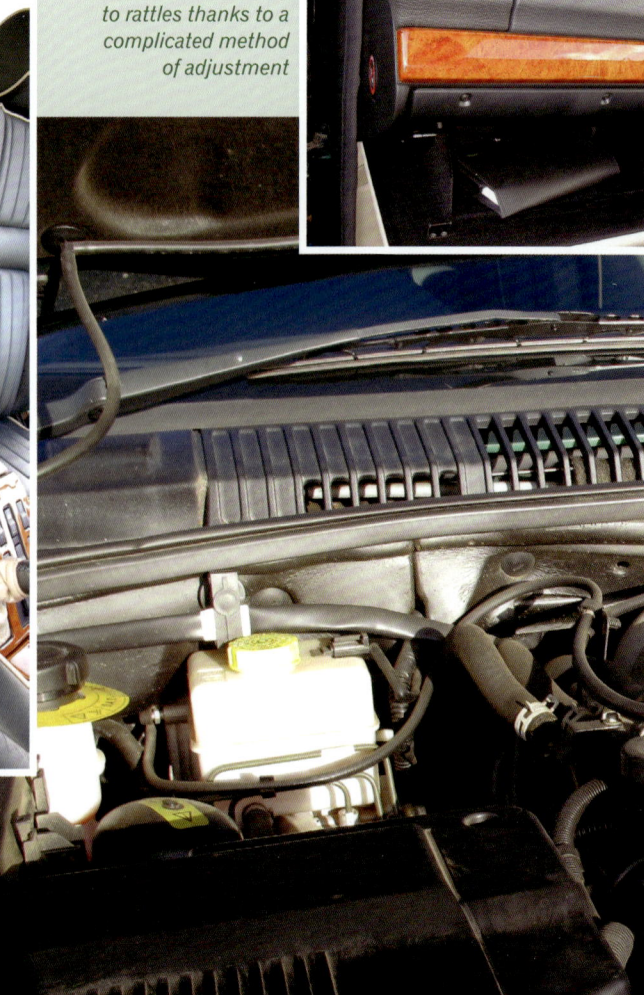

The rear seat centre armrest concealed twin retractable cup holders

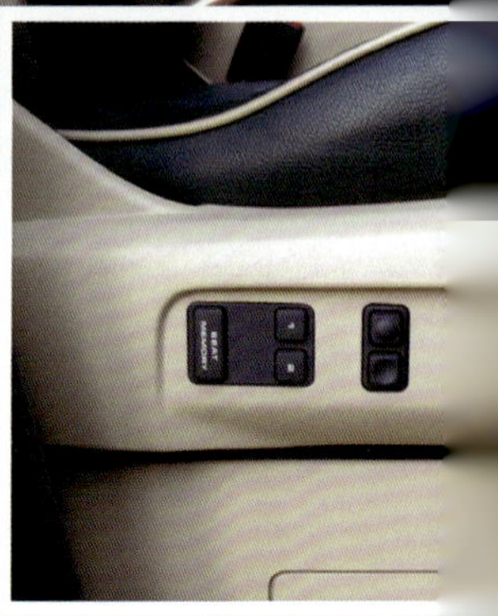

Range Rover - The Anniversary Guide

The Electronic Air Suspension (EAS) system had its own control module housed in the engine bay

The changes made to the 'Thor' V8 changed the under bonnet appearance drastically

This post-1999 model year vehicle has the revised V8 engine known as 'Thor'. Upgrades included a revised inlet tract arrangement to give more torque and a revised fuel injection system – changes which didn't need the earlier and distinctive cast alloy plenum

The sophisticated electrical system was protected by a large number of fuses, some of which were housed under the bonnet. Behind the fuse box are the cooling system header tank and the ABS module

The seat fitted on Vogue and Vogue SE models had a wide range of electric adjustment as well as memory positions that also altered the exterior mirrors to suit individual drivers

Range Rover - The Anniversary Guide

Range Rover Second Generation — Phase One

Technical Description

CHASSIS

Shaped ladder-frame chassis with a wider middle section and tapered front section for improved turning circle. Construction was of box section using micro-alloy steel of varying thickness (up to 4mm) to optimise weight, strength and torsional rigidity. The chassis featured collapsible 'crush cans' front and rear to absorb impact loads and reduce repair costs in the event of minor collision. Integral towers and mountings for suspension. Fully treated and painted to resist corrosion.

ENGINE

Three engine options were offered – 4.0-litre and 4.6-litre petrol and a 2.5-litre diesel.

The petrol engines were based on the long-standing V8 all-alloy engine, which was now a Land Rover design responsibility, but were heavily revised with a new stiffer block, lighter pistons and individually-balanced conrods to improve refinement. The ancillaries were driven by a new polyvee belt which reduced engine length, enabling it to be positioned further forward in the chassis. Camshaft profiles were also revised and a new Lucas GEMS electronic ignition system specified. The 4.6-litre version had a longer stroke with a different crankshaft and larger-diameter main and big end bearings.

The diesel engine was a bought-out six-cylinder unit from BMW. Block construction was of cast iron while the cylinder head was of aluminium. The engine also featured a turbocharger and intercooler. The fuel system was of the indirect injection type fed by a fully electronic Bosch pump. Compared with the unit normally fitted to BMW cars, the Range Rover application had reduced power but improved torque delivery and was modified to enable running at angles likely to be experienced off-road.

TRANSMISSION

Both 5-speed manual and 4-speed automatic gearboxes were offered but their availability differed across the model range. The 4.0-litre V8 was available with manual transmission and with an automatic gearbox while the 4.6-litre V8 was offered only with the automatic gearbox. The diesel was only available in manual form.

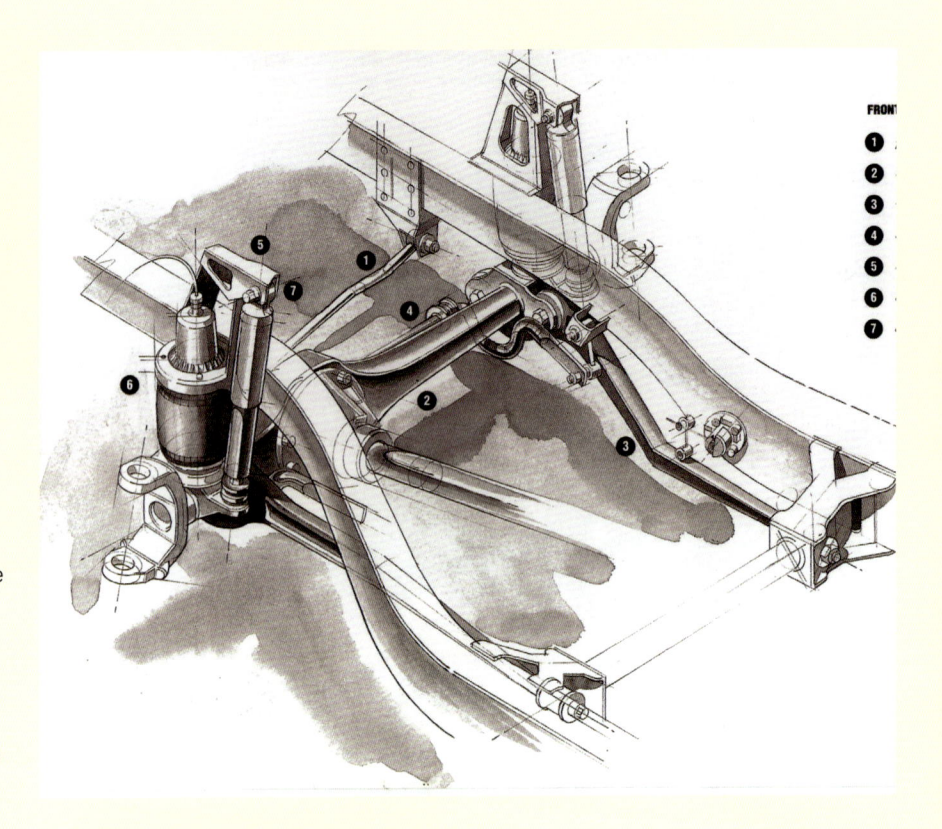

The manual gearbox was a development of Land Rover's R380 unit also used in the Discovery and the Defender although the gearbox specified with the diesel engine had a lower first gear ratio to compensate for the engine's torque delivery.

The automatic gearbox was sourced from ZF and was electronically-controlled to communicate with the engine to retard the ignition during gear changes to improve refinement.

The Borg-Warner two-speed chain drive transfer box provided permanent four-wheel drive with the slip between the axles controlled automatically by a viscous coupling. Speed changing was now achieved using an electric

The front suspension was designed to offer car-like handling attributes

motor. While on manual versions this was selected by a fascia-mounted switch, the automatic variants featured a new 'H-Gate' arrangement with the lever not only controlling the normal automatic gearbox modes but having the ability to change between high and low ranges in the neutral position. A 'Mode' switch allowed for the selection of a 'Sport' setting in high range or 'Manual' in low range which gave more control over gear selection.

Beam axles were fitted front and rear. Of a similar pressed-case with separate differential pinion housing design to other Land Rover axles, the front axle was new and had open steering joints to reduce cost and weight.

SUSPENSION

The only suspension offered was the new Electronic Air Suspension (EAS) system,

Technical Description

similar to, but an improvement on, that launched in the Range Rover Classic. It retained the five ride heights – Access, Low, Standard, High and Extended – but increased the options available to the driver and some of the height settings were revised. Operation was by a fascia-mounted rocker switch. During transition between heights a warning light built into the switch flashed, becoming steady when the height was established. Additional system information was also displayed on the Message Centre in the instrument cluster.

The Low height position was now 25mm (1 in) below the Standard ride height and was engaged automatically at speeds above 40 kp/h (25 mph) to improve stability and handling. It could now also be manually selected at any speed by the driver. Access mode was now 65mm (2.55 in) below Standard height and could be preselected before coming to a halt or for 40 seconds after engine switch off. The vehicle could also be manually held in Access height to enable the vehicle to be driven in restricted height areas although if speed exceeded 40 kp/h (25 mph), the vehicle would automatically rise to the Low position, returning to Access height once the speed dropped below 32 kp/h (20 mph).

The front suspension comprised the air springs, with the shock absorbers being mounted to their rear, attached to chassis-mounted towers. 'C-Spanner' type forward-facing forged radius arms mounted on rubber bushes located the axle assisted by a Panhard rod. There was also an anti-roll bar. At the rear, the shock absorbers were canted forwards of the air springs with location being by means of two lightweight composite radius arms and a Panhard rod. The radius arms were mounted using rubber bushes at the chassis end and sealed-for-life isolation rubbers at the axle. This arrangement negated the need for an anti-roll bar and allowed a measure of passive rear-end steering for improved handling. This also benefited from a reduction of the king pin offset on the front suspension geometry, a move that also improved the performance of the ABS braking system.

WHEELS AND TYRES

The wheels were cast alloy. Those specified for the 4.6 HSE were of a five-spoke design, 16 inches in diameter and eight inches in width. The tyres were of 255/65 R16 profile. The wheels for the 4.0 SE and 2.5 DSE were seven inches wide, of a five-hole design and fitted with 235/70 R16 tyres. The basic 4.0 and 2.5 DT models had three-spoke wheels of seven-inch width and were fitted with 235/70 R16 tyres. The wheels had a five-stud fixing and were offset to provide better front end suspension geometry.

BRAKING SYSTEM

Disc brakes were fitted all round, those at the front being ventilated. The front brakes also had larger calipers and braking effort was quoted as 67% front, 33% rear. The hydraulic system was dual line and featured four-channel ABS, the most advanced system on a four-wheel drive vehicle.

Electronic Traction Control (ETC) was fitted as standard on the 4.6 HSE and was optional on the other models. ETC acted on the rear wheels only, using the ABS sensors to detect a spinning wheel. A braking force was then applied to that wheel, encouraging torque transfer to the wheel with grip, to improve off-road capability.

STEERING

Steering was of the recirculating ball type with power assistance as standard on all models. The pump was engine-mounted and belt driven. The steering wheel was

The rear suspension featured innovative composite radius arms

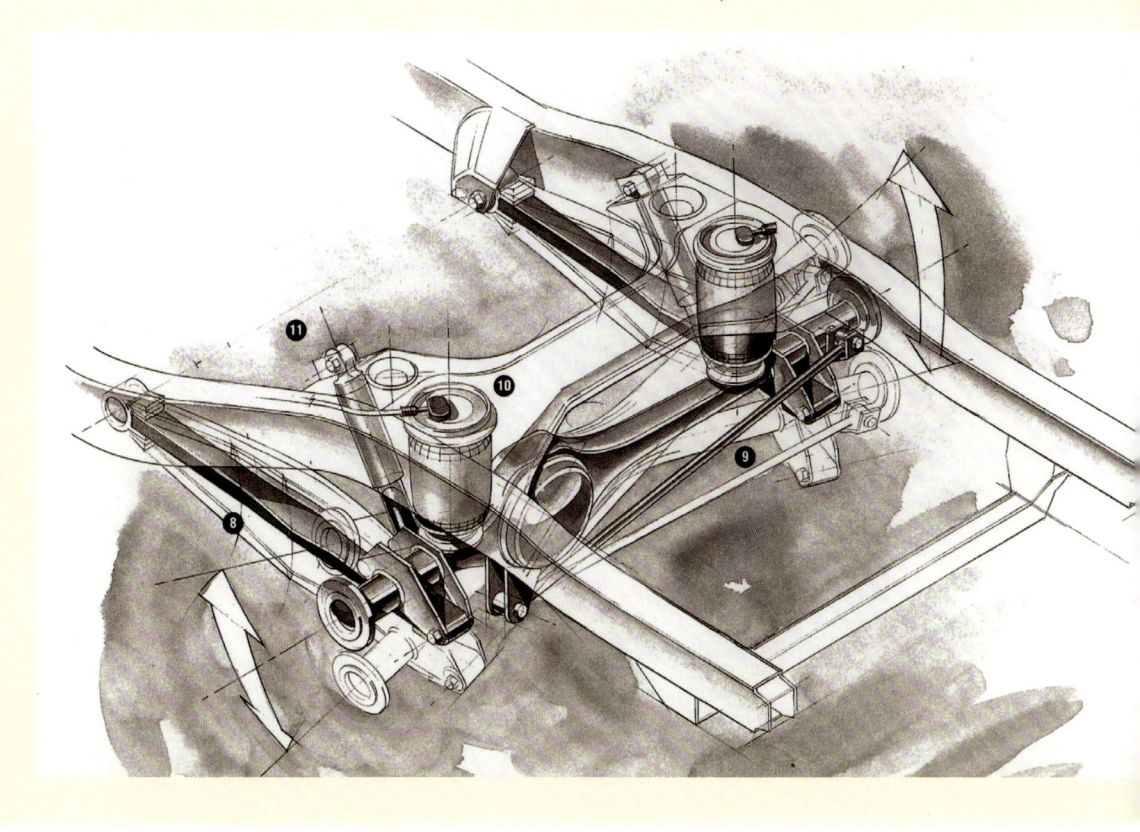

Range Rover - The Anniversary Guide

Technical Description

of a four-spoke design, incorporating a driver's air bag. It also housed switches to control the audio system and cruise control functions. The steering column was collapsible, and adjustable for reach and rake using a manually-operated lever.

The steering column housed twin stalks covering windscreen and rear tailgate wiper and washer functions as well as indicators and main beam operation. There was also a function to select information and settings within the Message Centre.

BODY

The body was of monocoque construction with structural panels pressed from double-sided zinc-coated steel to resist corrosion. The front wing outer panels, door skins and lower tailgate skin were in aluminium, the remaining skin panels being in double-sided zinc-coated steel. For ease of accident repair, the front wing panels and bonnet latching platform were bolt-on items, the remainder being designed for easy repair or replacement.

The glazing was semi-flush to improve airflow and hence refinement. The windscreen, rear quarter and tailgate glass was bonded to the structure to improve body stiffness and to improve airbag deployment performance. All door windows and the sun roof were electrically operated and included an 'anti-trap' function. The rear side windows incorporated screen-printed antennas for the radio system.

The body was constructed within the Body-In-White area at the Solihull factory from panels pressed at the Rover body plant at Swindon. Painting was done at the Solihull paint shop, specially re-furbished for the vehicle. Corrosion protection was achieved by an eight-stage zinc phosphate conversion process which was followed by PVC seam sealing and a primer coat applied using high voltage electrostatic equipment. Final colour coat was applied by the same method with an additional stone-chip resistant coating being added to vulnerable areas such as the sills.

The body was fitted to the chassis using compliant mounts to improve isolation from transmitted noise and vibration.

SEATING AND TRIM

The seats were of an all-new design to give improved lateral support and with longer cushions for thigh support. Both front seats were fitted with adjustable folding armrests. Another folding armrest was fitted for rear seat passengers. Adjustable head restraints were fitted to both front seats and to the outer rear seats.

HSE models were fitted with front seats having electrical operation of fore/aft adjustment, height, head restraint height, recline, front and rear tilt, and lumbar support. On the 4.6 HSE two individual seat settings (except for the lumbar support) could be stored in a memory along with the associated positions for the external mirrors and instrument panel dimmer settings. These settings could be recalled using a memory switch or, for the seat and mirror positions only, by the remote handset, two of which were supplied with the vehicle, each handset being

The monocoque body was constructed of galvanised steel while only the outer panels were pressed in Land Rover's signature aluminium

Technical Description

This ghosted cutaway illustration shows the complex construction of the New Range Rover

capable of individual programming.

On SE models, front seat adjustment was manual with a retractable, pump-action lever operating the height.

The rear seats had a deeper cushion for more thigh support and were wider than the previous model thanks to the lack of wheelarch intrusion afforded by the longer wheelbase. The rear seat had a 60/40 split to afford a versatile choice of loadspace/passenger accommodation and folded using a jack-knife system. The cushion incorporated the lower seat belt anchorages for outer and centre passengers with an interlock system preventing the back being raised unless the cushion was properly engaged. Outer passengers were provided with adjustable head restraints and there was a folding centre armrest.

The centre console blended into the fascia unit and was basically a plastic moulding with burr walnut trim. It housed a large ashtray with cigarette lighter and the main automatic gearbox 'H-Gate' control, the manual gear lever being encased in a leather gaiter. A cubby box was provided between the front seats and, on the 4.6 HSE, the lid was reversible to reveal four cup holders. The front face of the cubby box housed the window lift switches and controls for the sun roof when fitted. The handbrake lever was also mounted here, being trimmed with a leather gaiter. The rear face of the cubby box housed vents for the rear seat passengers with the trunking being incorporated into the centre console moulding. There was also a large ashtray and cigarette lighter.

The loadspace area was trimmed with fabric-covered boards to conceal the CD player and audio system bass woofer and

Range Rover - The Anniversary Guide

Technical Description

to provide access to the rear light bulbs. The loadspace cover was fabric-covered, resin-bonded board with moulded depressions for storage. It was foldable to ease access to the luggage area and could be stowed behind the rear seat.

There was a board in the loadspace floor to finish the compartment and to cover the spare wheel. It was provided with a strut to support it when open. Spare wheel extraction was aided by a strap to ease the wheel out of the compartment and onto the tailgate. The spare wheel compartment also housed a moulded tray for the vehicle tool kit.

Door trims were of foam-covered board with deep moulded pockets and plush inserts. The 4.6 HSE also had burr walnut inserts of wood veneer on an aluminium pressing to match the fascia. Puddle lamps were standard on

The fascia was much more car-like than earlier Range Rovers in an attempt to win customers from brands such as Jaguar and Mercedes

the front doors and also fitted to the rear doors of the 4.6 HSE. The 'D' post trim incorporated an adjustable mount for the rear seat outer passenger seat belt.

Roof trim was a fabric-covered one-piece moulding incorporating retractable grab handles, the volumetric alarm sensor and interior lights. A large glass tilt and slide, electrically-operated, sun roof with a retractable blind was available, being standard on the 4.6 HSE and optional on other models.

Technical Description

FASCIA AND INSTRUMENTS

The fascia was a large, full-width, foam-covered moulding handed for left- and right-hand drive and incorporating a passenger side airbag as standard. A removable trinket tray was mounted on its top face. A deep padded glove box was provided on the passenger side with a padded cover to make a knee bolster for impact zone protection of the driver's legs. The fascia also housed footwell illumination lamps.

The instrument pack included a rev. counter and a speedometer, the scaling of which varied according to market. These were flanked by a fuel gauge and water temperature gauge. A panel below the dials housed a Message Centre screen and two warning light clusters. The Message Centre showed 150 driver warning and information messages covering functions such as automatic gearbox selections, ride heights and speed – including the speed warning setting. It also alerted the driver to system failures – even including the need to replace the remote transmitter batteries.

A fascia-mounted panel included switches and warning lights for suspension height control, cruise control master on/off, hazard warning and auxiliary lights. On manual versions, the low-range selector switch was also positioned on the fascia. There was also a rotary master light switch.

Below the switch panel there was an analogue time clock and a small storage compartment. Further down and leading into the centre console was the radio/cassette player unit with the heater controls and front and rear heated screen switches.

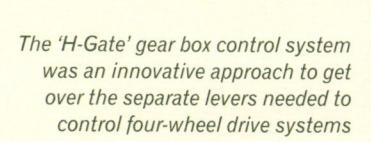

The 'H-Gate' gear box control system was an innovative approach to get over the separate levers needed to control four-wheel drive systems

Range Rover - The Anniversary Guide

Technical Description

HEATING AND VENTILATION

The heating and air conditioning system was of the combined type (HEVAC), supplied by Valeo and offered separate automatic temperature control for left and right hand occupants, the temperature selected being shown on a centre LCD display. In automatic mode, this brought the interior of the vehicle to the desired temperature as quickly as possible using the boost fan. Sensors detected both ambient temperature and solar load to achieve rapid establishment of the temperature and also provided a low temperature warning.

This automatic system was standard on the 4.6 HSE, 4.0 SE and 2.5 DSE models, the base 4.0 and 2.5 DT variants having manual temperature and distribution controls.

ELECTRICAL SYSTEM

The electrical system was extremely complex being based around the *Body electronic Control Module* (BeCM) which controlled all the interior and exterior electrical functions and interacted with all the other major functions of the vehicle. It also provided information to the driver's Message Centre. A key function of the BeCM was to record faults within the vehicle's systems so that these could be read by the service diagnostic system in order to cure problems quickly.

The security system was also complex and included perimetric and volumetric sensing in case of forced entry as well as an engine immobilisation system. The system was operated by a remote handset – two being supplied with the vehicle. One operation of the remote locked all the doors via the central locking system and activated the

The New Range Rover opted for more modern light units than its predecessor while the electrical system was extremely complex and initially troublesome

Technical Description

perimetric alarm while an additional operation also engaged a 'superlocking' system which prevented the doors from being unlocked from within the vehicle and engaged the volumetric alarm. The system also incorporated an automatic re-lock system and a mis-lock warning if a door or window was left open. The remotes also had a 'lazy locking' function where all doors and windows could be closed by an extended press of the remote button. On the 4.6 HSE, opening the doors using the remote also engaged the memory seat position assigned to that remote. If the remote was damaged, the vehicle could be unlocked and the engine immobilisation dis-engaged by using a key blade to operate a unique, four-digit Emergency Key Access (EKA) code.

LATER CHANGES

Soon after launch Land Rover took a decision to concentrate on a new model and so the Second Generation hardly changed throughout its lifetime.

ENGINE

Initially standard on 4.6-litre engine derivatives only, twin exhaust pipes were specified across the range to meet new noise regulations. This had a minor effect on power and torque output. The stainless steel finishers were deleted from the 4.6 and the new pipes concealed discretely behind the rear bumper.

TRANSMISSION

The automatic gearbox option was made available on the diesel-engined variants.

WHEELS AND TYRES

A new range of alloy wheels was introduced. By 1997 those available were as follows: the 7 x 16 inch 'Futura' three-spoke design, fitted with 235 section tyres, for the 4.0 and 2.5 DT models; the 'Pursuit' five-spoke design of the same size were standard on the 4.0 SE and 2.5 DSE; and the five-spoke 'Stratos' of 8-inch width, fitted with 255 tyres, were standard on the 4.6 HSE and optional on the other models.

The five-spoke 'Mondial' wheel was 8 inches wide and introduced an 18 inch wheel. Fitted with 255 low profile tyres, it was optional across the range. The 8 x 18 inch 'Triple Sport' fitted with 255 low profile tyres was offered as an accessory. All wheel and tyre options had an appropriate alloy spare wheel. Locking wheel nuts were now provided as standard.

BRAKING SYSTEM

Electronic Traction Control (ETC) was extended to act on all four wheels.

BODY

New colours were made available – see colour charts.

SEATING AND TRIM

New colours were introduced – see colour charts.

Considerable thought went into the appearance of the under bonnet area – the V8 engines having an attractive cast alloy plenum cover

Range Rover Second Generation — Phase One — Technical Data

Specification Sheets

GENERAL FEATURES

CONSTRUCTION
Four-door, five-seat body with clamshell opening tailgate. Steel substructure with alloy panels and bonded glass. High strength steel chassis with crush cans.

POWER UNITS
4.0-litre V8 petrol engine, 4.6-litre V8 petrol engine and 2.5-litre six-cylinder diesel engine

TRANSMISSION
Permanent four wheel drive. Five-speed manual gearbox (4.0-litre petrol or diesel only) or four-speed automatic gearbox with 'H-Gate' control. Chain-driven, two-speed transfer box with viscous coupled, automatically-locking centre differential driven transfer box with viscous-coupled, automatically-locking centre differential. Single reduction beam axles

SUSPENSION
Four-corner, variable-height, electonically-controlled air suspension with variable-rate air springs and hydraulic dampers. Front cast radius rods, Panhard rod and anti-roll bar at front, composite radius arms and Panhard rod at rear

STEERING
Power-assisted recirculating ball with hydraulic damper

BRAKING
Four-channel, four-wheel sensed ABS system with integrated four-wheel Electronic Traction Control

OTHER FEATURES
Sophisticated electrical system with Body Electrical Control Module (BeCM). Comprehensive security system. Driver and passenger airbags

	UNITS	4.0-Litre V8 Petrol Automatic	4.0-Litre V8 Petrol Manual	4.6-Litre V8 Petrol Automatic	2.5-Litre Diesel Manual
DIMENSIONS					
Overall Length	mm(in)	4713(185.6)	4713(185.6)	4713(185.6)	4713(185.6)
Overall Width (over mirrors)	mm(in)	1889(74.4)	1889(74.4)	1889(74.4)	1889(74.4)
Overall Height (nominal)	mm(in)	1817(71.6)	1817(71.6)	1817(71.6)	1817(71.6)
Wheelbase	mm(in)	2745(108)	2745(108)	2745(108)	2745(108)
Track Front/Rear	mm(in)	1540(60.6)/1530(60.2)	1540(60.6)/1530(60.2)	1540(60.6)/1530(60.2)	1540(60.6)/1530(60.2)
Luggage Capacity (Seat Up)	l(cu ft)	520(18.5)	520(18.5)	520(18.5)	520(18.5)
Luggage Capacity (Seat Folded)	l(cu ft)	1640(58.0)	1640(58.0)	1640(58.0)	1640(58.0)
WEIGHTS					
Kerb Weight (EEC)	kg(lb)	2100(4630)	2090(4608)	2220(4894)	2115(4663)
Gross Vehicle Weight	kg(lb)	2780(6129)	2780(6129)	2780(6129)	2780(6129)
Front Axle Maximum Weight	kg(lb)	1320(2910)	1320(2910)	1320(2910)	1320(2910)
Rear Axle Maximum Weight	kg(lb)	1840(4056)	1840(4056)	1840(4056)	1840(4056)
Maximum Payload	kg(lb)	603(1329)	603(1329)	603(1329)	596(1314)
Maximum On Road Trailer Weight	kg(lb)	3500(7716) with over-run brakes, 750(1653) unbraked			
Maximum Off Road Trailer Weight	kg(lb)	1000(2205) with over-run brakes, 500(1103) unbraked			
CAPABILITIES					
Drag Coefficient	Cd	0.38	0.38	0.38	0.38
Approach Angle (Maximum)	Deg	37 with suspension in high position, bib spoiler removed			
Under Body (Ramp) Angle (Maximum)	Deg	151 with suspension in high position			
Departure Angle (Maximum)	Deg	25 with suspension in high position			26 with suspension in high position
Turning Circle (Kerb to kerb)	mm(ft)	11,823(38.92)	11,823(38.92)	11,823(38.92)	11,823(38.92)
Wading Depth (Maximum)	mm(ft)	500(20)	500(20)	500(20)	500(20)

Range Rover - The Anniversary Guide

Specification Sheets

	UNITS	4.0-Litre V8 Petrol Automatic	4.0-Litre V8 Petrol Manual	4.6-Litre V8 Petrol Automatic	2.5-Litre Diesel Manual
PERFORMANCE					
Maximum Speed	kp/h(mph)	187(116)	190(118)	200(125)	170(105)
Acceleration 0 - 100 kp/h	secs	10.9	10.4	9.9	14
Acceleration 0 - 60 mph	secs	10.4	9.9	9.3	13
FUEL CONSUMPTION					
Urban Cycle (EC)	l/100km (mpg)	20.2(14.0)	18.6(15.2)	22.1(14.0)	10.9(25.8)
Constant 90 kph(56mph)	l/100km (mpg)	10.6(26.8)	10.4(27.2)	11.4(24.8)	7.5(37.9)
Constant 120 kph(75mph)	l/100km (mpg)	14.0(20.2)	13.5(21.0)	14.1(20.1)	11.2(25.3)
ENGINE					
Type		V8	V8	V8	In-line Six-Cylinder
Fuel		Petrol (Gasoline)	Petrol (Gasoline)	Petrol (Gasoline)	Diesel
Number of Cylinders		8	8	8	6
Number of Camshafts		1	1	1	1
Valves per Cylinder		2	2	2	2
Valve System		Push rods and rocker arms	Push rods and rocker arms	Push rods and rocker arms	Direct by overhead camshaft
Bore	mm(in)	94.0(3.70)	94.0(3.70)	94.0(3.70)	80.0(3.15)
Stroke	mm(in)	71.0(2.79)	71.0(2.79)	82.0(3.22)	82.8(3.60)
Capacity	cc(cu in)	3950(241)	3950(241)	4553(278)	2497(152)
Compression Ratio	:1	9	9	9	23
Cylinder Head Material		Aluminium alloy	Aluminium alloy	Aluminium alloy	Aluminium alloy
Cylinder Block Material		Aluminium alloy	Aluminium alloy	Aluminium alloy	Cast iron
Lubrication System		Wet sump pressure fed by rotor type oil pump. Sump intake with filter. Full flow cartridge filter			Gear type oil pump, oil cooler
Fuel System		Lucas electronic fuel injection with GEMS ECU, electric lift pump immersed in fuel tank			Bosch electronic type DDE 2.5
Ignition System		Lucas GEMS 8 engine management system with ECU. Lucas 2DIS2 coils, RN11YC spark plugs			N/A
Boost System		None	None	None	Mitsubishi TD04-11G4 turbocharger
Cold Start System		Automatic via ECU	Automatic via ECU	Automatic via ECU	Automatic with heater plugs
Air Cleaning System		Paper element	Paper element	Paper element	Paper element
Cooling System		Pressurised with crossflow radiator and remote header tank			Combined radiator, oil cooler and intercooler
Battery Capacity	Amp/hr	72	72	72	107
Max Power	kW(bhp)	140(188)	140(188)	165(221)	100(134)
At	rpm	4750	4750	4750	4400
Max Torque	Nm(lb/ft)	319(235)	319(235)	376(277)	270(199)
At	rpm	3000	3000	3000	2300

Range Rover - The Anniversary Guide

Range Rover Second Generation — Phase One — Technical Data

Specification Sheets

	UNITS	4.0-Litre V8 Petrol Automatic	4.0-Litre V8 Petrol Manual	4.6-Litre V8 Petrol Automatic	2.5-Litre Diesel Manual
TECHNOLOGIES					
Dual Line Braking System		Yes	Yes	Yes	Yes
Anti Lock Braking System (ABS)		Wabco four-channel, four-wheel sensed with electrically-driven pump.			
Electronic Traction Control (ETC)		Four-wheel system integrated with ABS			
Electronic Brakeforce Distribution (EBD)		No	No	No	No
Emergency Brake Assist (EBA)		No	No	No	No
Dynamic Stability Control (DSC)		No	No	No	No
Hill Descent Control (HDC)		No	No	No	No
Terrain Response™		No	No	No	No

NOTES

Data acquired from the best available sources but the publisher is not liable for any mistakes or omissions. Readers are advised to consult other sources e.g. manufacturer's workshop manuals before working on vehicles. The publication of performance and capability figures does not imply that this will be achieved in practice. Caution must be exercised in all driving activities especially off-road.

Units are expressed in the relevant international standard (SI). Where appropriate recognised conversion factors have been applied.

Specification Sheets

Range Rover - The Anniversary Guide

Range Rover Second Generation | Phase One | Technical Data

Chassis & Engine Numbers

CHASSIS and ENGINE NUMBERS

RANGE ROVER SECOND GENERATION PHASE 1

VEHICLE	PERIOD	MANUFACTURER	MODEL	TRIM CODE	STYLE	ENGINE CODE		TRANSMISSION CODE		MODEL YEAR		BUILD LOCATION
Range Rover P38A Second Generation	1994 - 2002	SAL	Land Rover LP	Range Rover A	Standard	M	P38A J	4.6-litre V8 Petrol	1	RHD Auto	M	1995	A	Solihull
						M	4.0-litre V8 Petrol	2	LHD Auto	T	1996		
						W	2.5-litre 6-cyl Diesel	3	RHD Manual	V	1997		
								4	LHD Manual	W	1998		
										X	1999		
										Y	2000		
										1	2001		
										2	2002		

The Second Generation (P38A) Range Rovers were identified using the 17-digit Vehicle Indentification Number (VIN) system. This consisted of a combination of letters and digits defining the vehicle type, engine fitted, transmission, model year and build location according to the table above. This was followed by a six-digit number unique to a particular vehicle. The VIN was stamped on a plate riveted inside the engine bay and on another plate visible through a gap in the lower windscreen masking on the left hand side ('Visible VIN').

PRICE LIST (UK)

RANGE ROVER SECOND GENERATION PHASE 1

DATE	MODEL	PRICE	NOTES
		£ Inc Car Tax and VAT	
June 1995	Range Rover 4.0	32,850	
	Range Rover 2.5 DT	32,850	
	Range Rover 4.0 SE	37,200	
	Range Rover 2.5 DSE	37,200	
	Range Rover 4.6 HSE	44,850	
OPTIONS			
	Automatic Transmission	1450	Standard on 4.6 HSE. Available late 1995 on diesel models
	Climate Control	2300	Standard on SE, DSE and HSE. Included heated seats and heated front screen
	Electronic Traction Control	500	Standard on 4.6 HSE
	Electronic Non Memory Seats	995	4.0 SE and 2.5 DSE only
	Electric Sun Roof	995	Standard on 4.6 HSE
	Mid Line ICE Upgrade	250	4.0 and 2.5 DT only
	Premium ICE Upgrade	1000	4.0 SE and 2.5 DSE only. Standard on 4.6 HSE
	18-inch Alloy Wheels (inc alloy spare)	1795	
	HSE Style Wheels	800	Standard on 4.6 HSE
	Alloy Spare Wheel	90	
	Cloth Seat Trim	nco	Standard on 4.0 and 2.5 DT

Colour & Trim

COLOUR & TRIM				
RANGE ROVER SECOND GENERATION PHASE 1				
YEAR	PAINTWORK		LRC NUMBER	NOTES
	COLOUR	TYPE		
1994	Alpine White	COB Solid	456	
	Arles Blue	COB Solid	424	
	Coniston Green	COB Solid	637	
	Portofino Red	COB Solid	390	
	Beluga Black	COB Solid	416	
	Avalon	COB Micatallic	575	
	Biarritz Blue	COB Micatallic	965	
	Caprice	COB Micatallic	533	
	Epsom Green	COB Micatallic	961	
	Montpellier	COB Micatallic	536	
	Sahara	COB Micatallic	583	
	Aspen Silver	COB Metallic	458	
	Niagara Grey	COB Metallic	574	
	Roman Bronze	COB Metallic	479	
	INTERIOR TRIM			
	COLOUR	MATERIAL		
	Granite	Cloth		
	Saddle	Cloth		
	Granite	Leather		
	Saddle	Leather		

Range Rover - The Anniversary Guide

COLOUR & TRIM

RANGE ROVER SECOND GENERATION PHASE 1

YEAR	PAINTWORK		LRC NUMBER	NOTES
	COLOUR	TYPE		
1994	Alpine White	COB Solid	456	
	Arles Blue	COB Solid	424	
	Coniston Green	COB Solid	637	
	Portofino Red	COB Solid	390	
	Beluga Black	COB Solid	416	
	Avalon	COB Micatallic	575	
	Biarritz Blue	COB Micatallic	965	
	Caprice	COB Micatallic	533	
	Epsom Green	COB Micatallic	961	
	Montpellier	COB Micatallic	536	
	Sahara	COB Micatallic	583	
	Aspen Silver	COB Metallic	458	
	Niagara Grey	COB Metallic	574	
	Roman Bronze	COB Metallic	479	

INTERIOR TRIM

	COLOUR	MATERIAL		
	Granite	Cloth		
	Saddle	Cloth		
	Granite	Leather		
	Saddle	Leather		

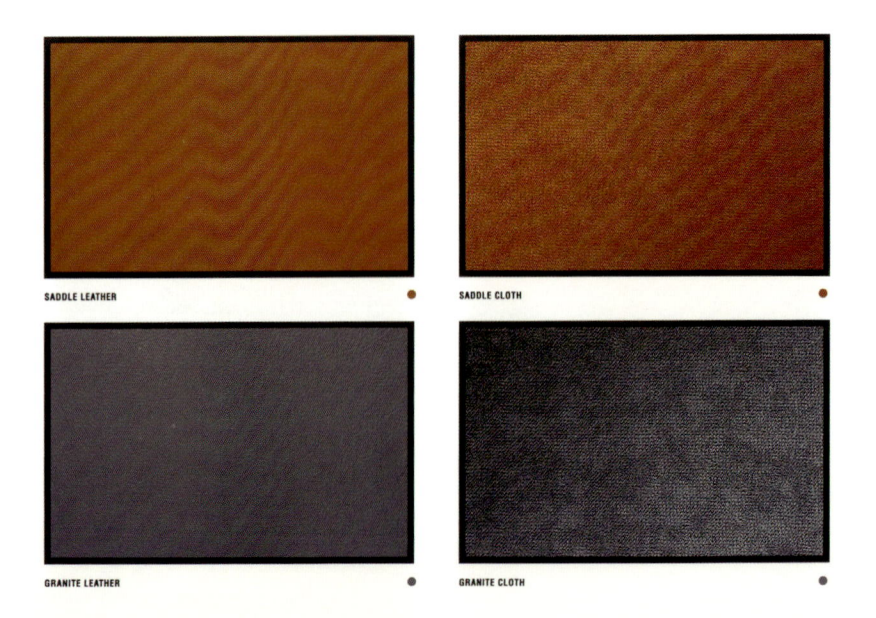

SADDLE LEATHER

SADDLE CLOTH

GRANITE LEATHER

GRANITE CLOTH

Range Rover - The Anniversary Guide

Colour & Trim

ALPINE WHITE
solid paint finish

ARLES BLUE
solid paint finish

ASPEN SILVER
clear over base metallic

AVALON
clear over base micatalic

BELUGA BLACK
clear over base solid

BIARRITZ BLUE
clear over base micatalic

CAPRICE
clear over base micatalic

CONISTON GREEN
solid paint finish

EPSOM GREEN
clear over base micatalic

MONTPELLIER
clear over base micatalic

NIAGARA
clear over base metallic

PORTOFINO RED
solid paint finish

ROMAN BRONZE
clear over base metallic

SAHARA
clear over base micatalic

Range Rover - The Anniversary Guide

Range Rover Second Generation — Phase One — Advertising

Advertising & Brochures

Range Rover advertising imagery was always superb but arguably reached its height with the Second Generation vehicle

The original 1994 launch publicity came as a boxed set of brochures covering all aspects of the vehicle including a specification sheet and accessories. The burnt orange colouring was a theme for the original vehicle's launch

Range Rover - The Anniversary Guide

Advertising & Brochures

The square brochures were a non-standard size so Land Rover marketing soon reverted to a more normal format

(Top right) Land Rover re-printed the Autocar special feature on the New Range Rover, packaging it with the rival Car magazine equivalent so that potential customers could see what the press thought of the new vehicle

(Right) Once again the US market could be relied upon to come up with innovative advertising pushing the 'Britishness' of their premium brand

Range Rover - The Anniversary Guide

109

Range Rover Second Generation | Phase One | Advertising

Advertising & Brochures

The 1997 brochure was a plush affair. Each Land Rover model now had its individual identifying colour banding, that for the Range Rover being, appropriately, an imperial purple

The spirit of individualism

With Autobiography, the Range Rover provides an entirely appropriate foreword to an essentially personal narrative. Here is an opportunity to create a vehicle that is precisely and particularly yours. The gleaming coach-painted body can reflect your unique choice of colour. The richly appointed leather and walnut interior will be tailored to your individual style. From world-class vision technology, to in-car navigation, the communications and entertainment systems can perfectly mesh with the way you live your life. A team of uniquely skilled craftsman will help you to ensure it will be your Autobiography. Ask your Land Rover dealer if you would like the full story.

While the 'Autobiography' programme had a brochure of its own, these were only produced in small numbers. This led to a page devoted to the scheme in the main brochure

110   Range Rover - The Anniversary Guide

Advertising & Brochures

Some of the wording in the brochures could be a little obscure

Real refinement holds the world in admiration

This moody mountain image of the Range Rover was used in a great deal of the Second Generation's publicity material

RANGE ROVER

Range Rover - The Anniversary Guide

Range Rover Second Generation — Phase Two

Technical Description

The 1999 model year changes were originally planned to be a major facelift for the Range Rover, introducing BMW engines – including a V12 petrol version – as well as a front-end styling change. There was also to be a completely revised interior and all-round independent suspension. However, the cost of the programme would have been not far short of that for a completely new model, so the changes were restricted to a minor facelift and power unit changes.

The model line-up was modified to 4.0 HSE, 2.5 DHSE and 4.6 Vogue variants. Styling changes were limited to revisions to the headlamps which had black areas added to the lens backing to accentuate the round portions of the lights themselves. The front indicator and side cluster went to a clear lens with coloured indicator bulbs to improve the appearance, while at the rear the indicator and reverse lamp portions of the cluster also had a clear lens, again with coloured indicator bulbs.

A planned facelift for 1999, including a new front end to accommodate a V12 petrol engine, was foregone in favour of a completely new vehicle. The Second Generation Range Rover was left with a few minor external changes including a revised headlamp arrangement to emphasise the round lights within the cluster

ENGINE

While the 2.5-litre diesel engine remained unchanged, both the 4.0-litre and 4.6-litre V8 petrol engines were considerably improved under a programme known as 'Thor'. The changes were designed to boost torque and improve refinement as well as introducing Bosch, a preferred BMW supplier, for electronic ignition systems. A key factor, and one immediately apparent on opening the bonnet, was the introduction of a new, long-tract inlet manifold in place of the central plenum chamber. This allowed each duct to be the optimum length for that particular cylinder, resulting in a claimed increase of peak torque of eight percent and a greatly improved torque delivery across a wider rev. range.

The engine management system moved from Lucas GEMS to Bosch's Motronic M5.2.1 and throttle response was improved by automatically re-mapping the engine's tuning to suit the prevailing driving conditions, whether on- or off-road. Land Rover called this 'Fast Throttle Control'. The ignition system was further enhanced by the fitment of twin coils, up-rated spark plugs and silicon plug leads. While Bosch themselves managed the 4.0-litre engine installation, the 4.6-litre programme was outsourced to Porsche. Both delivered a high quality system in line with the project's tight timescale.

Other changes included a new cast alloy sump to increase stiffness and reduce Noise, Vibration, and Harshness (NVH). The engine mounts were also re-positioned to further improve refinement.

WHEELS AND TYRES

Most wheels were re-styled. Those now available were the 'Lightning' five-spoke 8 x 16 inch wheel equipped with 255 section tyres, and offered as a no-cost option across the range. The 'Hurricane' 10-spoke 8 x 18 inch wheel with 255 section tyres was offered in several finishes depending on whether it was fitted to HSE or Vogue derivatives. The 'Comet' 8 x 18 inch wheel fitted with 255 section tyres was optional across the range.

STEERING

A wood and leather steering wheel was now standard on the Vogue and an option on HSE models.

BODY

Privacy glass for all windows behind the 'B/C' post was offered as an option.

SEATING AND TRIM

The front seats were modified to allow for the fitment of integral thorax air bags, along with associated changes to the seat belts including pre-tensioners. The standard leather seats had revised stitch patterns to increase the area of pleating and were offered in four colours with a choice of contrast piping on Lightstone

Technical Description

(see colour chart for details). Cloth-trimmed seats in three colours were offered as a no-cost option. A new Oxford leather trim, comprising a higher quality hide with a ruched appearance and softer foams was introduced as an option on all models. Four colours were available – the seats, however, were not piped so this option was not offered. Both driver's and passenger seats were electrically adjustable with memory seat and mirror positions offered on the driver's side.

When selected, the 'Oxford' leather option included matching panels on the door casings, on the cubby box lid and for the handbrake lever gaiter. A bright chrome surround was added to the gear lever control panel, and the handbrake release knob, gear lever selector knob and door handles were also in chrome. Vogue models had extra leather trim on the centre console and leather-covered door pulls.

FASCIA AND INSTRUMENTS

Graphics on the instruments and clock were revised and illuminated by green light. The In Car Entertainment system head unit was now sourced from Alpine and a harman/kardon® 11-speaker system specified, that fitted to the Vogue model having 12 speakers with Digital Sound Processing.

The Philips CARiN 2 plus satellite navigation system with a screen mounted above the heater controls was standard on the Vogue and optional on HSE models.

(Top) The original plans for 1999 also included a new fascia but with the cancellation of the programme, the original was retained. Originally featured on Autobiography vehicles, a wood and leather steering wheel was now available along with increased use of veneer on the centre stack – including a wooden gear lever

The heating and air conditioning system with automatic temperature control remained unchanged. It was an effective feature offering dual-level air flow directing warm air to the footwells and cooler air to the face-level vents

Range Rover - The Anniversary Guide

113

Specification Sheets

GENERAL FEATURES

CONSTRUCTION
Four-door, five-seat body with clamshell opening tailgate. Steel substructure with alloy panels and bonded glass. High strength steel chassis with crush cans.

POWER UNITS
Uprated (new ecu, inlet manifold and structural sump) 4.0-litre and 4.6-litre V8 petrol engine and 2.5-litre six-cylinder diesel engine

TRANSMISSION
Permanent four wheel drive. Four-speed automatic gearbox with 'H-Gate' control. Chain-driven, two-speed transfer box with viscous coupled, automatically-locking centre differential driven transfer box with viscous-coupled, automatically-locking centre differential. Single reduction beam axles

SUSPENSION
Four-corner, variable-height, electonically-controlled air suspension with variable-rate air springs and hydraulic dampers.

Front cast radius rods, Panhard rod and anti-roll bar at front, composite radius arms and Panhard rod at rear

STEERING
Power-assisted recirculating ball with hydraulic damper

BRAKING
Four-channel, four-wheel sensed ABS system with integrated four-wheel Electronic Traction Control

OTHER FEATURES
Sophisticated electrical system with Body Electrical Control Module (BeCM). Comprehensive security system. Driver and passenger airbags. New Twin Parabola headlamps

	UNITS	4.0-Litre V8 Petrol Automatic	4.6-Litre V8 Petrol Automatic	2.5-Litre Diesel Automatic
DIMENSIONS				
Overall Length	mm(in)	4713(185.6)	4713(185.6)	4713(185.6)
Overall Width (over mirrors)	mm(in)	1889(74.4)	1889(74.4)	1889(74.4)
Overall Height (nominal)	mm(in)	1817(71.6)	1817(71.6)	1817(71.6)
Wheelbase	mm(in)	2745(108)	2745(108)	2745(108)
Track Front/Rear	mm(in)	1540(60.6)/1530(60.2)	1540(60.6)/1530(60.2)	1540(60.6)/1530(60.2)
Luggage Capacity (Seat Up)	l(cu ft)	520(18.5)	520(18.5)	520(18.5)
Luggage Capacity (Seat Folded)	l(cu ft)	1640(58.0)	1640(58.0)	1640(58.0)
WEIGHTS				
Kerb Weight (EEC)	kg(lb)	2100(4630)	2220(4894)	2115(4663)
Gross Vehicle Weight	kg(lb)	2780(6129)	2780(6129)	2780(6129)
Front Axle Maximum Weight	kg(lb)	1320(2910)	1320(2910)	1320(2910)
Rear Axle Maximum Weight	kg(lb)	1840(4056)	1840(4056)	1840(4056)
Maximum Payload	kg(lb)	603(1329)	603(1329)	596(1314)
Maximum On Road Trailer Weight	kg(lb)	3500(7716) with over-run brakes, 750(1653) unbraked		
Maximum Off Road Trailer Weight	kg(lb)	1000(2205) with over-run brakes, 500(1103) unbraked		
CAPABILITIES				
Drag Coefficient	Cd	0.38	0.38	0.38
Approach Angle (Maximum)	Deg	37 with suspension in high position, bib spoiler removed		
Under Body (Ramp) Angle (Maximum)	Deg	151 with suspension in high position		
Departure Angle (Maximum)	Deg	25 with suspension in high position		26 with suspension in high position
Turning Circle (Kerb to kerb)	mm(in)	11,823(38.92)	11,823(38.92)	11,823(38.92)
Wading Depth (Maximum)	mm(in)	500(20)	500(20)	500(20)

Range Rover - The Anniversary Guide

Specification Sheets

	UNITS	4.0-Litre V8 Petrol Automatic	4.6-Litre V8 Petrol Automatic	2.5-Litre Diesel Automatic
PERFORMANCE				
Maximum Speed	kp/h(mph)	187(116)	196(122)	162(101)
Acceleration 0 - 100 kp/h	secs	12.2	9.9	17.5
Acceleration 0 - 60 mph	secs	11.4	9.3	16.0
FUEL CONSUMPTION				
Urban Cycle (EC)	l/100km (mpg)	21.7(13.0)	23.9(11.8)	14.5(19.5)
Extra Urban (EC)	l/100km (mpg)	11.5(24.5)	12.2(23.2)	9.6(29.5)
Combined (EC)	l/100km (mpg)	15.2(18.5)	16.4(17.2)	11.4(24.9)
CO_2 Emissions (EC)	g/km	385	398	304
City (EPA)	mpg(US)	13	12	N/A
Highway (EPA)	mpg(US)	17	15	N/A
ENGINE				
Type		V8	V8	In-line Six-Cylinder
Fuel		Petrol (Gasoline)	Petrol (Gasoline)	Diesel
Number of Cylinders		8	8	6
Number of Camshafts		1	1	1
Valves per Cylinder		2	2	2
Valve System		Push rods and rocker arms		Direct by overhead camshaft
Bore	mm(in)	94.0(3.70)	94.0(3.70)	80.0(3.15)
Stroke	mm(in)	71.0(2.79)	82.0(3.22)	82.8(3.60)
Capacity	cc(cu in)	3950(241)	4553(278)	2497(152)
Compression Ratio	:1	9	9	23
Cylinder Head Material		Aluminium alloy	Aluminium alloy	Aluminium alloy
Cylinder Block Material		Aluminium alloy	Aluminium alloy	Cast iron
Lubrication System		Wet sump pressure fed by rotor type oil pump. Sump intake with filter. Full flow cartridge filter		Gear type oil pump, oil cooler
Fuel System		Bosch Motronic M5.2.1 engine management system, electric lift pump immersed in fuel tank		Bosch electronic type DDE 2.5
Ignition System		Bosch Motronic M5.2.1, RC11PYB4 spark plugs		N/A
Boost System		None	None	Mitsubishi TD04-11G4 turbocharger
Cold Start System		Automatic via ECU	Automatic via ECU	Automatic with heater plugs
Air Cleaning System		Paper element	Paper element	Paper element
Cooling System		Pressurised with crossflow radiator and remote header tank		Combined radiator, oil cooler and intercooler
Battery Capacity	Amp/hr	72	72	107
Max Power	kW(bhp)	136(182)	160(215)	102(137)
At	rpm	4750	4750	4400
Max Torque	Nm(lb/ft)	340(251)	400(295)	270(199)
At	rpm	3000	2600	2300

Range Rover - The Anniversary Guide

Range Rover Second Generation — Phase Two — Technical Data

Specification Sheets

TECHNOLOGIES	UNITS	4.0-Litre V8 Petrol Automatic	4.6-Litre V8 Petrol Automatic	2.5-Litre Diesel Automatic
Dual Line Braking System		Yes	Yes	Yes
Anti Lock Braking System (ABS)		Wabco four-channel, four-wheel sensed with electrically-driven pump.		
Electronic Traction Control (ETC)		Four-wheel system integrated with ABS		
Electronic Brakeforce Distribution (EBD)		No	No	No
Emergency Brake Assist (EBA)		No	No	No
Dynamic Stability Control (DSC)		No	No	No
Hill Descent Control (HDC)		No	No	No
Terrain Response™		No	No	No

NOTES

Data acquired from the best available sources but the publisher is not liable for any mistakes or omissions. Readers are advised to consult other sources e.g. manufacturer's workshop manuals before working on vehicles. The publication of performance and capability figures does not imply that this will be achieved in practice. Caution must be exercised in all driving activities especially off-road.

Units are expressed in the relevant international standard (SI). Where appropriate recognised conversion factors have been applied.

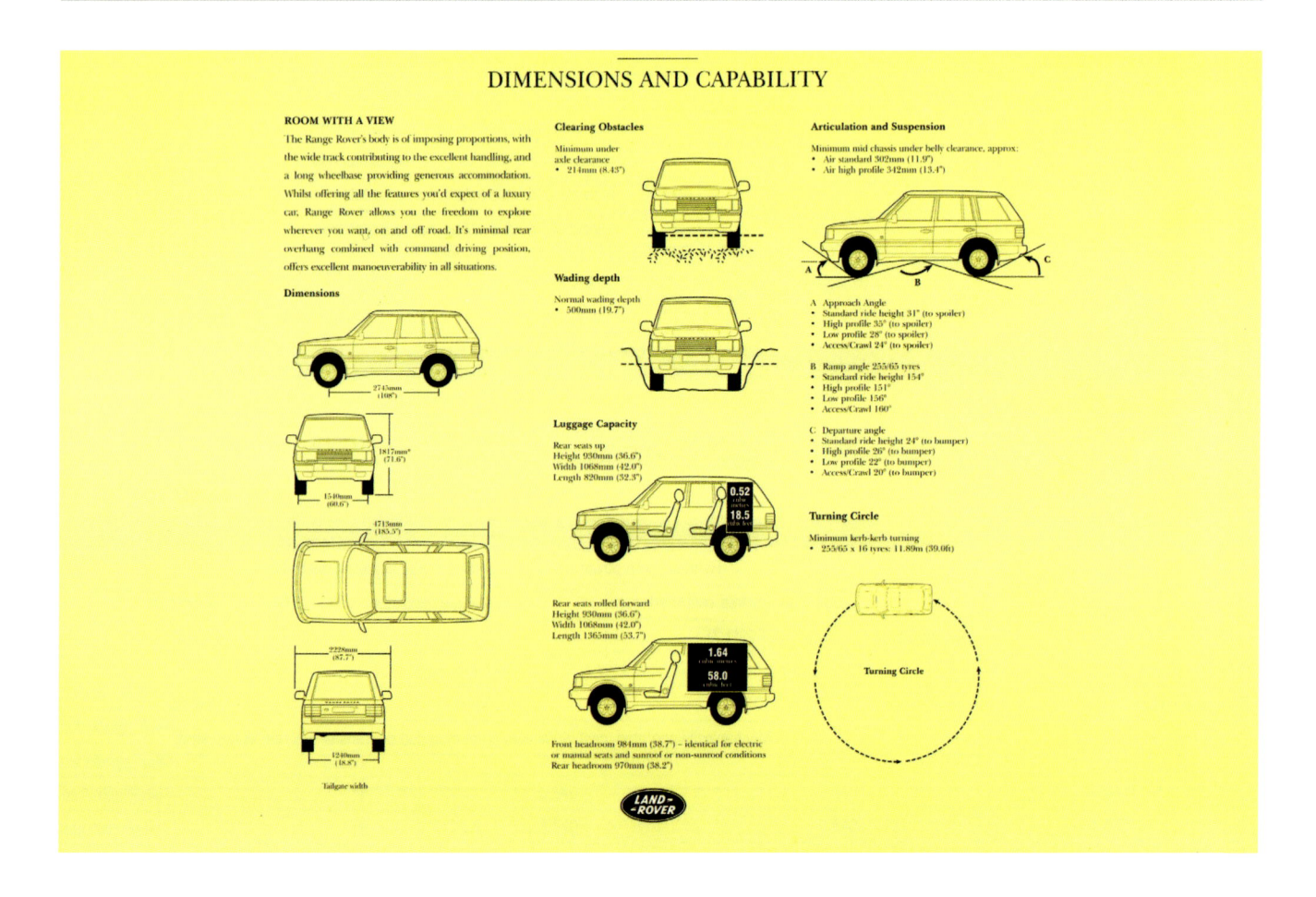

DIMENSIONS AND CAPABILITY

ROOM WITH A VIEW

The Range Rover's body is of imposing proportions, with the wide track contributing to the excellent handling, and a long wheelbase providing generous accommodation. Whilst offering all the features you'd expect of a luxury car, Range Rover allows you the freedom to explore wherever you want, on and off road. It's minimal rear overhang combined with command driving position, offers excellent manoeuverability in all situations.

Dimensions
- 2745mm (108")
- 1817mm (71.6")
- 1540mm (60.6")
- 4713mm (185.5")
- 2226mm (87.7")
- 1240mm (48.8")
- Tailgate width

Clearing Obstacles

Minimum under axle clearance
- 214mm (8.43")

Wading depth

Normal wading depth
- 500mm (19.7")

Luggage Capacity

Rear seats up
- Height 930mm (36.6")
- Width 1068mm (42.0")
- Length 820mm (32.3")
- 0.52 cubic metres / 18.5 cubic feet

Rear seats rolled forward
- Height 930mm (36.6")
- Width 1068mm (42.0")
- Length 1365mm (53.7")
- 1.64 cubic metres / 58.0 cubic feet

Front headroom 984mm (38.7") – identical for electric or manual seats and sunroof or non-sunroof conditions
Rear headroom 970mm (38.2")

Articulation and Suspension

Minimum mid chassis under belly clearance, approx:
- Air standard 302mm (11.9")
- Air high profile 342mm (13.4")

A Approach Angle
- Standard ride height 31° (to spoiler)
- High profile 35° (to spoiler)
- Low profile 28° (to spoiler)
- Access/Crawl 24° (to spoiler)

B Ramp angle 255/65 tyres
- Standard ride height 154°
- High profile 151°
- Low profile 156°
- Access/Crawl 160°

C Departure angle
- Standard ride height 24° (to bumper)
- High profile 26° (to bumper)
- Low profile 22° (to bumper)
- Access/Crawl 20° (to bumper)

Turning Circle

Minimum kerb-kerb turning
- 255/65 x 16 tyres: 11.89m (39.0ft)

Specification Sheets

Range Rover - The Anniversary Guide

Range Rover Second Generation — Phase Two — Technical Data

Chassis & Engine Numbers

CHASSIS and ENGINE NUMBERS

RANGE ROVER SECOND GENERATION PHASE 2

VEHICLE	PERIOD	MANUFACTURER	MODEL	TRIM CODE	STYLE	ENGINE CODE		TRANSMISSION CODE		MODEL YEAR		BUILD LOCATION
Range Rover P38A Second Generation	1994 - 2002	SAL	Land Rover	LP	Range Rover	A Standard	M P38A	J 4.6-litre V8 Petrol	1 RHD Auto	M 1995	A Solihull
								M 4.0-litre V8 Petrol	2 LHD Auto	T 1996	
								W 2.5-litre 6-cyl Diesel	3 RHD Manual	V 1997	
									4 LHD Manual	W 1998	
										X 1999	
										Y 2000	
										1 2001	
										2 2002	

The Second Generation (P38A) Range Rovers were identified using the 17-digit Vehicle Indentification Number (VIN) system. This consisted of a combination of letters and digits defining the vehicle type, engine fitted, transmission, model year and build location according to the table above. This was followed by a six-digit number unique to a particular vehicle. The VIN was stamped on a plate riveted inside the engine bay and on another plate visible through a gap in the lower windscreen masking on the left hand side ('Visible VIN').

PRICE LIST (UK)

RANGE ROVER SECOND GENERATION PHASE 2

DATE	MODEL	PRICE	NOTES
		£ Inc Car Tax and VAT	
1999	Range Rover 2.5DT	39,645	
	Range Rover 4.0 Auto	41,000	
	Range Rover 2.5 DSE	42,705	
	Range Rover 4.0 SE Auto	44,060	
	Range Rover 2.5D HSE	47,805	
	Range Rover 4.6 HSE	51,170	
OPTIONS			
	Automatic Transmission	1530	Standard on petrol models and 2.5D HSE
	Electric Memory Seats	1075	Not available on 2.5DT and 4.0. Standard on 2.5D HSE and 4.6 HSE
	Electric Sunroof	1075	Standard on 2.5D HSE and 4.6 HSE
	Premium harman/kardon ICE upgrade	1075	Not available on 2.5DT and 4.0. Standard on 2.5D HSE and 4.6 HSE
	Hurricane 18-inch alloy wheels (inc alloy spare)	1970	
	Mondial 18-inch alloy wheels (inc alloy spare)	1970	
	Lightning 16-inch wheels (inc alloy spare)	885	Standard on 2.5D HSE and 4.6 HSE
	Heated seats and front windscreen	540	2.5DT and 4.0 only - standard on other models
	Micatallic/Metallic Paint	nco	
	Cloth Seat Trim	nco	Standard on 2.5DT and 4.0

Colour & Trim

COLOUR & TRIM				
\multicolumn{5}{c}{RANGE ROVER SECOND GENERATION PHASE 2}				
YEAR	PAINTWORK		LRC NUMBER	NOTES
	COLOUR	TYPE		
2000	Caledonian Blue	COB Solid	507	
	Chawton White	COB Solid	603	
	Coniston Green	COB Solid	570	
	Rutland Red	COB Solid	607	
	Epsom Green	COB Micatallic	961	
	Java Black	COB Micatallic	697	
	Oxford Blue	COB Micatallic	602	
	Rioja Red	COB Micatallic	601	
	Woodcote Green	COB Micatallic	623	
	Blenheim Silver	COB Metallic	642	
	Charleston Green	COB Metallic	610	
	Cobar Blue	COB Metallic	624	
	Niagara Grey	COB Metallic	574	
	White Gold	COB Metallic	618	
\multicolumn{5}{c}{INTERIOR TRIM}				
	COLOUR	MATERIAL		
	Ash Grey	Cloth		
	Dark Granite	Cloth		
	Walnut	Cloth		
	Ash Grey	Leather		
	Dark Granite	Leather		
	Lightstone	Leather		
	Walnut	Leather		

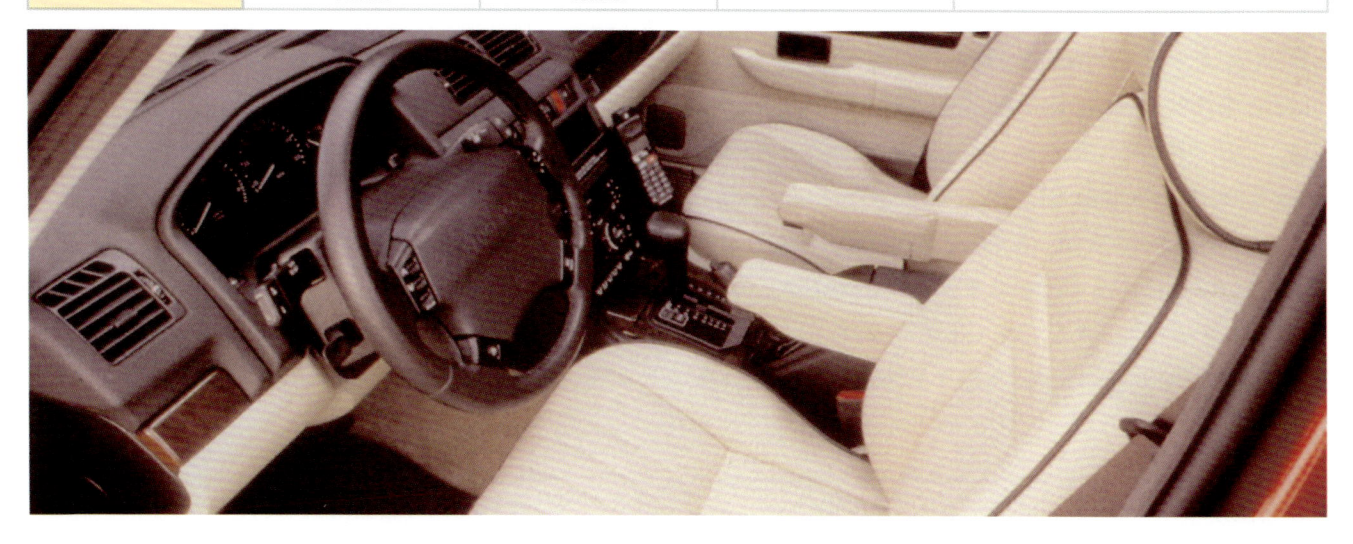

Range Rover - The Anniversary Guide

Colour & Trim

COLOUR & TRIM

RANGE ROVER SECOND GENERATION PHASE 2

YEAR	PAINTWORK		LRC NUMBER	NOTES
	COLOUR	TYPE		
2001	Caledonian Blue	COB Solid	507	
	Chawton White	COB Solid	603	
	Coniston Green	COB Solid	570	
	Rutland Red	COB Solid	607	
	Epsom Green	COB Micatallic	961	
	Java Black	COB Micatallic	697	
	Alveston Red	COB Metallic	696	
	Blenheim Silver	COB Metallic	642	
	Bonatti Grey	COB Metallic	916	
	Icelandic Blue	COB Metallic	621	
	Monte Carlo Blue	COB Metallic	608/9	Differs by application/technology
	Oslo Blue	COB Metallic	644	
	White Gold	COB Metallic	618	

INTERIOR TRIM

	COLOUR	MATERIAL		
	Darkstone	Cloth		
	Granite	Cloth		
	Walnut	Cloth		
	Ash	Leather		Either smooth with contrasting piping or ruched 'Oxford' leather
	Granite	Leather		Either smooth with contrasting piping or ruched 'Oxford' leather
	Lightstone	Leather		Either smooth with contrasting piping or ruched 'Oxford' leather
	Walnut	Leather		Either smooth with contrasting piping or ruched 'Oxford' leather

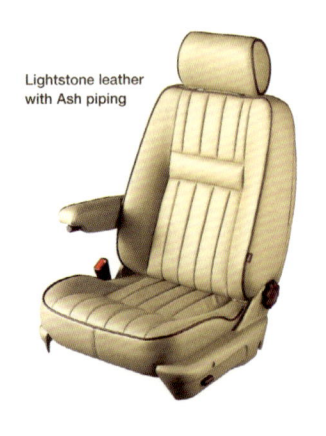

Lightstone leather with Ash piping

Ash leather with Ash piping

Granite leather with Ash piping

Walnut leather with Ash piping

Colour & Trim

Rutland Red (-)

Alveston Red (Red)

Caledonian Blue (-)

White Gold (Red, Green)

Blenheim Silver (Red, Green)

Chawton White (Green)

Oslo Blue (Blue)

Icelandic Blue (Blue)

Monte Carlo Blue (Blue)

Java Black (Red)

Bonatti Grey (Red)

The colour range covered 11 external paint finishes including solid, micatallic, and metallic colours. All used Clear Over Base (COB) technology where a coat of clear lacquer was applied over a matt base coat. The leather trim was offered in either the standard smooth finish or in ruched Oxford leather with a revised stitching pattern

Range Rover - The Anniversary Guide

123

| Range Rover Second Generation | Phase Two | Advertising |

Advertising & Brochures

The 2000 brochure featured the limited edition Westminster model on its dramatic cover

The last brochure for the Second Generation Range Rover featured the vehicle set, appropriately, against a sunset

Advertising & Brochures

The later Second Generation Range Rover brochures featured a separate specification leaflet held in a pocket in the back cover. They were often purloined for the information held, leaving potential customers in the dark over the vehicle's capabilities

Land Rover was by now rapidly expanding other aspects of its powerful brand. This included promoting the Land Rover Experience (which would eventually have nine centres around the UK with other locations in Europe, the US and South Africa), the Land Rover Gear range of clothing and branded goods and the Adventures holiday programme

Range Rover Second Generation | Phase Two | Advertising

Advertising & Brochures

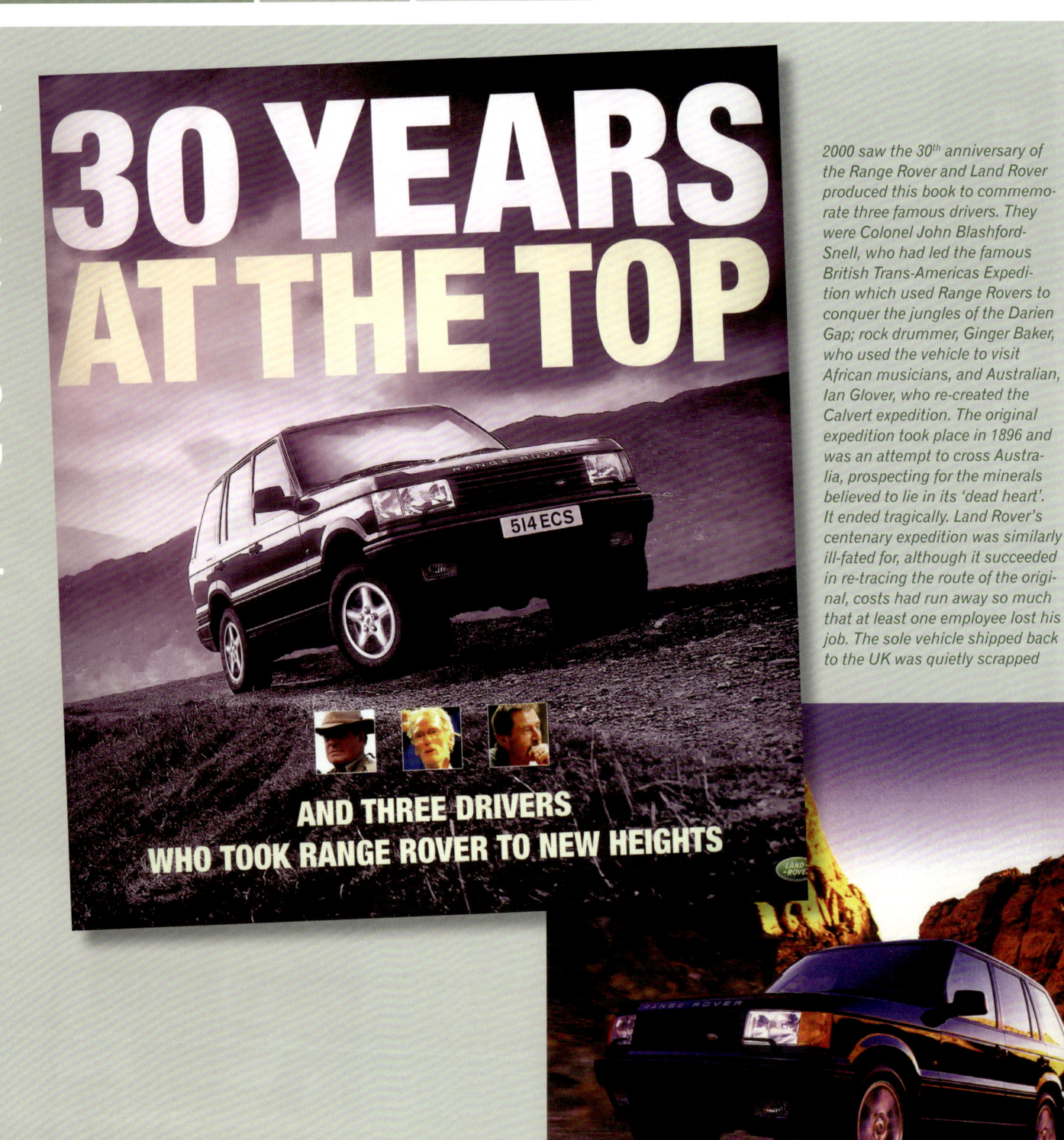

30 YEARS AT THE TOP
AND THREE DRIVERS WHO TOOK RANGE ROVER TO NEW HEIGHTS

2000 saw the 30th anniversary of the Range Rover and Land Rover produced this book to commemorate three famous drivers. They were Colonel John Blashford-Snell, who had led the famous British Trans-Americas Expedition which used Range Rovers to conquer the jungles of the Darien Gap; rock drummer, Ginger Baker, who used the vehicle to visit African musicians, and Australian, Ian Glover, who re-created the Calvert expedition. The original expedition took place in 1896 and was an attempt to cross Australia, prospecting for the minerals believed to lie in its 'dead heart'. It ended tragically. Land Rover's centenary expedition was similarly ill-fated for, although it succeeded in re-tracing the route of the original, costs had run away so much that at least one employee lost his job. The sole vehicle shipped back to the UK was quietly scrapped

126

Range Rover - The Anniversary Guide

Advertising & Brochures

Getting full marks for consistency, Land Rover of North America played the British card to the end in promoting the 'peerless' Range Rover

Accessories had, since Discovery, been designed alongside the main vehicle programmes to ensure fit and finish consistent with the Range Rover itself. This 2001 dated brochure included a choice of wheels and exterior protection as well as racks for mountain bikes and skis

The Range Rover. Anything less, is.

"Foie gras again?" "Do we have to sit in the skybox?" and "I settled for the Range Rover" are comments you'll never hear. Because there are some things people can't get enough of.

Like the Range Rover's smoother-than-silk ride, courtesy of its electronic air suspension and permanent four-wheel drive. And the 14-gauge boxed steel frame, and driver and front-passenger side airbags, which make you feel as safe as a knight in a suit of armor.

On top of that, the Range Rover has dual climate controls, 10-way power adjustable leather seats, and a 12-speaker, six-disc CD auto-changer audio system.

A vehicle this capable and luxurious is fit for a king. Which explains why there's been a Land Rover in the Royal Family since 1948. So for more information, visit us at www.Best4x4.LandRover.com or call 1-800-FINE 4WD.

After driving a Range Rover, you'll find it difficult to drive anything else. Because sometimes only the foie gras will do.

Always use your seatbelts. SRS/airbags alone do not provide sufficient protection.

Accessories
RANGE ROVER

Range Rover - The Anniversary Guide

127

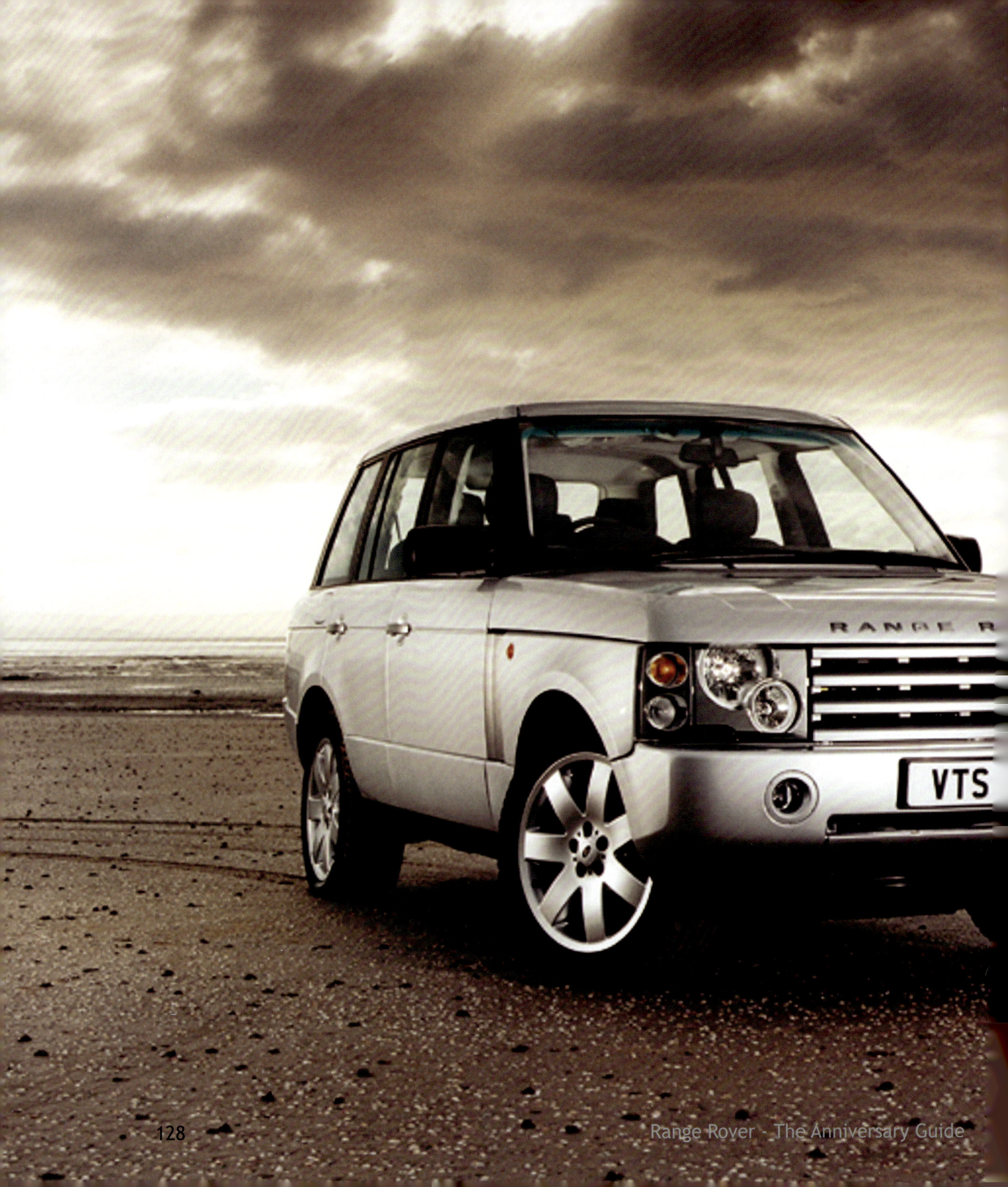
RANGE R
VTS

Range Rover - Third Generation

A Brief History

Even before the New Range Rover – as the P38A was christened - was launched in 1994, work had begun on a comprehensive mid-life update. With the acquisition of the Rover Group by BMW, this grew into a major change incorporating new BMW engines, including a V12. Associated revisions to enable them to be packaged led to a new front end treatment while a major upgrade to the interior was also planned.

BMW board member for product, Wolfgang Reitzle, was not convinced that the facelifted model would hold its own in the luxury vehicle sector where, despite its obvious off-road credentials, it would compete with vehicles such as the BMW 7-Series, Mercedes S-Class and the Jaguar XJ range – all of which had outstanding on-road handling. In addition, Mercedes with the M-Class and, especially, BMW with the X5, were about to define another 4 x 4 market sub-sector, with offerings that BMW dubbed 'Sports Activity Vehicles' (SAVs). Here, ultimate off-road capability was sacrificed to improve on-road performance. The BMW X5, with a driveline based on that used earlier in a 5-Series Touring with four-wheel drive, was offered with a range of performance engines and, like the Mercedes M-Class, made in America. Reitzle felt that the money could be better spent on a completely new vehicle rather than a facelift.

A team was put together to scope out the new vehicle, which would effectively be the ultimate luxury off-roader. Members included David Sneath, who was developing the facelift project, designer, Don Wyatt, who had also worked on cars projects

Range Rover Third Generation

including the MG RV8, and American marketing man, Paul Ferriaolo. The fourth member of the team was Alistair Patrick from manufacturing who would eventually be responsible for the new vehicle's innovative production facility.

To make its mark in the luxury car sector, it was virtually a given that the vehicle must have independent suspension and, ideally, monocoque construction to provide the stiffness essential to positive handling. With the CB40 programme - the Freelander - featuring both these attributes, it was no longer unthinkable that a Land Rover product could only be defined by beam axles and a separate chassis.

However, the new Range Rover, now known as L30 in the BMW model-numbering system, must be an all-conquering off-roader too as it was to bear the Land Rover badge. This dictated a two-speed transfer box, not a feature of the BMW X5, and also a variable-height air suspension system which had become a Range Rover trademark, following its introduction on the 'Classic' in 1992, and was the only system offered on the New Range Rover.

Independent suspension had been for many years derided by Land Rover as having many disadvantages when driving off road. This was initially a reaction to the Land-Rover's once deadly rival, the Austin Gypsy, which had such a

Given free rein, Don Wyatt's design team came up with some exciting themes for the L30. One strong influence was the Riva Aquarama power boat with its tapering lines evident in the side rendering. These were carried through to the production vehicle, although in a more subtle form

A Brief History

system, but had become endemic to the company's philosophy. The Freelander, which was a catalyst in this sea-change, had started life as a Rover Cars project and was designed more as an SAV rather than a fully-capable off-roader.

The breakthrough came with the concept of 'cross-linking' the air springs. With this system, under certain conditions, air could be fed from one spring to the other on the same axle. As one spring was forced upwards by the terrain, the air, instead of being vented to let the wheel act independently and running the risk of grounding the vehicle, was transferred to the other wheel through an electronically-controlled valve. This forced the opposite wheel down, mimicking the action of a beam axle and increasing its ground pressure to improve traction.

Power would obviously come from BMW's superb range of engines, with the 4.4-litre V8 being chosen for the petrol derivative and the six-cylinder in-line 3.0-litre diesel as its alternative. With high aspirations for the L30, it was also designed around the BMW V12 petrol engine. In an innovative move which was to cause trouble later, the front axle drive shaft ran through the engine sump. The transmission incorporated a Torsen® torque biasing differential to distribute the drive between the front and rear axles. While the petrol-engined derivative used a ZF automatic gearbox, the diesel employed a General Motors unit. Both had five speeds with 'Steptronic' manual over-ride and were the only transmissions offered.

While the L30 project team illustrated the importance of off-road capability for a Land Rover on a specially-prepared course in the Black Forest, work began on the styling of the new vehicle. As before, no-one was in any doubt that re-designing an iconic vehicle was a difficult prospect. It soon became clear that, especially to meet the requirements for wheel travel with the proposed suspension system, the new vehicle would be larger than its predecessor. It was equally clear that it must incorporate the design cues such as the 'clamshell' bonnet and 'floating' roof that had become synonymous with a Range Rover. Chief designer, Don Wyatt, issued a brief to a variety of designers both inside and outside the Rover Group who produced large scale models for an initial theme selection to be made.

A design by Phil Simmons, inspired by the Italian Riva Aquarama power

Final theme selection was done using scale models. A design by Phil Simmons won through and this model shows the distinctive Range Rover 'floating roof' as well as the side 'gills' of the production vehicle. While the brutal styling was muted for the final vehicle, it retained significant 'presence'

Range Rover - The Anniversary Guide

Range Rover Third Generation

boat, soon emerged as a favourite. While Reitzle demanded a run-off with a competing design from BMW's Munich studio, the Simmons theme was selected eventually, albeit in a less sensational style more suited to production.

While some of the interior proposals had very dramatic structural themes, it was a design by Gavin Hartley that was ultimately chosen. Like Simmons, Hartley was also inspired by marine themes, with his design owing much to the interiors of luxury yachts. Hartley paid great attention to the tactility of his interior, choosing textures again inspired by the winches and fittings used on racing yachts.

Wolfgang Reitzle increasingly began to see the L30 as his own personal project, often referring to it as "my baby" and often visiting the project team to view progress. But Reitzle was not just a product man – he was a member of BMW's Supervisory Board. Things had begun to go wrong at BMW – its share price was falling, thanks to the problems with the Rover Group, now known as 'The English Patient' after a popular contemporary film. Astonishingly, Bernd Pischetsrieder, proponent of BMW's acquisition of the Rover Group, had virtually killed off the 'Last Chance Saloon' – the Rover 75 – at birth by stating at its launch press conference in Birmingham that manufacturing cars in Britain had no future and the Rover Group faced massive cutbacks.

His plan to save the company was rejected at a BMW board meeting and he resigned. His successor was intended to be Reitzle but, following an indecisive vote at the same dramatic gathering, his appointment was not supported by the head of the Supervisory Board and he too resigned. He soon re-surfaced as the head of the Ford Motor Company's Premier Automotive Group which then encompassed the British brands of Aston Martin and Jaguar as well as Swedish firm Volvo, and the American luxury nameplate, Lincoln.

But the problems at the Rover Group continued with a battle with the UK Government over funding for the intended replacement for the mid-range Rover 25 and 40 models, code-named R30 and planned to be built at Longbridge. Fearing a re-birth of British Leyland, the then Chancellor of the Exchequer, Gordon Brown, was reluctant to release funding which, in any case, may not have been acceptable within the rules of the European Community. By now there was a real possibility that Rover's problems could bring down the whole BMW Group, so they determined to pull the plug on the English Patient's life support system. In an embarrassing confusion, MG Rover was eventually sold to the Phoenix partnership, led by former Land Rover Managing Director, John Towers. MG Rover staggered along for five years before finally folding – the reasons for their final demise being subject to a lengthy Government enquiry.

Prototypes were subjected to intensive testing in all extremes of climate

To fund the dowry being given to anyone who would take MG Rover off their hands, BMW, in a surprise move, sold Land Rover to the Ford Motor Company. The brand joined the Premier Automotive Group (PAG), headed by BMW's former employee, Reitzle. He was back in the nursery looking after his baby, now re-christened L322 in the Ford model code system.

By the time of the acquisition, the development and production engineering of the L322 were well advanced with the facilities for the new vehicle laid down in Solihull's South Works. A key factor in the negotiations between Ford and BMW, L322 owed more to German, rather than American, production methods and had a very different supplier base structure. The vehicle also employed many components – including engines – used in other BMW products and security of supply was a major issue in the 'due diligence' conducted by Ford.

The launch of the Range Rover was going to be the first all-new model début following Ford's acquisition of Land Rover. With its position as the leading luxury 4 x 4, it was to be a lavish affair with no expense spared. Indeed, Land Rover staff were being encouraged to "think like winners" and it seemed that the days of austerity were over. The vehicle was first introduced to the press in November 2001 at the Design Museum in London with Reitzle proudly presenting

(Above) Wolfgang Reitzle was re-united with his pet project in time for its press début at the London Design Museum

The press launch took place in Scotland where the Range Rover was put through its paces both on- and off-road

Range Rover - The Anniversary Guide

133

Range Rover Third Generation

the vehicle that he had helped to create.

In a bold move, the main international press launch was planned to take place in Scotland in the first few weeks of 2002. Delegates were flown to RAF Kinloss and, following a presentation in one of the base's bomb-proof aircraft hangers, the test route began by driving over the building's sloping roof. The event included on- and off-road driving through the spectacular Scottish winter landscape with guests being accommodated over night in the luxury surroundings of Skibo Castle. The dealer event took place in Italy with the Range Rover's off-road prowess being demonstrated over land near Lake Garda and on a specially-prepared course built in a quarry.

It was now quite obvious that the Range Rover name had enough presence to be a brand, not just a vehicle. This was revealed first in 2004 when the Range Stormer concept vehicle was unveiled at the Detroit Motor Show. This stunning design, actually built on a Second Generation Range Rover platform by Geoff Upex's team at Gaydon, featured frameless doors that swung upwards and forwards to open, while the body, echoing strong Range Rover design cues, featured a full-length glass roof.

Another key innovation was Terrain Response™, designed to optimise the vehicle's characteristics to suit a variety

The Range Stormer concept vehicle proved that the Range Rover name could be applied to other models

134

Range Rover - The Anniversary Guide

A Brief History

of conditions selected by the driver. While Terrain Response™ made its production début later that year with the Discovery 3, a new model to the Range Rover brand emerged the following year in the shape of the Range Rover Sport. While based on a common platform with the Discovery 3, Mike Sampson's dramatic design was every inch a Range Rover and the Range Rover Sport was destined to become the most successful Land Rover model up to that time.

Naturally, Ford was anxious to free themselves of the burden of having to buy engines from BMW and determined to employ their own engines as soon as possible. The front drive shaft arrangement caused difficulties in packaging new units and also caused some customer issues due to its tendency to transmit vibrations, notably with the diesel engine.

By 2005 these issues had been resolved and the BMW petrol engine was replaced by not one, but two engines – both units originally designed for Jaguar, Land Rover's sister company in a revised Premier Automotive Group structure. By now, things had become tough for Ford as well. Deprived of his main supporter, Jac Nasser – who had been ousted in a Ford management shake-up - Reitzle had now also left the Premier Automotive Group to head up fork lift truck manufacturer, Linde.

One power unit was a straight replacement for the BMW petrol engine in the form of a 4.4-litre, all-alloy V8 engine with variable valve timing that produced 15 kW (20 bhp) more power than its predecessor. The other petrol choice was a supercharged 4.2-litre V8

The arrival of the Jaguar-based supercharged V8 engine led to the introduction of mesh grille and side vents

Range Rover - The Anniversary Guide

Range Rover Third Generation

producing 291 kW (390 bhp) – a massive 35% increase over the old BMW engine. Though a new, Land Rover-developed diesel engine was waiting in the wings, the 3.0-litre BMW oil burner was retained. Naturally, the engines received special treatment to enable them to withstand Land Rover duty cycles and had revised sumps to accommodate the Range Rover's unique front axle arrangement.

These petrol engines were mated to a new, six-speed ZF automatic gearbox, featuring 'Command Shift', as the manual over-ride control was now called, 'Steptronic' being a BMW-registered term. The Torsen® centre differential was also replaced by an electronically-controlled unit for improved management of torque distribution. The diesel driveline remained unchanged.

Along with the new engines came a re-styled front bumper with a mesh grille, while mesh 'power vents' replaced the 'gills' on the vehicle's flanks. The light units were also revised to allow for the new, swivelling, adaptive headlamps and the vehicle's equipment levels were updated.

It would take another two years for the Ford-based power train line-up to be completed. The 3.6-litre TDV8 diesel engine was based on the 2.7-litre V6 used in the Discovery 3, Range Rover Sport, and Jaguar and Peugeot cars. The engines were part of a co-operative venture between Ford and Peugeot to develop a range of in-line and Vee engines. However, design leadership of the Vee-configured power units was in the hands of Jaguar and Land Rover, who were by now sharing design teams on specific vehicle systems. Echoing their Peugeot lineage, they were known as the 'Lion' engines.

Although based on the V6, the TDV8 was a very different engine. The Compacted Graphite (CG) cast iron block was computer designed to achieve maximum strength and stiffness while keeping weight to a minimum. The TDV8 had a 90° configuration between the cylinder banks, rather than the 60° of the V6, so that each engine had the optimum slope for its arrangement. This ensured maximum refinement from the outset. The engine was fed by twin variable nozzle turbochargers that had to be slung under the cylinder heads due to the steep Vee of the engine. This required a special oil supply system to ensure constant lubrication for the turbochargers under Range Rover operating conditions.

The TDV8 offered 54% more power and 64% more torque than the earlier BMW six-cylinder diesel, as well as returning a significantly better fuel consumption. Developing 200 kW (268 bhp), this made the V8 naturally-aspirated petrol engine virtually redundant and it was soon dropped from the range.

The TDV8 used the ZF six-speed automatic gearbox and electronically-controlled centre differential introduced earlier on the petrol-engined derivatives. This also enabled the Range Rover to be fitted with Land Rover's

Terrain Response™ was introduced with the TDV8 engine

Terrain Response™ which optimised the characteristics of the engine, transmission and other vehicle systems to the conditions facing the driver who could select from five 'Special Programs' using a control knob, now mounted on the centre console.

Land Rover was by now facing another change of ownership. Ford had been facing problems even before the global economic downturn caused by the banking crisis. In order to save the company, it had decided to concentrate on its core business, in the

The 2010 model year introduced a 'virtual' instrument panel and a dual-view centre display

process divesting itself of some of the acquisitions made in happier times. First to go was Aston Martin, in 2007. Rumours soon abounded that Jaguar and Land Rover, now effectively combined, were also up for sale. Tata Motors of India soon emerged as front runners, eventually acquiring the marques in June 2008. Jaguar Land Rover was soon faced with a major financial crisis as the credit crunch began to bite. While billions of pounds were handed out to failed banks, UK Prime Minister, Gordon Brown, who as Chancellor had refused backing for Rover, was equally unwilling to help Jaguar Land Rover. Fortunately, other investors could see the value in the company and new owners, Tata, were able to finance both day-to-day operations and a forward model programme using private resources.

The first fruits came in 2009 for the 2010 model year. The Range Rover received a new, 5.0-litre V8 supercharged petrol engine to replace the 4.2-litre unit. Using the latest technology, the new power unit not only gave nearly 30% more power but also improved fuel consumption and reduced emissions. Along with the new engine came a styling facelift including a new front bumper, headlamp and grille treatment. The Range Rover now had a 30cm (12in) Thin Film Transistor (TFT) display with 'virtual' dials to replace the conventional instrument pack, while a dual view centre screen, enabling the driver and front passenger to see different displays, was a world first.

At the same time as the 2010 model year Range Rover was revealed to the press, Land Rover announced that a fourth addition to the Range Rover model line-up would be built at its Halewood plant from 2011. Based on the LRX concept car, first shown in 2008, the new vehicle would feature advanced construction techniques and new hybrid technology to reduce its environmental impact. It would also be considerably smaller and lighter than previous Range Rovers.

Work was also proceeding on a replacement for the current generation of Range Rovers with styling themes being selected at the Gaydon design studio under the direction of Gerry McGovern, Land Rover's new design director. While still behind a veil of secrecy, the new Range Rover will no doubt share the same design DNA created by its seminal predecessor 40 years ago.

Range Rover - The Anniversary Guide

BODY AND CHASSIS

The Third Generation Range Rover (known as L30 under the BMW Group model designation system and L322 under the Ford system) abandoned the separate body and chassis used on previous models in favour of a monocoque body which achieved stiffness levels of 32,500 Nm per degree to enhance its off-road ability but also to offer class-leading levels of on-road refinement and handling. Special consideration was given to the capability of towing a 3.5 tonne trailer and to be able to withstand snatch recovery shock loads.

The main monocoque structure comprising the floor, engine bay, pillars, roof and rear wings was of zinc-coated, high-strength steel. The tailgate upper and lower assemblies were also steel, while the bonnet and front wings were of aluminium. The bonnet featured one of the largest deep-draw pressings in Europe – even more remarkable for being in aluminium. It was claimed to be half the weight of a steel equivalent. The doors were a mixture of aluminium castings, extrusions and pressings – even including the side intrusion bars. Use of the material was estimated to save 40 kg of weight. The doors had a plastic lower cladding-panel to protect against damage from stone chips, off-road obstacles or other minor knocks. There was provision for a sliding sun roof.

Front and rear steel subframes, produced using hydroforming techniques, acted as mounts for the suspension.

Special attention was paid to the 'ground plane' underneath the vehicle to protect vital components, such as the engine, suspension and fuel tank, with Kevlar shields. This also aided off-road performance by smoothing the underside to prevent snagging on rough terrain.

Body panels were pressed at a new stamping facility built at the Solihull plant which also provided components for the new MINI being built at Oxford by BMW. The shell was assembled at a new body-in-white (BIW) shop built within Solihull's East Works although the all-alloy doors were supplied as fully built-up units from a sub-contractor.

The completed body was finished in the facility built for the Freelander programme of 1997 with 12 colour options being available.

All fixed glazing was bonded to the structure, the front windscreen being laminated with a shade band, while both front and rear screens were heated. Radio and television antennae were screen printed onto the rear side windows. Windows and the sun roof were electrically operated and featured an 'anti-trap' mechanism.

ENGINE

Two engine options – a V8 petrol and six-cylinder diesel - were offered, both from the BMW range. The design of the engine bay allowed for the fitment of a V12 petrol engine at a later date.

The petrol engine was the BMW M62 4.4.-litre V8 with variable camshaft control (single VANOS). This power unit was of all-alloy construction with twin camshafts and 32 valves.

The body was an immensely strong monocoque but was clad with Land Rover's signature aluminium

The diesel engine was the BMW M57 3.0-litre direct injection inline six-cylinder with variable nozzle turbocharger and intercooler. It had a cast-iron block and aluminium cylinder head. The camshaft was chain driven with 24 valves.

Both engines used electronic throttle control with dual maps designed to give faster response on-road and more control off-road. Both engines – particularly the diesel – were modified to suit Land Rover off-road performance parameters.

TRANSMISSION

Automatic transmission was standard. The petrol engine version used a five-speed gearbox by ZF while the diesel version used a GM unit. Both versions featured a manual override system using the BMW-named Steptronic at launch although this was later dubbed Command Shift when Land Rover's right to use the BMW trademark

Technical Description

lapsed under Ford ownership.

The two-speed transfer box used a chain drive with a single offset shaft with torque distribution being controlled by a Torsen® torque-biasing differential. Normal torque distribution was 50:50 but the differential had a maximum torque bias ratio of 2:1. Range change used synchromesh and a electric motor driven shift to allow swapping between high and low ranges on the move, provided the main gearbox was in neutral. High to Low shifts could be made at speeds up to 16 kp/h (10 mph) while Low to High changes could be made up to 48 kp/h (30 mph).

Both front and rear propshafts were of the high angle, high plunge type to maximise axle articulation.

With independent suspension, the rear differential housing was mounted to the rear subframe while the front unit was mounted directly to the engine sump, one of the driveshafts passing through the sump itself.

SUSPENSION

Independent suspension with air springs was used all-round. The front suspension comprised a MacPherson strut with an air spring and telescopic hydraulic damper. The front suspension geometry used a virtual double centre double joint MacPherson strut with two ball joints at the end of the suspension arms. This arrangement increased the king-pin inclination angle and gave negative ground level offset. Combined with the use of drive shafts with high articulation joints, total front wheel travel was 270mm (10.6in). There was also an anti-roll bar mounted on the front subframe and linked to the suspension struts.

The rear suspension was of the double wishbone type mounted to the rear subframe with air springs and separate hydraulic dampers mounted forward of the springs. There was also a subframe-mounted anti-roll bar.

The system employed cross link valves in air lines linking the left and right hand air springs. When on road, these valves were shut enabling each wheel to act independently and to stiffen the suspension to improve ride and handling. The suspension system employed 'Terrain Sensing Software' to determine off-road conditions. Under certain circumstances, this let the valves open allowing air to pass from one side to the other. This allowed more compliance to enable the wheels to fully articulate and to increase ground pressure – in this way mimicking the effect of a beam axle.

Air was provided by a compressor motor housed in the spare wheel stowage area in the boot. The tubular

(Below left) The petrol engine was BMW's well-known 4.4-litre V8

(Below) While the diesel alternative was a six-cylinder 3.0-litre unit, also from BMW

Range Rover - The Anniversary Guide

Technical Description

reservoir was made from aircraft-grade aluminium and incorporated the five-way valve block, controlled by the system's own electronic management unit.

The system had a number of heights, either automatic or selected by the driver. Normal height was employed during on-road driving with an automatic lowering (by 23mm [0.91in]) to the Cruise position during sustained high speeds. Access mode reduced vehicle height by 43mm (1.69in) from Normal for ease of ingress and egress. This could also be locked for manoeuvring in reduced height areas such as car parks. The vehicle would automatically revert to Normal height at a given speed after warning the driver. The Access position could be pre-selected, allowing the vehicle to gradually fall as it slowed down so as to be in the Access position as it reached a standstill. An Off Road position raised the vehicle by 52mm (2.05in) from Normal and could be selected by the driver to increase ground clearance, improve approach and departure angles, and allow a greater wading depth. Use of wheel height and other sensors enabled an automatic emergency off-road height to be provided to reduce the chance of the vehicle grounding.

WHEELS AND TYRES

All wheels were aluminium and a full-size alloy spare wheel was provided. The standard wheel on all models except the Vogue petrol was an 18-inch twin-spoke design fitted with 255/16 R18 tyres. The Vogue petrol was fitted with a 19-inch, six-spoke wheel with 255/55 R19 tyres. An 18-inch, five-spoke design fitted with 255/60 R18 tyres was available across the range. Later (from June 2002) a 20-inch, seven-spoke wheel fitted with 255/50 R20 tyres was available as an accessory for petrol models only. Other tyre proposals included a Goodyear MTR type (later used on G4 Challenge vehicles) and a sand tyre.

The spare wheel had a harness system to aid extraction from the stowage well.

BRAKING SYSTEM

The vehicle was fitted with large-diameter disc brakes all-round, those at the front being ventilated, with the rear brakes having an integral drum for the park brake. The foundation braking system was of the latest ABS type and included a number of supplementary functions. These included Emergency Brake Assist (EBA) which increased brake pressure in the case of an emergency stop and Electronic Brakeforce Distribution (EBD) which ensured equal braking pressure front and rear to keep the vehicle stable under braking.

The foundation braking system also supported other dynamic features. This included Dynamic Stability Control (DSC) which automatically applied differential braking pressure in an attempt to keep the vehicle under control if adhesion was likely to be lost when cornering. This feature also reduced engine torque to supplement the braking action and this effect could be switched off to prevent it being a disadvantage when driving off road. Another feature was Electronic Traction Control (ETC) which applied a braking force to a slipping wheel to prevent drive being lost and to transfer torque to a wheel with grip. First developed for the Freelander but also used on the Discovery Series II and BMW X5, the vehicle was also equipped with Hill Descent Control (HDC). This applied a braking force automatically to reduce speed and improve control on downhill gradients.

STEERING

Rack and pinion power-assisted steering, manufactured by ZF, was fitted. It used the Servotronic speed-sensitive system to provide greater assistance at lower speeds to aid manoeuvring.

The collapsible steering column

Cross-linking the air suspension from side to side was the key to on- and off-road performance

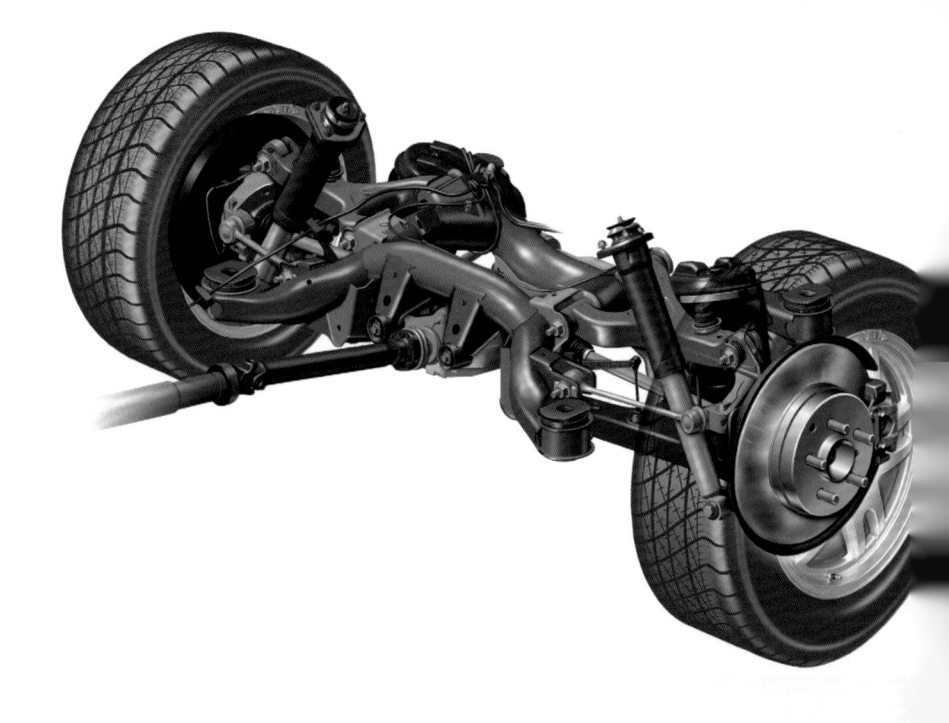

Technical Description

featured electronic adjustment for reach and tilt that was coupled to the seat and mirror memory system. The column automatically rose when the key was removed to aid driver access and egress. The ignition key was located on the fascia, column locking being achieved electronically.

The four-spoke steering wheel had a leather-covered rim capable of being heated. The wheel housed controls for the audio system, telephone system, voice recognition, cruise control and steering wheel heating as well as horn buttons. The driver's air bag was also located here.

Twin column stalks controlled the direction indicators, dip and main beam as well as the front and rear wiper and washer systems. One stalk also provided the control to access the information display. There was also a knob for column adjustment.

SEATING AND TRIM

The seats were of a new design and comprised separate driver and passenger front seats and a three-person rear bench seat with a central folding armrest. The rear seat was foldable with a 60:40 split. It also had a hatch for the stowage of skis, a ski bag being standard on Vogue models and optional for other

The fascia owed much to influences from power boats and luxury yachts

Range Rover - The Anniversary Guide

141

Range Rover Third Generation — Phase One

Technical Description

derivatives. The rear central armrest also incorporated twin cup holders capable of accommodating a range of beverage containers. Rear seats provided ISO mountings for child seats on the two outer positions with staples mounted on the back for tethers. Driver and front passenger seats were heated on the HSE model (optional on SE) while the Vogue had heated front and rear outer seats.

Standard trim for SE and HSE models was Blenheim leather while HSE models were fitted with Oxford leather, Contour seats with split backs offering a wider range of adjustment. Front seat adjustment was electric and linked to the memory system which also provided automatic setting of the external mirrors and steering column. Both front seats had adjustable armrests.

The floor was trimmed in a moulded pile carpet. Interior colourway options offered a wide range of colours for seats, piping, carpet and veneers.

The centre console incorporated a large cubby box with a double lid that

The seats were extremely supportive and had a wide range of power adjustment

Technical Description

The L30/322 Range Rover was a very complex vehicle as revealed by this cutaway

also offered a housing for an integrated mobile phone handset. The centre console housed the gear lever, which had a leather gaiter, as well as a cigar lighter, ignition key, paddle switches for the high/low transfer box change and Hill Descent Control, as well as having coin and oddment trays. The handbrake lever emerged from the front face of the cubby box and also had a leather gaiter. There was a large ashtray.

The loadspace area was trimmed with moulded panels with a carpet finish. The side panels were removable to allow access for bulb changing and equipment. There was a carpet-covered board covering the spare wheel well which was fitted with a lifting handle and support strut. The spare wheel compartment also housed the tool kit and the detachable towing ball. A falling panel filled the gap between the tailgate and the body when the tailgate was open. The floor was fitted with four folding chrome 'D' rings to use with luggage restraining nets or straps. There were also a number of hooks around the loadspace area for use with accessory nets. This loadspace area was illuminated and provided with a power outlet for use with portable fridges, compressors, etc. The area was covered by a folding, fabric-covered board which could be removed to maximise the loadspace area. A retractable mesh screen was provided that hooked into locations in the headlining to protect occupants from falling luggage.

The door trims were of foam and vinyl-covered board; the front door trims included side impact protection air bags for the driver and front passenger. The door trims also housed speakers for the in-car entertainment system and window lift switches, that on the driver's side including switches for all windows, the disabling switch for the rear windows, mirror adjustment and suspension Access position pre-selector.

The roof trim comprised fabric-covered mouldings and housed a complex system of interior lighting for both front and rear seat passengers including 'waterfall' lighting which constantly provided a low level of illumination. The roof and 'A' pillar also concealed head impact air bags and curtains for both front and outer rear seat passengers for protection from impact or injury from flying glass in the case of a roll over accident. The interior mirror was of the automatic dipping type.

FASCIA AND INSTRUMENTS

The fascia was of a striking design featuring strong horizontal and vertical styling features. The interior design team were inspired by top-end Hi-Fi equipment and the materials used on yachts and power boats, the Italian Riva being cited as an influence for both the exterior and interior design treatment. This led to a combination of metallic finishes with real wood veneers.

The design featured a topper panel attached with exposed fixings, a central core housing the glove box and knee bolster panels, veneered end caps and a vertical centre stack flanked by wood veneer cheeks that appeared to run continuously through the fascia to the centre console.

A key feature of the fascia design was a windscreen LCD monitor which was capable of displaying a TV picture or Teletext as well as satellite navigation maps and information. The display

Range Rover - The Anniversary Guide

Range Rover Third Generation | Phase One

Styling Concepts

Mike Sampson.

This rendering of the final design was done by Mike Sampson in 2001 just as production was about to commence

This bold design still echoes Range Rover themes and was done by Julian Quincy

Styling Concepts

This design was by Mike Sampson and was the second Land Rover studio theme. The front end graphics were very strong and, according to Don Wyatt, could have led to a common theme for Land Rover vehicles. Some elements can be seen in Freelander 2 and the 2010 model year Range Rover

These interior sketches are by Alan Sheppard who, says Don Wyatt, had a deep understanding of luxury products – something which had a deep impact on the final design

Range Rover - The Anniversary Guide

| Range Rover Third Generation | Phase One |

Styling Concepts

Seen in the Gaydon Design and Engineering Centre (GDEC) in August 1997, this was the clay model of Phil Simmons' design for the final exterior theme selection

Interior theme selection took place in November 1997. This was the model for Alan Sheppard's proposal. Like the final design, it featured strong horizontal and vertical lines with exposed fixings

Range Rover - The Anniversary Guide

Styling Concepts

With the last Range Rover 'Classic' and a Second Generation Range Rover in the background, the contenders for the theme selection for their successor lined up on !st August 1997. From left they are: Mike Sampson and Paul Hanstock's design, the proposal from the BMW Munich design studio, Phil Simmons' winning theme and the offering from the Design Works studio

This was the second side of the Phil Simmons theme and, according to Don Wyatt, the preferred option thanks to its cleaner lines and, compared with earlier designs from Phil Simmons, a true floating roof with a blacked out 'E' pillar

Range Rover - The Anniversary Guide

Range Rover Third Generation — Phase One — Technical Data

Specification Sheets

GENERAL FEATURES

CONSTRUCTION
Four-door, five-seat body with clamshell opening tailgate. Steel monocoque body with aluminium doors, bonnet and front wings. Steel front and rear subframes.

POWER UNITS
4.4-litre V8 petrol engine, 3.0-litre six-cylinder diesel engine

TRANSMISSION
Permanent four wheel drive. Five-speed automatic gearbox with Steptronic. Chain-driven, two-speed transfer box with Torsen centre differential. Open drive shaft axles with front differential mounted to engine sump

SUSPENSION
Four-corner, variable-height, electonically-controlled interlinked air suspension with variable-rate air springs and hydraulic dampers. MacPherson strut front suspension with negative ground offset. Double wishbone rear suspension

STEERING
Speed-sensitive power-assisted rack and pinion

BRAKING
ABS with Electronic Traction Control, Dynamic Stability Control, Hill Descent Control, Electronic Brakeforce Distribution and Emergency Brake Assist

OTHER FEATURES
GPS navigation system with widescreen TV monitor. Bi-Xenon headlights. Front, thorax and head protection airbags

	UNITS	4.4-Litre V8 Petrol Automatic	3.0-Litre Diesel Automatic
DIMENSIONS			
Overall Length	mm(in)	4972(195.8)	4972(195.8)
Overall Width (over mirrors)	mm(in)	2192(86.3)	2192(86.3)
Overall Height (max)	mm(in)	1902(74.9)	1902(74.9)
Wheelbase	mm(in)	2880(113.3)	2880(113.3)
Track Front/Rear	mm(in)	1629(64.1)/1625(64.0)	1629(64.1)/1625(64.0)
Luggage Capacity (Seat Up)	l(cu ft)	997(35.2)	997(35.2)
Luggage Capacity (Seat Folded)	l(cu ft)	2122(74.9)	2122(74.9)
WEIGHTS			
Kerb Weight (EEC) min	kg(lb)	2440(5380)	2435(5368)
Gross Vehicle Weight	kg(lb)	3050(6724)	3050(6724)
Front Axle Maximum Weight	kg(lb)	1530(3373)	1530(3373)
Rear Axle Maximum Weight	kg(lb)	1850(4079)	1850(4079)
Maximum Payload	kg(lb)	610(1344)	615(1356)
Maximum On Road Trailer Weight	kg(lb)	3500(7716) with over-run brakes, 750(1653) unbraked	
Maximum Off Road Trailer Weight	kg(lb)	1000(2205) with over-run brakes, 500(1103) unbraked	
CAPABILITIES			
Drag Coefficient	Cd	0.39	0.39
Approach Angle (Maximum)	Deg	34 with suspension at off-road height	34 with suspension at off-road height
Under Body (Ramp) Angle (Maximum)	Deg	150 with suspension at off-road height	150 with suspension at off-road height
Departure Angle (Maximum)	Deg	26.6 with suspension at off-road height (no tow bar)	
Gradient Climbable (Maximum)	Deg	45 (drive through)	45 (drive through)
Sideslope Angle (Maximum)	Deg	35	35
Turning Circle (Kerb to kerb)	mm(in)	11.6(38.1))	11.6(38.1))
Wading Depth (Maximum)	mm(in)	700(27.6)	700(27.6)

Specification Sheets

	UNITS	4.4-Litre V8 Petrol Automatic	3.0-Litre Diesel Automatic
PERFORMANCE			
Maximum Speed	kp/h(mph)	208(130)	179(111)
Acceleration 0 - 100 kp/h	secs	9.2	13.6
Acceleration 0 - 60 mph	secs	8.7	12.7
FUEL CONSUMPTION			
Urban Cycle (EC)	l/100km (mpg)	22.2(12.7)	14.4(19.6)
Extra Urban (EC)	l/100km (mpg)	12.6(22.4)	9.4(30.1)
Overall (EC)	l/100km (mpg)	16.2(17.4)	11.3(25.0)
CO_2 Emissions (EC)	g/km	389	299
City (EPA)	mpg(US)	12	N/A
Highway (EPA)	mpg(US)	17	N/A
ENGINE			
Type		V8	In-line Six-Cylinder
Fuel		Petrol (Gasoline)	Diesel
Number of Cylinders		8	6
Number of Camshafts		4	2
Valves per Cylinder		4	4
Valve System		Twin overhead camshafts	Twin overhead camshafts
Bore	mm(in)	92.0(3.62)	84.0(3.31)
Stroke	mm(in)	82.7(3.42)	88.0(3.47)
Capacity	cc(cu in)	4398(268)	2926(179)
Compression Ratio	:1	10	18
Cylinder Head Material		Aluminium alloy	Aluminium alloy
Cylinder Block Material		Alusil aluminium alloy	Cast iron
Lubrication System		Chain driven oil pump immersed in sump	Chain driven oil pump immersed in sump
Fuel System		Bosch 7.2 ECU, electric lift pump immersed in fuel tank	Bosch electronic type DD4.0
Ignition System		Distributorless via ECU. Electronic throttle. Drag torque control	N/A
Boost System		None	Exhaust driven turbocharger with Variable Nozzle Turbine (VNT)
Cold Start System		Automatic via ECU	Automatic with heater plugs
Air Cleaning System		Paper element	Paper element
Cooling System		Cross flow with aluminium radiator	Cross flow with aluminium radiator
Battery Capacity	Amp/hr	90(110 optional)	96(110 optional)
Max Power	kW(bhp)	210(282)	130(174)
At	rpm	5400	4000
Max Torque	Nm(lb/ft)	440(325)	390(288)
At	rpm	3600	2000

Range Rover - The Anniversary Guide

PRICE LIST (UK)

RANGE ROVER THIRD GENERATION PHASE 1

DATE	MODEL	PRICE	NOTES
		£ Inc Car Tax and VAT	
February 2004	Range Rover Td6 SE	45,995	
	Range Rover V8 SE	50,995	
	Range Rover Td6 HSE	48,995	
	Range Rover V8 HSE	53,995	
	Range Rover Td6 Vogue	49,995	
	Range Rover V8 Vogue	53,995	
	OPTIONS		
	Six disc CD Autochanger	350	Standard on HSE and Vogue models
	11-Speaker Hi-Fi System	495	SE models only
	Hi-Fi system with digital sound processor	625	HSE models only
	Hi-Fi system with digital sound processor	1095	SE models only
	TV/Navigation system	2500	Standard on Vogue models
	Cellular telephone system with voice recognition	1150	
	Cloth Seat Trim	nco	Not available on Vogue models
	Electrochromatic door mirrors	200	Standard on Vogue models
	Auto dipping interior mirrors and powerfold exterior mirrors	300	Standard on HSE and Vogue models
	18-inch five-spoke alloy wheels	nco	
	19-inch six-spoke alloy wheels	2000	Standard on V8 Vogue. Not available on Td6 models
	Cherry wood trim	nco	
	Burr wood trim	nco	
	Privacy glass	450	
	Electric sunroof	1075	Standard on Vogue models
	Seat heating - front	320	Standard on HSE, not available on Vogue models
	Cold weather pack - heated rear seats, steering wheel and ski bag	595	HSE models only
	Ski bag	100	Vogue models only
	Climate control heated windscreen	350	In lieu of rain sensing windscreen
	Remote park heating	750	
	Park distance control	525	Standard on HSE and Vogue models
	Headlamp wash wipe	250	Standard on HSE and Vogue models
	Detachable tow bar	595	
	Drop plate tow bar	595	
	Warning triangle	30	
	First aid kit	30	

Specification Sheets

Range Rover - The Anniversary Guide

Range Rover Third Generation | Phase One | Advertising

Advertising & Brochures

The main customer brochure for the launch of the Third Generation Range Rover was a multi-part publication with supplements covering pricing information, colour charts and the vehicle's specification

Like other aspects of the Range Rover's press launch, the press kit was a lavish affair, picking up on the different textures in the vehicle. Freed from its sleeve, the booklet folded out to reveal a glossy press brochure and a CD of images and text

Advertising & Brochures

Launch imagery was dark and classy using advanced digital techniques

THE NEW RANGE ROVER.

HIGHER GROUND.

What defines the evolution of a world-class vehicle? The ability to scale new heights. And when you experience the new 2003 Range Rover, getting there is as rewarding as being there. With a new cross-linked Electronic Air Suspension that provides unprecedented comfort and capability over almost any terrain. And the special alchemy of its luxurious waterfall-lit wood and leather interior that indulges the soul. No wonder Car and Driver magazine selected it "Best Luxury Sport-Utility Vehicle." The new Range Rover for 2003. From Land Rover. The most well-traveled vehicles on earth.

RANGE ROVER • FREELANDER • DISCOVERY

THE LAND ROVER EXPERIENCE

Early US advertising picked up on the award won by the vehicle from Car and Driver *magazine*

Range Rover - The Anniversary Guide

159

| Range Rover Third Generation | Phase One | Advertising |

Advertising & Brochures

RANGE ROVER
The inside story of Britain's brand new 4x4 hero
AN AUTOCAR BOOK

In the UK, Autocar produced a special book celebrating the launch of the vehicle. This included coverage of a trip to Andorra in a prototype vehicle by Ben Oliver, accompanied by the author, then Land Rover PR Manager, and David Sneath, Programme Manager. Photography was by David Shephard

Range Rover - The Anniversary Guide

Advertising & Brochures

The customer brochure pack included details of the 12 exterior colours offered at launch together with a variety of interior and trim finishes. The customer's selection was guided by a chart showing available matches together with 'Designer's Choice' combinations

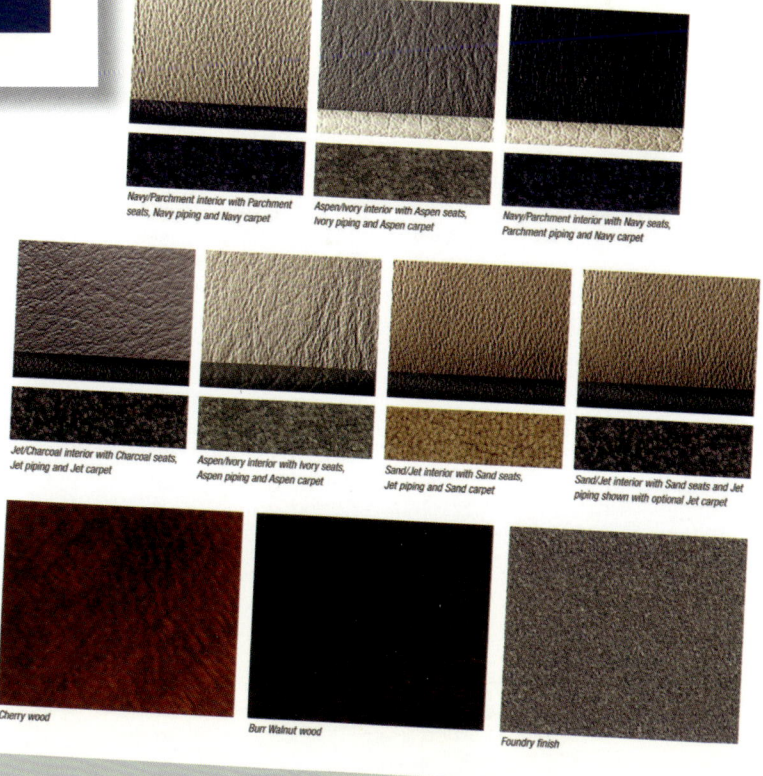

Exterior colours:
- Chawton White (Solid)
- Zambezi Silver (Metallic)
- White Gold (Metallic)
- Epsom Green (Micatallic)
- Giverny Green (Micatallic)
- Icelandic Blue (Metallic)
- Bonatti Grey (Metallic)
- Java Black (Pearlescent)
- Alveston Red (Micatallic)
- Adriatic Blue (Micatallic)
- Oslo Blue (Micatallic)
- Monte Carlo Blue (Micatallic)

Interior trim combinations:
- Navy/Parchment interior with Parchment seats, Navy piping and Navy carpet
- Aspen/Ivory interior with Aspen seats, Ivory piping and Aspen carpet
- Navy/Parchment interior with Navy seats, Parchment piping and Navy carpet
- Jet/Charcoal interior with Charcoal seats, Jet piping and Jet carpet
- Aspen/Ivory interior with Ivory seats, Aspen piping and Aspen carpet
- Sand/Jet interior with Sand seats, Jet piping and Sand carpet
- Sand/Jet interior with Sand seats and Jet piping shown with optional Jet carpet

Wood/finish:
- Cherry wood
- Burr Walnut wood
- Foundry finish

Range Rover - The Anniversary Guide

Range Rover Third Generation | Phase Two

Technical Description

Land Rover under Ford ownership were obviously keen to avoid the costs associated with buying in BMW power units and by 2005 (2006 model year) were able to introduce a face-lifted version of the Range Rover with petrol engines derived from the Jaguar range and which were also used in the Discovery 3 and Range Rover Sport. The opportunity was also taken to refresh the exterior design and to revise the transmission on the petrol engine derivatives.

BODY AND CHASSIS

A new bumper design was introduced across the range with V8 supercharged models also getting a new mesh-design front grille. The supercharged version also gained side 'power vents' in place of the original 'gill' design. The headlamps were revised on all models to allow for swivelling adaptive front lamps while the tail lamp design was also updated.

Laminated front side window glass was introduced to reduce noise, along with a re-profiling of the 'A' posts to smooth airflow and reduce wind noise.

ENGINE

Two new engines were introduced – a 4.4-litre V8 naturally-aspirated and a 4.2-litre V8 supercharged unit. Both engines were derived from those used on the Jaguar car range. The 4.4-litre V8 was also used in the Discovery 3 while both engines were used in the Range Rover Sport.

The 4.4-litre V8 naturally-aspirated engine was of all-alloy construction and featured a structural sump to allow for the passage of one of the drive shafts – an unwanted hang over

The major change for the second phase of the Third Generation Range Rover was the introduction of new, Jaguar-derived V8 petrol engines. This was accompanied by a minor styling facelift including a new grille

from the original design. Like its BMW predecessor, it featured variable inlet valve timing with four valves per cylinder.

The 4.2-litre V8 force-fed engine employed a top-mounted Eaton supercharger with twin meshing impellors that were PTFE coated to improve charge pressure. Before entering, the air was passed through twin intercoolers to optimise the charge – these had their own cooling matrix in front of the main radiator, the circuit having its own electric pump. The cylinder block liners had wider walls to improve the strength

Range Rover - The Anniversary Guide

Technical Description

of the block which resulted in the reduced capacity compared with the naturally aspirated engine. The pistons also had a revised bowl profile while the injectors were of increased capacity. Valve timing was fixed.

Both engines were modified from the units used in Jaguar cars to suit Land Rover operating conditions. The engine management system was re-mapped to give more torque at lower speeds while the oil sumps were bigger with the oil pump being modified to a more efficient design – a modification which was subsequently employed on Jaguar engines. The front crankshaft seal was modified with an additional sealing bead, and a mud flinger and labyrinth was fitted to prevent contamination in off-road conditions. The cooling fan was of the electro-mechanical type and was only engaged when required.

TRANSMISSION

The petrol engines were married to a new six-speed ZF automatic gearbox, replacing the earlier five-speed unit. The Torsen® centre differential was also replaced with an electronically-controlled unit which allowed more flexibility in torque split between the front and rear axles.

The older arrangement was retained for the diesel model.

SUSPENSION

The air suspension system was modified and re-programmed to improve on- and off-road performance and ride comfort. The V8 Supercharged variant had revisions to provide

The 4.2-litre V8 supercharged petrol engine used an Eaton blower with its own twin intercoolers

Range Rover - The Anniversary Guide

Range Rover Third Generation | **Phase Two**

Technical Description

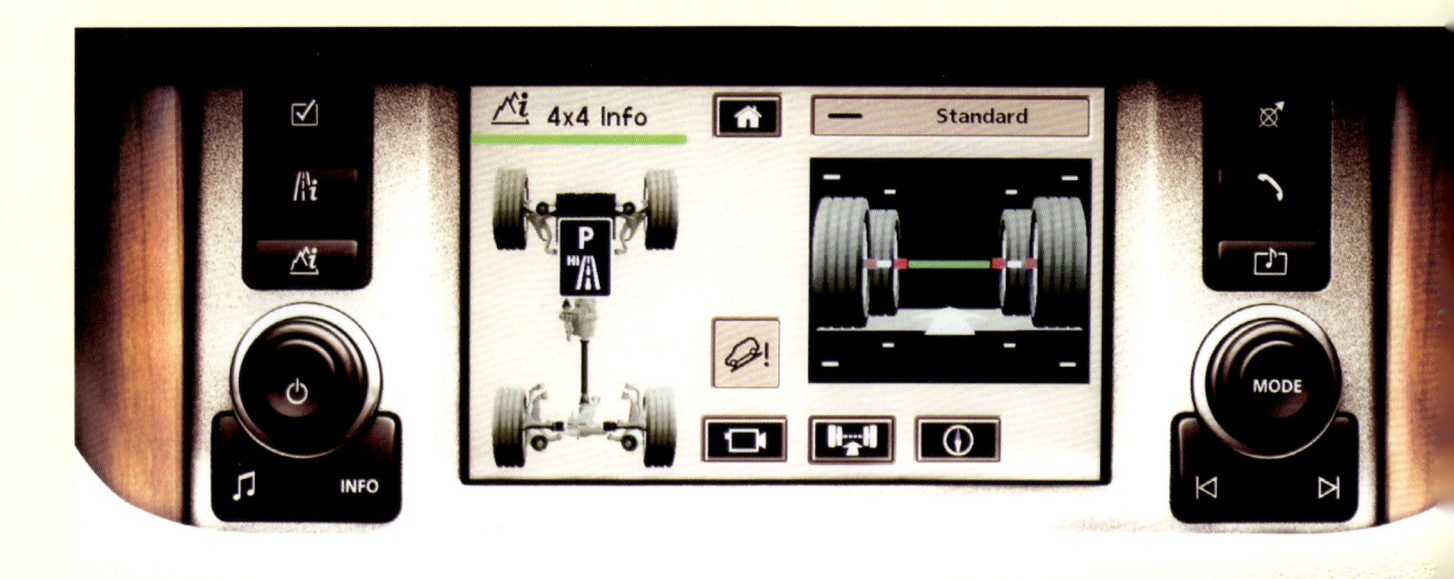

flatter handling for improved high speed, on-road performance.

WHEELS AND TYRES

New styles of 18- and 19-inch wheels were introduced with the V8 Vogue getting a new 20-inch seven-spoke wheel fitted with 255/50 R20 tyres. The V8 Vogue Supercharged was fitted with unique 20-inch nine-spoke wheels equipped with 255/50 R20 tyres, both 20-inch tyres coming from Dunlop.

BRAKING SYSTEM

V8 Supercharged vehicles received a new Brembo four-piston front brake system with fixed calipers. The ventilated front discs were enlarged to match the new brakes.

FASCIA AND INSTRUMENTS

A saddle stitch feature line was added to the fascia topper panel.

ELECTRICAL SYSTEM

Adaptive front headlamps were introduced. These had swivelling Xenon light units, supplemented by sideward-facing corner lights that were lit as lock was applied to illuminate kerb corners.

A new, touch screen display was introduced which enabled direct control

A new transfer box with an electronically-controlled centre differential allowed for the introduction of a 4 x 4 information screen – but only on the petrol-engined versions

of the audio, navigation, phone, on-board computer and a new 4x4 information screen which showed the status of the system – this was not available on diesel variants which retained the earlier Torsen® centre differential. The new screen enabled a reduction in the buttons surrounding the display. New control knobs were also introduced, the combination leading to a considerable tidying up of the centre fascia area.

164   Range Rover - The Anniversary Guide

Technical Description

A reversing camera was introduced, with the display appearing automatically on the fascia screen when reverse was selected. Tyre pressure monitoring was also re-introduced following its earlier disappearance due to frequent spurious warnings.

Also made available was a rear seat entertainment system with screens built into the front seat headrests. Operated by a remote control, this featured a six-disc DVD auto-changer with the soundtrack being delivered by wireless headphones. There were also sockets for other inputs such as MP3 players and games consoles.

The telephone system was upgraded to include Bluetooth® enabled phones to be used while SMS texts could now be sent using a keyboard on the touch screen when cradle-mounted phones were fitted.

(Top) The steering wheel had its original thin rim – designed for delicate Japanese hands – beefed up for the 2006 model year

As if it were needed, the rev. counter reminded the driver of the fact the V8 engine was supercharged

Range Rover - The Anniversary Guide

165

Range Rover Third Generation — Phase Two — Technical Data

Specification Sheets

GENERAL FEATURES

CONSTRUCTION
Four-door, five-seat body with clamshell opening tailgate. Steel monocoque body with aluminium doors, bonnet, and front wings. Steel front and rear subframes

POWER UNITS
New 4.2-litre V8 supercharged petrol engine, new 4.4-litre V8 petrol engine, 3.0-litre six-cylinder diesel engine

TRANSMISSION
Permanent four wheel drive. Six-speed (petrol) or five-speed (diesel) automatic gearbox with 'Command Shift' over-ride. Chain-driven, two-speed transfer box with electonically-controlled (petrol) or Torsen (diesel) centre differential. Open drive shaft axles with front differential mounted to engine sump

SUSPENSION
Four-corner, variable-height, electonically-controlled interlinked air suspension with variable-rate air springs and hydraulic dampers. MacPherson strut front suspension with negative ground offset. Double wishbone rear suspension

STEERING
Speed-sensitive power-assisted rack and pinion

BRAKING
ABS with Electronic Traction Control, Dynamic Stability Control, Hill Descent Control, Electronic Brakeforce Distribution, and Emergency Brake Assist

OTHER FEATURES
GPS navigation system with widescreen TV monitor. 4x4 information screen. Bi-Xenon headlights. Front, thorax and head protection airbags

	UNITS	4.4-Litre V8 Petrol Automatic	4.2-Litre V8 Supercharged Automatic	3.0-Litre Diesel Automatic
DIMENSIONS				
Overall Length	mm(in)	4972(195.8)	4972(195.8)	4972(195.8)
Overall Width (over mirrors)	mm(in)	2192(86.3)	2192(86.3)	2192(86.3)
Overall Height (max)	mm(in)	1902(74.9)	1902(74.9)	1902(74.9)
Wheelbase	mm(in)	2880(113.3)	2880(113.3)	2880(113.3)
Track Front/Rear	mm(in)	1629(64.1)/1625(64.0)	1629(64.1)/1625(64.0)	1629(64.1)/1625(64.0)
Luggage Capacity (Seat Up)	l(cu ft)	997(35.2)	997(35.2)	997(35.2)
Luggage Capacity (Seat Folded)	l(cu ft)	2122(74.9)	2122(74.9)	2122(74.9)
WEIGHTS				
Minimum Kerb Weight (EEC)	kg(lb)	2592(5714)	2680(5908)	2545(5611)
Gross Vehicle Weight	kg(lb)	3100(6834)	3100(6834)	3050(6724)
Front Axle Maximum Weight	kg(lb)	1530(3373)	1530(3373)	1530(3373)
Rear Axle Maximum Weight	kg(lb)	1850(4079)	1850(4079)	1850(4079)
Maximum Payload	kg(lb)	508(1120)	420(926)	505(1113)
Maximum On Road Trailer Weight	kg(lb)	3500(7716) with over-run brakes, 750(1653) unbraked		
Maximum Off Road Trailer Weight	kg(lb)	1000(2205) with over-run brakes, 500(1103) unbraked		
CAPABILITIES				
Drag Coefficient	Cd	0.39	0.39	0.39
Approach Angle (Maximum)	Deg	34 with suspension at off-road height		
Under Body (Ramp) Angle (Maximum)	Deg	150 with suspension at off-road height		
Departure Angle (Maximum)	Deg	26.6 with suspension at off-road height (no tow bar)		
Gradient Climbable (Maximum)	Deg	45 (drive through), 35 (continuous)		
Sideslope Angle (Maximum)	Deg	35	35	35
Turning Circle (Kerb to kerb)	mm(in)	11.6(38.1)	12.6(41.30)	11.6(38.1)

Range Rover - The Anniversary Guide

Specification Sheets

	UNITS	4.4-Litre V8 Petrol Automatic	4.2-Litre V8 Supercharged Automatic	3.0-Litre Diesel Automatic
Wading Depth (Maximum)	mm(in)	700(27.6)	700(27.6)	700(27.6)
PERFORMANCE				
Maximum Speed	kp/h(mph)	200(124)	210(130)	179(111)
Acceleration 0 - 100 kp/h	secs	8.7	7.5	13.6
Acceleration 0 - 60 mph	secs	8.3	7.1	12.7
FUEL CONSUMPTION				
Urban Cycle (EC)	l/100km (mpg)	21.2(13.4)	22.4(12.6)	14.4(19.6)
Extra Urban (EC)	l/100km (mpg)	11.4(24.9)	12.2(23.1)	9.4(30.1)
Combined (EC)	l/100km (mpg)	14.9(18.9)	16.0(17.7)	11.3(25.0)
CO_2 Emissions (EC)	g/km	352	376	299
City (EPA)	mpg(US)	12	12	N/A
Highway (EPA)	mpg(US)	18	18	N/A
ENGINE				
Type		V8	V8	In-line 6
Fuel		Petrol (Gasoline)	Petrol (Gasoline)	Diesel
Number of Cylinders		8	8	6
Number of Camshafts		4	4	2
Valves per Cylinder		4	4	4
Valve System		Twin overhead camshafts	Twin overhead camshafts	Twin overhead camshafts
Bore	mm(in)	88.0(3.47)	86.0(3.39)	84.0(3.31)
Stroke	mm(in)	90.3(3.56)	90.3(3.56)	88.0(3.47)
Capacity	cc(cu in)	4394(268)	4197(256)	2926(179)
Compression Ratio	:1	11	9	18
Cylinder Head Material		Aluminium alloy	Aluminium alloy	Aluminium alloy
Cylinder Block Material		Aluminium alloy	Aluminium alloy	Cast iron
Lubrication System		Frame mounted oil pump in sump, chain driven	Frame mounted oil pump in sump, chain driven	Chain driven oil pump immersed in sump
Fuel System		Denso PAN PAG EMS Generation 1	Denso PAN PAG EMS Generation 1	Bosch electronic type DD4.0
Ignition System		Distributorless via ECU. Electronic throttle. Drag torque control	Distributorless via ECU. Electronic throttle. Drag torque control	N/A
Boost System		None	Eaton supercharger	
Cold Start System		Automatic via ECU	Automatic via ECU	Automatic with heater plugs
Air Cleaning System		Paper element	Paper element	Paper element
Cooling System		Cross flow with aluminium radiator	Cross flow with aluminium radiator	Cross flow with aluminium radiator
Battery Capacity	Amp/hr	90	90	90
Max Power	kW(bhp)	225(302)	291(390)	130(174)
At	rpm	5750	5750	4000
Max Torque	Nm(lb/ft)	440(325)	560(413)	390(288)
At	rpm	4000	3500	2000

Range Rover - The Anniversary Guide

Specification Sheets

	UNITS	4.4-Litre V8 Petrol Automatic	4.2-Litre V8 Supercharged Automatic	3.0-Litre Diesel Automatic
Electronic Traction Control (ETC)		Four-wheel system integrated with ABS		
Electronic Brakeforce Distribution (EBD)		Yes	Yes	Yes
Emergency Brake Assist (EBA)		Yes	Yes	Yes
Dynamic Stability Control (DSC)		Yes	Yes	Yes
Hill Descent Control (HDC)		Yes	Yes	Yes
Terrain Response™		No	No	No
NOTES				

Data acquired from the best available sources but the publisher is not liable for any mistakes or omissions. Readers are advised to consult other sources e.g. manufacturer's workshop manuals before working on vehicles. The publication of performance and capability figures does not imply that this will be achieved in practice. Caution must be exercised in all driving activities especially off-road.
Units are expressed in the relevant international standard (SI). Where appropriate recognised conversion factors have been applied.

Swivelling Bi-Xenon adaptive front headlamps were another innovation

Specification Sheets

CHASSIS and ENGINE NUMBERS

RANGE ROVER THIRD GENERATION PHASE 2

VEHICLE	PERIOD	MANUFACTURER	MODEL	TRIM CLASS	BODY STYLE	ENGINE CODE		TRANSMISSION CODE		MODEL YEAR		BUILD LOCATION
Range Rover L30/L322	2002 on	SAL	Land Rover	LM Range Rover	A Standard	M 4-Door	C	3.0-litre 6-cyl diesel (BMW)	3	RHD Auto	5	2005	A	Solihull
							3	4.2-litre V8 petrol supercharged	4	LHD Auto				
							5	4.4-litre V8 petrol NA						

The Range Rover (L30/L322) is identified using the 17-digit Vehicle Indentification Number (VIN) system. This consists of a combination of letters and digits defining the vehicle type, engine fitted, transmission, model year and build location according to the table above. This is followed by a six-digit number unique to a particular vehicle. The VIN was stamped on a plate riveted inside the engine bay and on another plate visible through a gap in the lower windscreen masking on the left hand side ('Visible VIN').

A touch screen display allowed for a cleaning up of the centre fascia area

Range Rover - The Anniversary Guide

COLOUR & TRIM

RANGE ROVER THIRD GENERATION PHASE 2 2005 - 2007

YEAR	PAINTWORK		LRC NUMBER	NOTES
	COLOUR	TYPE		
2005	Alveston Red	COB Metallic	696	
	Bonatti Grey	COB Metallic	916	
	Buckingham Blue	COB Metallic	588	
	Cairns Blue	COB Metallic	849	
	Giverny Green	COB Metallic	734	
	Java Black	COB Metallic	697	
	Maya Gold	COB Metallic	846	Only available before October 2005
	Tonga Green	COB Metallic	904	
	Zambezi Silver	COB Metallic	798	
	Chawton White	COB Solid	603	

INTERIOR TRIM

	COLOUR	MATERIAL		
	Aspen	Leather		
	Charcoal	Leather		
	Ivory	Leather		
	Navy	Leather		
	Parchment	Leather		
	Sand	Leather		

Colour & Trim

Advertising & Brochures

For the launch of the new Jaguar-derived V8 naturally-aspirated and supercharged engines, Land Rover produced an expensive, case-bound hardback book as a customer brochure. Expensive to produce, relatively few were printed and they are now collectors' items

The press kit for the 2006 model year, while not as lavish as that issued at the vehicle's launch, was still impressive in an age where the press could expect little more than a CD. It included quotes from Matthew Taylor, Land Rover's Managing Director stating that the arrival of the new engines reinforced the Range Rover's status "at the head of the premium SUV sector"

Advertising & Brochures

The hardback brochure soon gave way to a cheaper soft cover version that included this colour guide

By now Land Rover had a new marketing strap line 'GO BEYOND' which featured on all the company's literature as well as appearing as a slogan on branded goods

Range Rover - The Anniversary Guide

Range Rover Third Generation | Phase Two | Advertising

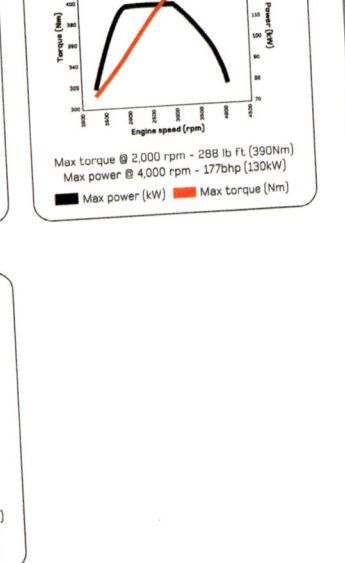

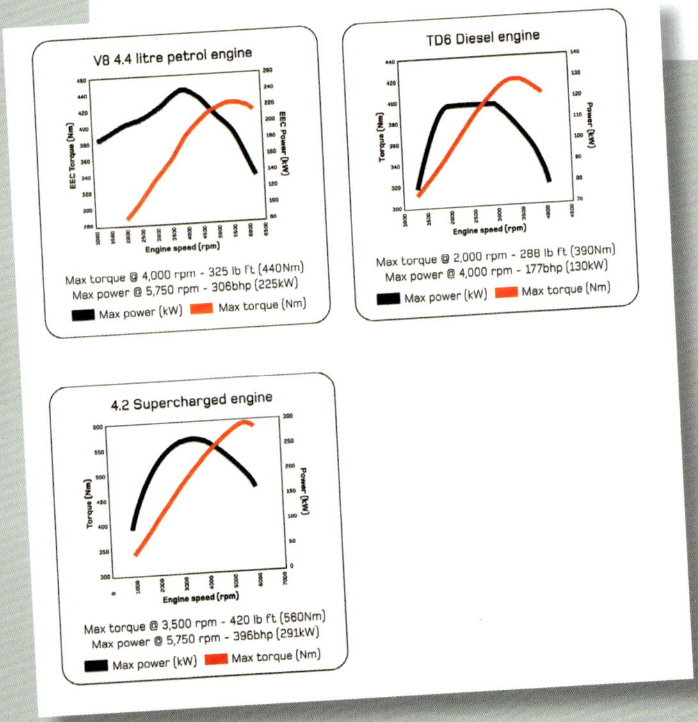

Advertising & Brochures

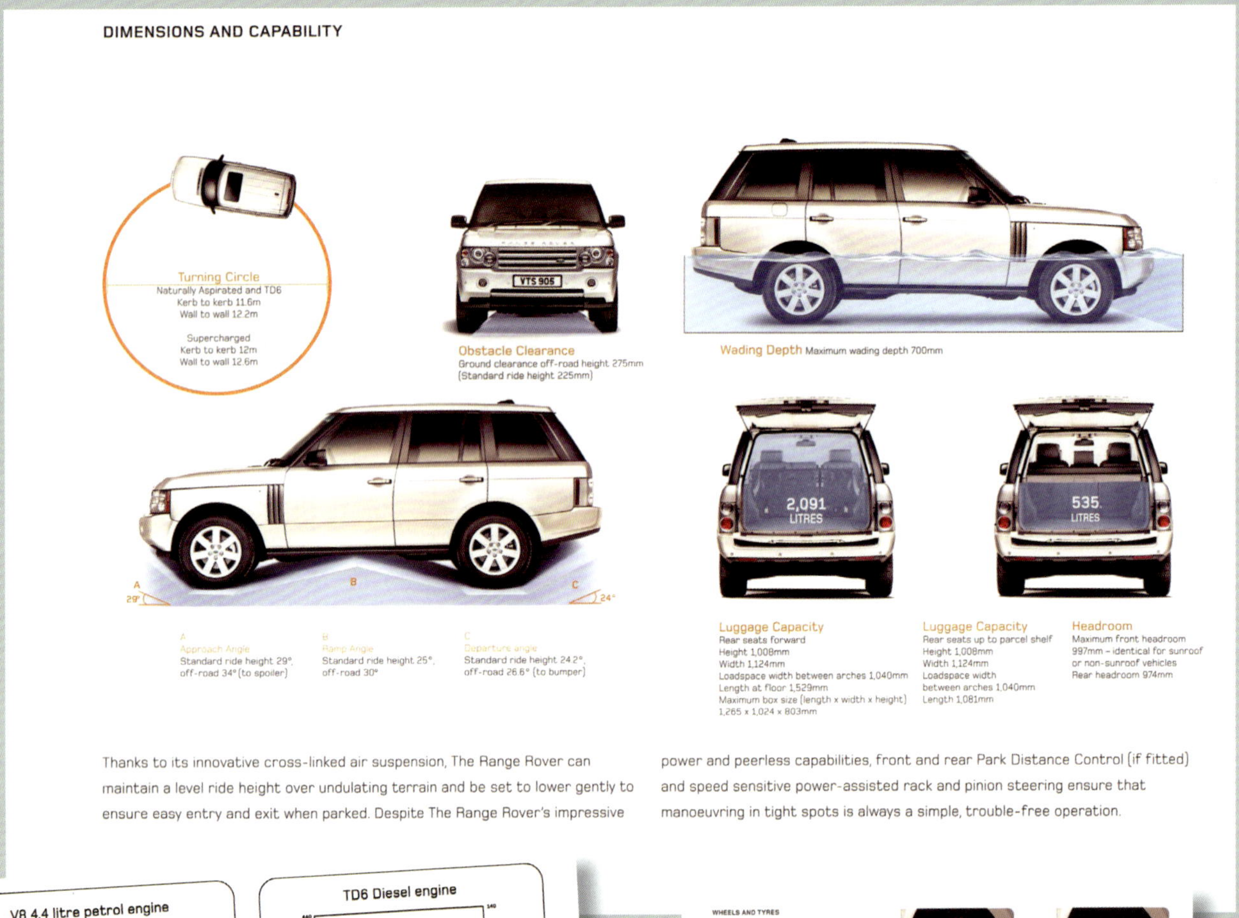

DIMENSIONS AND CAPABILITY

Turning Circle
Naturally Aspirated and TD6
Kerb to kerb 11.6m
Wall to wall 12.2m

Supercharged
Kerb to kerb 12m
Wall to wall 12.6m

Obstacle Clearance Ground clearance off-road height: 275mm (Standard ride height 225mm)

Wading Depth Maximum wading depth 700mm

A Approach Angle Standard ride height 29°, off-road 34° (to spoiler)

B Ramp Angle Standard ride height 25°, off-road 30°

C Departure angle Standard ride height 24.2°, off-road 26.6° (to bumper)

Luggage Capacity — 2,091 litres
Rear seats forward
Height 1,008mm
Width 1,124mm
Loadspace width between arches 1,040mm
Length at floor 1,529mm
Maximum box size (length x width x height) 1,265 x 1,024 x 803mm

Luggage Capacity — 535 litres
Rear seats up to parcel shelf
Height 1,008mm
Width 1,124mm
Loadspace width between arches 1,040mm
Length 1,081mm

Headroom Maximum front headroom 997mm – identical for sunroof or non-sunroof vehicles. Rear headroom 974mm.

Thanks to its innovative cross-linked air suspension, The Range Rover can maintain a level ride height over undulating terrain and be set to lower gently to ensure easy entry and exit when parked. Despite The Range Rover's impressive power and peerless capabilities, front and rear Park Distance Control (if fitted) and speed sensitive power-assisted rack and pinion steering ensure that manoeuvring in tight spots is always a simple, trouble-free operation.

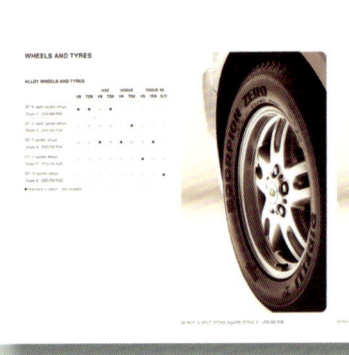

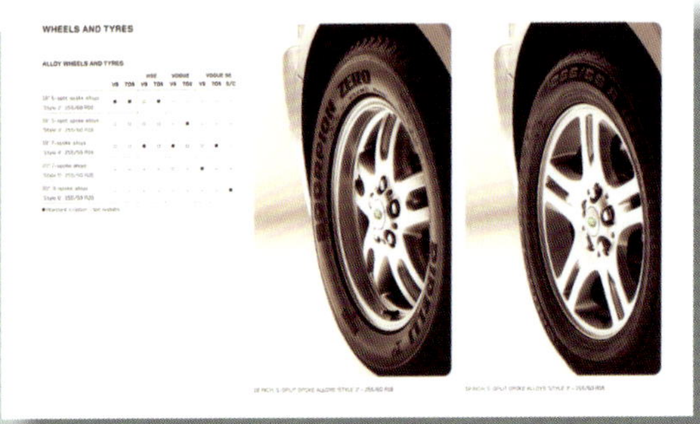

V8 4.4 litre petrol engine
Max torque @ 4,000 rpm - 325 lb ft (440Nm)
Max power @ 5,750 rpm - 306bhp (225kW)

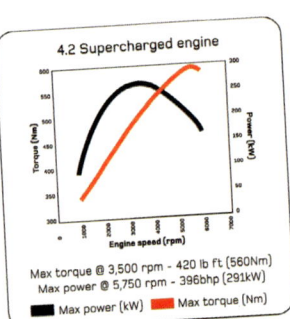

TD6 Diesel engine
Max torque @ 2,000 rpm - 288 lb ft (390Nm)
Max power @ 4,000 rpm - 177bhp (130kW)

4.2 Supercharged engine
Max torque @ 3,500 rpm - 420 lb ft (560Nm)
Max power @ 5,750 rpm - 396bhp (291kW)

WHEELS AND TYRES

176

Range Rover - The Anniversary Guide

Advertising & Brochures

With its new Jaguar-derived petrol engines, the Range Rover got a new mesh grille and side vents, the grille dramatically setting off its pocketed front light arrangement

Range Rover - The Anniversary Guide

Range Rover Third Generation — Phase Three

Range Rover Walkaround

Despite a minor revision to the bumper, the 2008 model closely resembled the vehicle at the time of its launch in 2001

A heavily slatted grille had been a Range Rover signature for years. The Land Rover 'jewel' badge also went back to the re-branding exercise of the late 1980s

A change to the front headlamp unit was required to accommodate the Bi-Xenon adaptive lights that swivelled as the vehicle turned a corner

With such a large vehicle, the luggage space was equally massive. It was fully trimmed and shaped to maximise loading capacity

Range Rover - The Anniversary Guide

'Grand Black Lacquer' had been used on the Range Rover Linley but was brought in as a mainstream option

The spare wheel was housed in a well under the luggage compartment along with the tool kit and towing attachment if specified. A prop kept the lid open while, as on earlier vehicles, the wheel rested on a harness that could be used to aid its extraction

Against a suitably stately background, the Range Rover shows off its lines reflecting the influences of earlier generations such as the 'clamshell' bonnet, 'floating roof' and strong horizontal feature lines

Range Rover - The Anniversary Guide

Range Rover Third Generation | Phase Three

Range Rover Walkaround

The rear aspect on such a large vehicle provides designers with a significant challenge to prevent it looking too bulky. The Range Rover pulls it off with its 'floating' roof, large lamp clusters and strong lines

The fitment of Terrain Response™ required revisions to the centre console. Range Rover designers paid particularly attention to the tactile appeal of the driver interface by selecting premium materials and finishes

The rear of the centre console is a significant structure housing the operating knobs for the rear climate control, vents and connections for external entertainment equipment

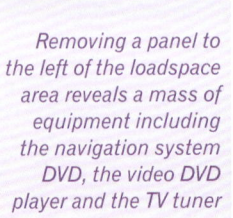

Removing a panel to the left of the loadspace area reveals a mass of equipment including the navigation system DVD, the video DVD player and the TV tuner

182   Range Rover - The Anniversary Guide

The glove box area houses the CD player for the audio system as well as the Venture-Cam™ camera which re-charges itself from its special housing

The steering wheel houses the controls for the cruise control, and the audio and phone systems. It is also heated. By 2008, the rim was considerably more bulky than that of the original model

The Rear Screen Entertainment system included twin screens for the rear passengers. These were fed by the DVD player in the loadspace compartment or by external systems such as games machines

The folding centre armrest of the rear seat houses not only beverage holders but has a useful storage area – including a place for the rear entertainment system remote. With many Range Rover owners being chauffeur-driven, a respectable working area in the rear is essential

...pired by marine themes, the ...ge Rover features gently ...ing lines to give it presence ...le subtly concealing its bulk

Range Rover - The Anniversary Guide

183

Range Rover Third Generation — Phase Three

Range Rover Walkaround

The ambience formed by the use of premium materials is an essential part of the Range Rover experience

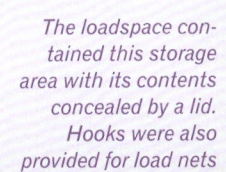

The loadspace contained this storage area with its contents concealed by a lid. Hooks were also provided for load nets

The headphones were housed in their own special case which fitted into the rear door pocket. The control for the rear entertainment system fitted into the centre armrest

The TDV8 was a magnificent power unit, returning respectable fuel consumption while offering impressive power and torque

184 Range Rover - The Anniversary Guide

The rear seats had an asymmetric split and could be folded flat…

…or fully jackknifed to maximise load space

The ski bag reveals BMW's influence on the design but many Range Rover owners enjoyed the sport. The bag allowed skis to be carried inside the vehicle and prevented snow and dirt from entering the passenger compartment

VentureCam™ could be used to scout out the track ahead by sending a signal back to the vehicle that could be seen on the fascia display. The system could also be configured to receive signals from home security systems

Range Rover - The Anniversary Guide

185

Specification Sheets

Range Rover Third Generation | Phase Three | Technical Data

GENERAL FEATURES

CONSTRUCTION
Four-door, five-seat body with clamshell opening tailgate. Steel monocoque body with aluminium doors, bonnet, and front wings. Steel front and rear subframes

POWER UNITS
New 4.2-litre V8 supercharged petrol engine, new 4.4-litre V8 petrol engine, new 3.6-litre, twin-turbocharged, V8 diesel engine

TRANSMISSION
Permanent four wheel drive. Six-speed automatic gearbox with 'Command Shift' over-ride. Chain-driven, two-speed transfer box with electronically-controlled centre differential. Open drive shaft axles with front differential mounted to engine sump

SUSPENSION
Four-corner, variable-height, electonically-controlled interlinked air suspension with variable-rate air springs and hydraulic dampers. MacPherson strut front suspension with negative ground offset. Double wishbone rear suspension

STEERING
Speed-sensitive power-assisted rack and pinion

BRAKING
ABS with Electronic Traction Control, Dynamic Stability Control, Hill Descent Control, Electronic Brakeforce Distribution and Emergency Brake Assist

OTHER FEATURES
GPS navigation system with widescreen TV monitor. 4x4 information screen. Bi-Xenon headlights. Front, thorax and head protection airbags. Terrain Response

	UNITS	4.4-Litre V8 Petrol Automatic	4.2-Litre V8 Supercharged Automatic	3.6-Litre Diesel Automatic
DIMENSIONS				
Overall Length	mm(in)	4972(195.8)	4972(195.8)	4972(195.8)
Overall Width (over mirrors)	mm(in)	2192(86.3)	2192(86.3)	2192(86.3)
Overall Height (max)	mm(in)	1902(74.9)	1902(74.9)	1902(74.9)
Wheelbase	mm(in)	2880(113.3)	2880(113.3)	2880(113.3)
Track Front/Rear	mm(in)	1629(64.1)/1625(64.0)	1629(64.1)/1625(64.0)	1629(64.1)/1625(64.0)
Luggage Capacity (Seat Up)	l(cu ft)	997(35.2)	997(35.2)	997(35.2)
Luggage Capacity (Seat Folded)	l(cu ft)	2122(74.9)	2122(74.9)	2122(74.9)
WEIGHTS				
Minimum Kerb Weight (EEC)	kg(lb)	2592(5714)	2680(5908)	2710(5975)
Gross Vehicle Weight	kg(lb)	3100(6834)	3100(6834)	3200(7055)
Front Axle Maximum Weight	kg(lb)	1530(3373)	1530(3373)	1530(3373)
Rear Axle Maximum Weight	kg(lb)	1850(4079)	1850(4079)	1850(4079)
Maximum Payload	kg(lb)	508(1120)	420(926)	490(1080)
Maximum On Road Trailer Weight	kg(lb)	3500(7716) with over-run brakes, 750(1653) unbraked		
Maximum Off Road Trailer Weight	kg(lb)	1000(2205) with over-run brakes, 500(1103) unbraked		
CAPABILITIES				
Drag Coefficient	Cd	0.39	0.39	0.39
Approach Angle (Maximum)	Deg	34 with suspension at off-road height		
Under Body (Ramp) Angle (Maximum)	Deg	150 with suspension at off-road height		
Departure Angle (Maximum)	Deg	26.6 with suspension at off-road height (no tow bar)		
Gradient Climbable (Maximum)	Deg	45 (drive through), 35 (continuous)		
Sideslope Angle (Maximum)	Deg	35	35	35
Turning Circle (Kerb to kerb)	mm(in)	12.0(39.0)	12.0(39.0)	12.0(39.0)
Wading Depth (Maximum)	mm(in)	700(27.6)	700(27.6)	700(27.6)

Specification Sheets

	UNITS	4.4-Litre V8 Petrol Automatic	4.2-Litre V8 Supercharged Automatic	3.6-Litre Diesel Automatic
PERFORMANCE				
Maximum Speed	kp/h(mph)	200(124)	210(130)	200(124)
Acceleration 0 - 100 kp/h	secs	8.7	7.5	9.2
Acceleration 0 - 60 mph	secs	8.3	7.1	8.6
FUEL CONSUMPTION				
Urban Cycle (EC)	l/100km (mpg)	21.2(13.4)	22.4(12.6)	14.4(19.6)
Extra Urban (EC)	l/100km (mpg)	11.4(24.9)	12.2(23.1)	9.2(31.2)
Combined (EC)	l/100km (mpg)	14.9(18.9)	16.0(17.7)	11.3(25.0)
CO_2 Emissions (EC)	g/km	352	376	299
City (EPA)	mpg(US)	12	12	N/A
Highway (EPA)	mpg(US)	18	18	N/A
ENGINE				
Type		V8	V8	V8
Fuel		Petrol (Gasoline)	Petrol (Gasoline)	Diesel
Number of Cylinders		8	8	8
Number of Camshafts		4	4	4
Valves per Cylinder		4	4	4
Valve System		Twin overhead camshafts	Twin overhead camshafts	Twin overhead camshafts
Bore	mm(in)	88.0(3.47)	86.0(3.39)	81.0(3.19)
Stroke	mm(in)	90.3(3.56)	90.3(3.56)	88.0(3.47)
Capacity	cc(cu in)	4394(268)	4197(256)	3630(222)
Compression Ratio	:1	10.75	9.1	18.1
Cylinder Head Material		Aluminium alloy	Aluminium alloy	Aluminium alloy
Cylinder Block Material		Aluminium alloy	Aluminium alloy	Cast iron
Lubrication System		Frame mounted oil pump in sump, chain driven	Frame mounted oil pump in sump, chain driven	Oil pump driven by crankshaft nose
Fuel System		Denso PAN PAG EMS Generation 1		Siemens pcr2.4
Ignition System		Distributorless via ECU. Electronic throttle. Drag torque control		N/A
Boost System		None	Eaton supercharger	Twin turbochargers
Cold Start System		Automatic via ECU	Automatic via ECU	Automatic with heater plugs
Air Cleaning System		Paper element	Paper element	Paper element
Cooling System		Cross flow with aluminium radiator	Cross flow with aluminium radiator	Cross flow with aluminium radiator
Battery Capacity	Amp/hr	90	90	90
Max Power	kW(bhp)	225(302)	291(390)	200(268)
At	rpm	5750	5750	4000
Max Torque	Nm(lb/ft)	440(325)	560(413)	640(472)
At	rpm	4000	3500	2000

Range Rover - The Anniversary Guide

Range Rover Third Generation — Phase Three — Technical Data

Specification Sheets

	UNITS	4.4-Litre V8 Petrol Automatic	4.2-Litre V8 Supercharged Automatic	3.6-Litre Diesel Automatic
CAPACITIES				
Engine Oil Sump and Filter	l(Imp Gall) [US Gall]	8.0(1.76)[2.11]	10.9(2.4)[2.88]	9.9(2.18)[2.62]
Cooling Circuit	l(Imp Gall) [US Gall]	15.0(3.30)[3.96]	16.0(3.52)[4.23]	14.0(3.08)[3.70]
Fuel Tank (Maximum Usable)	l(Imp Gall) [US Gall]	104.5(23)[27.6]	104.5(23)[27.6]	104.5(23)[27.6]
TRANSMISSION				
Type		ZF6HP26 6-Speed		
Flywheel		Fluid torque converter with lock up		
Gearbox Type		Automatic with 'Command Shift'		
Number of Forward Gears		6	6	6
Selection Mechanism		Remote lever with 'sport' setting and 'Command Shift' manual override		
Transfer Box Type		Chain drive, permanent four wheel drive		
Number of Ratios		2	2	2
Selection Mechanism		Motor driven operated by console mounted switch		
Slip Control System		Electronically-controlled variable differential		
Front Prop Shaft Type		Open with rubber coupling at rear, shrouded spline connection to front differential		
Rear Prop Shaft Type		Open split shafts with centre rubber bush bearing. CV joint connections to transfer box and rear differential		
Front Axle Type		Single reduction mounted onto engine sump, open drive shafts		
Rear Axle Type		Single reduction, open drive shafts	Single reduction, open drive shafts	Single reduction, open drive shafts
Wheel Type		Cast alloy, J-type rim.	Cast alloy, J-type rim.	Cast alloy, J-type rim.
Wheel Size - Standard	in	18 x 7.5	20 x 8.5	18 x 7.5
Wheel Size - Options	in	18 x 8, 19 x 8, 20 x 8.5 (Accessory)	N/A	19 x 8
Tyre Size - Standard		255/60R18	255/50R20	255/60R18
Tyre Size - Options		255/55R19, 255/55R19, 255/50R20 (Acc)	N/A	255/55R19
RATIOS				
1st Gear Ratio	:1	4.171	4.171	4.171
2nd Gear Ratio	:1	2.340	2.340	2.340
3rd Gear Ratio	:1	1.521	1.521	1.521
4th Gear Ratio	:1	1.143	1.143	1.143
5th Gear Ratio	:1	0.867	0.867	0.867
6th Gear Ratio	:1	0.691	0.691	0.691
Reverse Gear	:1	3.403	3.403	3.540
High Range Ratio	:1	1.000	1.000	1.000
Low Range Ratio	:1	2.930	2.930	2.930
Front Axle Ratio	:1	3.730	3.730	3.730
Rear Axle Ratio	:1	3.730	3.730	3.730
1st Gear Ratio Overall High Range	:1	15.558	15.558	15.558

Specification Sheets

	UNITS	4.4-Litre V8 Petrol Automatic	4.2-Litre V8 Supercharged Automatic	3.6-Litre Diesel Automatic
2nd Gear Ratio Overall High Range	:1	8.728	8.728	8.728
3rd Gear Ratio Overall High Range	:1	5.673	5.673	5.673
4th Gear Ratio Overall High Range	:1	4.263	4.263	4.263
5th Gear Ratio Overall High Range	:1	3.234	3.234	3.234
6th Gear Ratio Overall High Range	:1	2.577	2.577	2.577
Reverse Gear Overall High Range	:1	12.693	12.693	13.204
1st Gear Ratio Overall Low Range	:1	45.584	45.584	45.584
2nd Gear Ratio Overall Low Range	:1	25.574	25.574	25.574
3rd Gear Ratio Overall Low Range	:1	16.623	16.623	16.623
4th Gear Ratio Overall Low Range	:1	12.492	12.492	12.492
5th Gear Ratio Overall Low Range	:1	9.475	9.475	9.475
6th Gear Ratio Overall Low Range	:1	7.552	7.552	7.552
Reverse Gear Overall Low Range	:1	37.191	37.191	38.688
SUSPENSION				
Front Suspension Type		MacPherson strut with air springs and hydraulic dampers. Negative ground level offset. Anti roll bar		
Rear Suspension Type		Double wishbone with air springs and hydraulic dampers.		
Front Springs		Interlinked, electonically-controlled variable-rate air springs		
Rear Springs		Interlinked, electonically-controlled variable-rate air springs		
Front Dampers		Telescopic, double acting, non-adjustable		
Rear Dampers		Telescopic, double acting, non-adjustable		
Anti Roll Bar Diameter Front	mm(in)	30(1.18)	30(1.18)	30(1.18)
Anti Roll Bar Diameter Rear	mm(in)	N/A	N/A	N/A
STEERING				
Type		ZF speed proportional power assisted rack and pinion		
Assistance		Belt driven pump	Belt driven pump	Belt driven pump
Number of Turns Lock to Lock		3	3	3
BRAKES				
Type		Hydraulic with power assistance and ABS. Self adjusting discs all-round.		
Front Disc Type		Cast iron, ventilated		
Front Disc Diameter	mm(in)	344(13.54)	360(14.17)	344(13.54)
Rear Disc Type		Cast iron, ventilated	Cast iron, ventilated	Cast iron, ventilated
Rear Disc Diameter	mm(in)	354(13.94)	354(13.94)	354(13.94)
Park Brake Type		Mechanically operated drum integral with rear discs		
TECHNOLOGIES				
Dual Line Braking System		Yes	Yes	Yes
Anti Lock Braking System (ABS)		Bosch DSC8	Bosch DSC8	Bosch DSC8
Electronic Traction Control (ETC)		Four-wheel system integrated with ABS		

Range Rover - The Anniversary Guide

Range Rover Third Generation — Phase Three — Technical Data

Specification Sheets

	UNITS	4.4-Litre V8 Petrol Automatic	4.2-Litre V8 Supercharged Automatic	3.6-Litre Diesel Automatic
Electronic Brakeforce Distribution (EBD)		Yes	Yes	Yes
Emergency Brake Assist (EBA)		Yes	Yes	Yes
Dynamic Stability Control (DSC)		Yes	Yes	Yes
Hill Descent Control (HDC)		Yes	Yes	Yes
Terrain Response™		Yes	Yes	Yes

NOTES

Data acquired from the best available sources but the publisher is not liable for any mistakes or omissions. Readers are advised to consult other sources e.g. manufacturer's workshop manuals before working on vehicles. The publication of performance and capability figures does not imply that this will be achieved in practice. Caution must be exercised in all driving activities especially off-road.
Units are expressed in the relevant international standard (SI). Where appropriate recognised conversion factors have been applied.

CHASSIS and ENGINE NUMBERS

RANGE ROVER THIRD GENERATION PHASE 3

VEHICLE	PERIOD	MANUFACTURER	MODEL	TRIM CLASS	BODY STYLE	ENGINE CODE		TRANSMISSION CODE		MODEL YEAR		BUILD LOCATION	
Range Rover L30/L322	2002 on	SAL	Land Rover LM	A Standard	M 4-Door	2	3.6-litre V8 diesel	3	RHD Auto	6	2006	A	Solihull
						3	4.2-litre V8 petrol supercharged	4	LHD Auto	7	2007		
						5	4.4-litre V8 petrol NA			8	2008		
						7	3.6-litre V8 diesel with DPF						

The Range Rover (L30/L322) is identified using the 17-digit Vehicle Indentification Number (VIN) system. This consists of a combination of letters and digits defining the vehicle type, engine fitted, transmission, model year and build location according to the table above. This is followed by a six-digit number unique to a particular vehicle. The VIN was stamped on a plate riveted inside the engine bay and on another plate visible through a gap in the lower windscreen masking on the left hand side ('Visible VIN').

Specification Sheets

Range Rover - The Anniversary Guide

Range Rover Third Generation | Phase Three | Advertising

Advertising & Brochures

THE RANGE ROVER
A LAND ROVER GUIDE

The brochure for the 2008 model year Range Rover was effectively done in two parts – one of which was this slimmed down 'Guide' to the vehicle

The Guide included a chart of the available exterior colours – now trimmed down to 10 – as well as the choice of interior trim

EXTERIOR COLOURS: ALASKA WHITE (SOLID), ATACAMA SAND (METALLIC), BUCKINGHAM BLUE (METALLIC), CAIRNS BLUE (METALLIC), LUCERNE GREEN (METALLIC), JAVA BLACK (METALLIC), RIMINI RED (METALLIC), STORNOWAY GREY (METALLIC), TONGA GREEN (METALLIC), ZERMATT (METALLIC)

INTERIOR TRIMS: ASPEN, STORM, IVORY, JET, NAVY, PARCHMENT, SAND
INTERIOR FINISHES: BURR WALNUT, CHERRY WOOD, GRAND BLACK LACQUER, GRANITE
AUTOBIOGRAPHY FINISHES: LINED OAK ANTHRACITE, ASH BURR, BURR MAPLE PRUSSIAN BLUE, VAVONA BURL AMBER

194   Range Rover - The Anniversary Guide

Advertising & Brochures

The main brochure for 2008 featured an almost impressionist image of the main light unit on its cover while other photography sought to associate the Range Rover's interior with the country house lifestyle

Range Rover - The Anniversary Guide

Range Rover Third Generation | Phase Three | Advertising

Advertising & Brochures

Range Rover marketing imagery was always sophisticated echoing the peerless nature of the vehicle and its customers. But it had a sporty side too, picked up by inset details such as the Brembo front brakes

Range Rover - The Anniversary Guide

Advertising & Brochures

WADING DEPTH Maximum wading depth 700mm

20 INCH, 9-SPOKE ALLOYS 'STYLE 6' – 255/50 R20

20 INCH, POLISHED 10-SPOKE ALLOYS

19 INCH, 7-SPOKE ALLOYS 'STYLE 4' – 255/55 R19

20 INCH, 7-SPOKE ALLOYS 'STYLE 5' – 255/50 R20

The choice of wheels added a lot to the final appearance of the Range Rover and, for 2008, included a 20-inch polished variant. Whether many owners chose to subject this pricey option to the 700 mm (27.5 in) maximum wading depth possible with the vehicle in off-road height mode is doubtful

Range Rover - The Anniversary Guide

BODY AND CHASSIS

For the 2010 model year, the Range Rover received extensive, but subtle, design changes to enhance the vehicle's style and bring in some contemporary detailing.

The headlamp units were slightly narrowed and featured a 'Three Finger' design cue that was carried around the vehicle. Further definition was provided by LED 'signature lights'. The front grille was made slightly deeper, its outline being more defined, and its mesh design featured three horizontal bars, further emphasising the 'Three Finger' theme. The front bumper was of a new, smoother outline, recessed at the top to accommodate the deeper grille, and had a revised lower air intake defined by a strong horizontal bar. The front fog lamps were also moved away from the bumper, now being mounted in the lower air intake area. The new front bumper was designed with front wheel deflectors to reduce drag.

The side air intakes were re-styled, again echoing the 'Three Finger' design theme, a feature also carried through to the revised rear light clusters.

ENGINE

A new 5.0-litre V8 supercharged petrol engine was offered alongside the 3.6-litre V8 diesel power unit. The new petrol engine was designed in-house by Jaguar Land Rover and was also used in Jaguar car models and the Range

The 2010 model year vehicle introduced a new front grille, bumper and light units featuring a 'three finger' styling theme. This introduced a 'hierarchy' in the Range Rover model line-up with the Range Rover Sport carrying a similar theme but with only two style lines

Technical Description

Rover Sport. It offered improvements in fuel consumption and reduced emissions in relation to its predecessor. Compared with the Jaguar unit, the engine used in the Range Rover had a deeper sump to cope with the extreme angles encountered during off-road driving as well as to accommodate the front differential, an arrangement carried over from the original design.

Of all-alloy construction, the new engine featured direct fuel injection to maximise control over the combustion cycle. Fuel was supplied by twin, engine-driven, high-pressure pumps and, with direct injection cooling the induction charge, the compression ratio could be raised to further improve fuel economy. The combustion characteristics were manipulated during the warm-up phase to speed catalyst warm-up and reduce emissions. The engine featured variable camshaft timing with profile switching on all four camshafts.

The supercharger was a Roots type, twin vortex system feeding the engine through twin intercoolers which had their own cooling circuit. The supercharger and its attendant induction system were packaged in the Vee of the engine to keep the engine height low. The design of the supercharger and the intake system was such that the system was virtually silent in operation.

TRANSMISSION

While a six-speed automatic transmission was retained, it was now of the revised and more refined ZF 6HP28 type. The gearbox was tuned to complement the characteristics of the new 5.0-litre supercharged petrol engine with earlier torque converter lock-up. This reduced slip losses, improving fuel consumption and reducing emissions. To exploit the engine's power, the new gearbox had an intelligent 'Sport' mode.

The 3.6-litre turbocharged V8 diesel engine continued to be mated with the ZF 6HP26 gearbox.

The Sand and Rock Crawl programmes of the Terrain Response™ system were refined to enhance the vehicle's capabilities. The Sand programme had the benefit of Sand Launch Control to limit wheel spin and consequent

The 2010 model year saw the introduction of the 5.0-litre version of the supercharged V8 petrol engine. This Land Rover image in fact shows the version fitted to the Range Rover Sport as it lacks the distinctive Range Rover sump arrangement

Range Rover - The Anniversary Guide

'digging in' to soft surfaces while the Rock Crawl programme was revised to modify brake and traction control response times to prevent 'roll off' when negotiating slippery rocks.

SUSPENSION

For the 2010 model year the Range Rover was fitted with the Adaptive Dynamics system which used electronically-controlled variable dampers. The conventional shock absorbers were replaced by Bilstein DampTronic™ units which used variable valves to alter the settings in response to the virtually continual monitoring of damper pressure on each wheel. By modelling the reaction over a variety of surfaces, both on- and off-road, the system was able to predict the correct damper response to a given situation and alter the vehicle's handling accordingly.

BRAKING SYSTEM

The braking system for the V8 petrol supercharged model was uprated to include larger front ventilated discs and a unique, aluminium, six-piston, opposed-action monoblock caliper arrangement developed by Brembo™. Larger, solid discs were also fitted at the rear.

The stability control system was improved by the addition of Enhanced Understeer Control which introduced automatic braking into the torque reduction aspect of the system. Roll Stability Control used very rapid,

Adaptive Dynamics features a Bilstein shock absorber with variable valve adjustment. Predictive electronic control ensured that the Range Rover's response to a variety of on- and off-road conditions was optimised

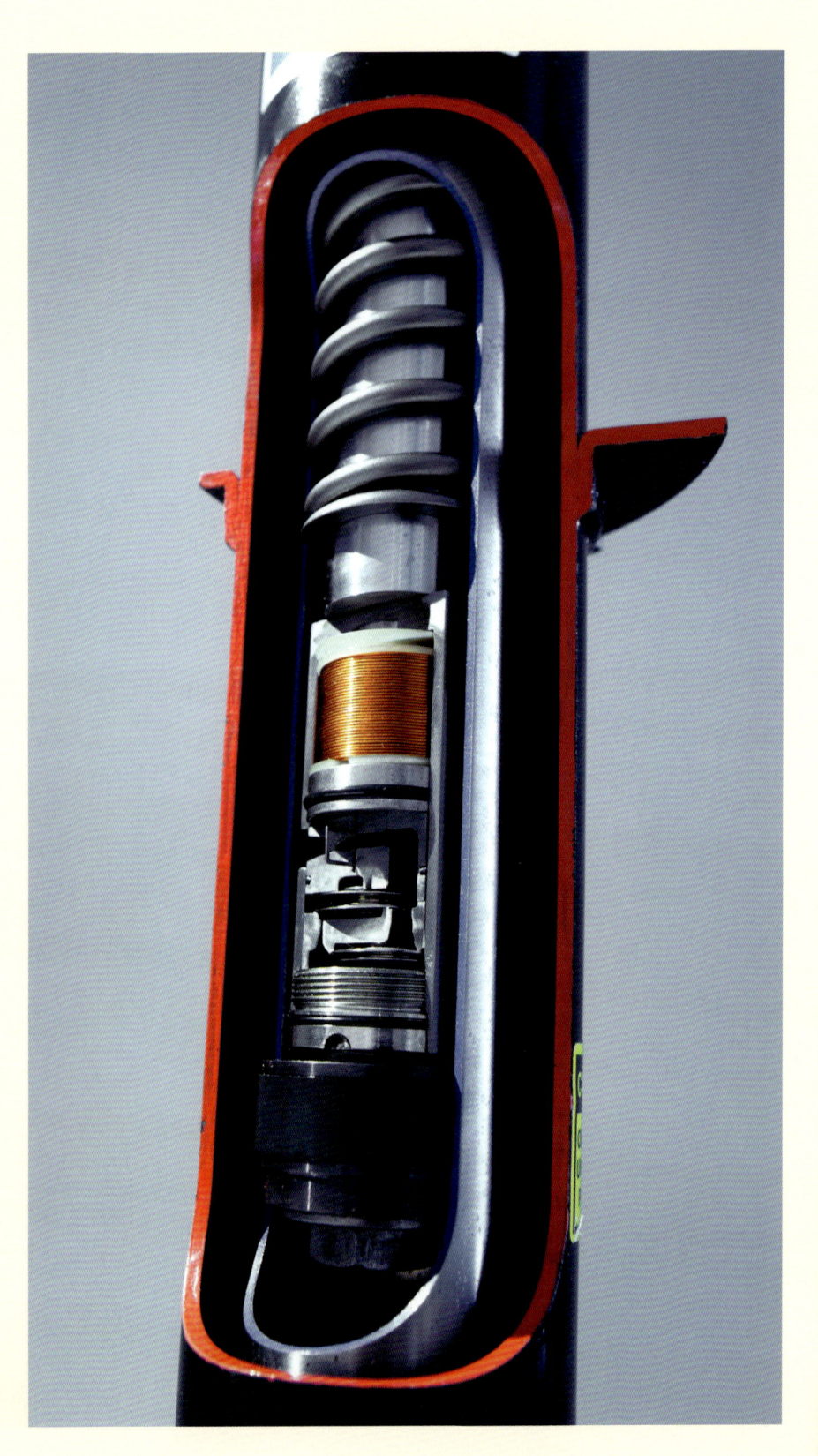

Technical Description

wheel-specific braking actions to reduce speed and marginally widen the cornering radius if a potential roll-over situation was detected. Trailer Stability Assist used automatic braking interventions, coupled with reducing engine torque to reduce swing induced by an unstable trailer. The Hill Descent Control system was improved by the addition of Gradient Release Control which prevented sudden accelerations on steep angles by automatically releasing the brakes smoothly.

An enhanced Emergency Brake Assist system was fitted to vehicles equipped with Adaptive Cruise Control.

SEATING AND TRIM

The new Autobiography trim level introduced a hand-sewn, luxury-grade leather headlining with matching panels on the door casings. Body pillars were also leather trimmed.

The waterfall lighting was enhanced to improve night time illumination of the interior.

FASCIA AND INSTRUMENTS

The surrounds to the fascia buttons were changed to a satin chrome finish and a new engine start/stop button was added.

The instrument pack was replaced by a 300 mm (12in) Thin Film Transistor (TFT) screen which featured 'virtual' instruments and an information area that could be customised by the driver to present essential information and personally prioritised data such as audio and telephone displays. The screen was controlled by command buttons on a revised steering wheel.

The virtual dials comprised a rev. counter and a speedometer with water temperature and fuel gauges.

For 2010, the fascia design was further cleaned up with control of several functions reverting to the dual-view touch screen. A 'smart' key allowed for a push button engine start/stop function

Range Rover - The Anniversary Guide

The speedometer had a single scale appropriate to the market but an alternative digital scale could also be displayed. When a Terrain Response™ setting was selected in low range, the speedometer display moved to reveal the 4 x 4 Information screen.

ELECTRICAL SYSTEM

The electrical system was totally upgraded for the 2010 model year with a high-speed Controlled Area Network (CAN) system with a fibre-optic Media Orientated System Transport (MOST) network serving the infotainment systems. The charging system incorporated Intelligent Power System Management which allowed the alternator to charge the battery when it was most economical to do so such as when coasting rather than during acceleration.

The front headlamps were provided with Automatic High Beam Assist which automatically turned on the lamps' high beam when light levels fell to a preset level. The system automatically reverted to dipped beam when oncoming traffic was detected.

The Range Rover was equipped with Adaptive Cruise Control which used a radar scanning beam to detect vehicles moving in the same direction and then kept the vehicle at a preset variable distance using acceleration, deceleration and braking.

The centre fascia display was upgraded to feature (for the first time in any vehicle) dual-view Parallax Barrier screen technology which enabled the passenger and the driver to view different images. This enabled, for example, the passenger to watch a DVD movie while the driver could view satellite navigation information. The screen was also coated to reduce glare.

The touch screen command logic was changed to enable a reduction in the 'hard' buttons around the screen.

The screen was used as a display for a new Surround Camera System which had five digital cameras mounted around the vehicle to provide 360-degree coverage. A variety of visual modes

The TFT 'virtual' instrument pack was a significant innovation and enabled a wide range of information to be displayed including this reminder of how to start the vehicle

Technical Description

could be selected using the display's touch screen. The system also provided a Towing Assist function which used a digitally-enhanced image from the rear-facing cameras to provide an undistorted image of a trailer behind the vehicle. Guide lines projected onto the screen allowed the driver to accurately hitch-up to a trailer. A variety of trailer types and sizes could be selected from a menu to provide accurate positioning.

The satellite navigation system was now served by a hard drive rather than by DVD. This enabled faster route calculation, greater map coverage and improved reliability. The display was also changed to provide improved guidance instructions.

A new portable audio interface allowed connectively to a number of personal audio devices such as MP3 players and it could also accommodate USB memory sticks. One of the ports was dedicated to the Apple iPod™. This was exclusive to Land Rover and was designed to prevent the device coming loose when subject to the stresses of off-road driving.

(Top) At the time of its introduction, the dual-view centre display screen was a world first, offering the opportunity for the front seat passenger to watch the TV or movies while the driver could view, for example, the navigation screen, undisturbed

In 2010, Land Rover enhanced the rear seat passengers' experience with a package including reclining rear seats with a heating or cooling facility, revised rear head restraints, and enhanced sound proofing. The controls mounted in the rear doors operated the rear seat recline

Range Rover - The Anniversary Guide

203

Range Rover Third Generation — Phase Four

Range Rover Walkaround

Although the styling changes for 2010 model year, were subtle, they were sufficient to give the head-on appearance a radical new look

The 'mesh' effect on the front grille came in with the original V8 supercharged model but was now introduced across the range. The subtle angling of the grille outline can be seen on other Land Rover models

The light units were revised to reflect the 'three finger' theme and to introduce LED 'signature' lights around the main units

For the 2010 model year, the interior materials were upgraded. This is an Autobiography model

204   Range Rover - The Anniversary Guide

The front end changes preserved the presence and stature of the third generation Range Rover but significantly enhanced its 'static dynamics'. As part of Land Rover's drive towards 'e_Terrain Technologies', it also improved the drag coefficient

The 'three finger' theme was carried around the vehicle, including the rear light units

The Autobiography model is fitted with 20-inch 'Style 11' wheels as standard. A polished silver option of the same wheel is also available

Range Rover - The Anniversary Guide

205

Range Rover Third Generation — Phase Four

Range Rover Walkaround

Apart from the new light units, the rear appearance was little changed for the 2010 model year

The 'virtual' speedometer on the new TFT display moved aside to reveal a repeat of the 4 x 4 information screen also shown on the centre screen

Apart from the specification of new materials, the centre console was little changed for 2010. The new engine stop/start button on the fascia rail replaced the key operated switch and was matched by the button to open the glove box

The dual-view screen enabled the front seat passenger to view the TV screen while the driver saw other information such as the navigation system

Range Rover - The Anniversary Guide

Plenty of information was displayed on firing up the ignition. The speedometer was presented in the appropriate units for the vehicle's destination market. Other units were presented on a digital sub scale when programmed by the driver

The steering wheel – here the wood and leather version of the Autobiography derivative – gained new controls to operate the TFT display information and the in-car entertainment system

...viously keyed to Land ...er's personalisation pro-...mme, the Autobiography ...e was applied to a spe- ...derivative with a series of ...que features and options ...he 2010 model year

The 2010 model year vehicle featured a new hard disc navigation system for more information and a quicker response

Black leather head lining had been a feature of the Range Rover Linley of 10 years before but was now used on the 2010 Autobiography model

Range Rover - The Anniversary Guide 207

Specification Sheets

Range Rover Third Generation — Phase Four — Technical Data

GENERAL FEATURES

CONSTRUCTION
Four-door, five-seat body with clamshell opening tailgate. Steel monocoque body with aluminium doors, bonnet, and front wings. Steel front and rear subframes.

POWER UNITS
New 5.0-litre V8 supercharged petrol engine, new 5.0-litre V8 petrol engine, 3.6-litre, twin-turbocharged, V8 diesel engine

TRANSMISSION
Permanent four wheel drive. Six-speed automatic gearbox with 'Command Shift' over-ride. Chain-driven, two-speed transfer box with electronically-controlled centre differential. Open drive shaft axles with front differential mounted to engine sump

SUSPENSION
Four-corner, variable-height, electonically-controlled interlinked air suspension with variable-rate air springs and hydraulic dampers. MacPherson strut front suspension with negative ground offset. Double wishbone rear suspension

STEERING
Speed-sensitive power-assisted rack and pinion

BRAKING
ABS with Electronic Traction Control, Dynamic Stability Control, Hill Descent Control, Electronic Brakeforce Distribution and Emergency Brake Assist

OTHER FEATURES
GPS navigation system with dual-screen TV display. TFT instrument display. Bi-Xenon headlights. Front, thorax and head protection airbags. Terrain Response Adaptive Dynamics, Adaptive Cruise Control, Blind Spot Monitoring and Surround Camera System

	UNITS	5.0-Litre V8 Petrol	5.0-Litre V8 Supercharged Automatic	3.6-Litre Diesel Automatic
DIMENSIONS				
Overall Length	mm(in)	4972(195.8)	4972(195.8)	4972(195.8)
Overall Width (over mirrors)	mm(in)	2192(86.3)	2192(86.3)	2192(86.3)
Overall Height (max)	mm(in)	1902(74.9)	1902(74.9)	1902(74.9)
Wheelbase	mm(in)	2880(113.3)	2880(113.3)	2880(113.3)
Track Front/Rear	mm(in)	1629(64.1)/1625(64.0)	1629(64.1)/1625(64.0)	1629(64.1)/1625(64.0)
Luggage Capacity (Seat Up)	l(cu ft)	997(35.2)	997(35.2)	997(35.2)
Luggage Capacity (Seat Folded)	l(cu ft)	2122(74.9)	2122(74.9)	2122(74.9)
WEIGHTS				
Minimum Kerb Weight (EEC)	kg(lb)	2615(5765)	2710(5975)	2744(6050)
Gross Vehicle Weight	kg(lb)	3200(7055)	3200(7055)	3200(7055)
Front Axle Maximum Weight	kg(lb)	1530(3373)	1530(3373)	1530(3373)
Rear Axle Maximum Weight	kg(lb)	1850(4079)	1850(4079)	1850(4079)
Maximum Payload	kg(lb)	585(1290)	490(1080)	456(1005)
Maximum On Road Trailer Weight	kg(lb)	3500(7716) with over-run brakes, 750(1653) unbraked		
Maximum Off Road Trailer Weight	kg(lb)	1000(2205) with over-run brakes, 500(1103) unbraked		
CAPABILITIES				
Drag Coefficient	Cd	0.39	0.39	0.39
Approach Angle (Maximum)	Deg	34 with suspension at off-road height	34 with suspension at off-road height	34 with suspension at off-road height
Under Body (Ramp) Angle (Maximum)	Deg	150 with suspension at off-road height	150 with suspension at off-road height	150 with suspension at off-road height
Departure Angle (Maximum)	Deg	26.6 with suspension at off-road height (no tow bar)		
Gradient Climbable (Maximum)	Deg	45 (drive through), 35 (continuous)	45 (drive through), 35 (continuous)	45 (drive through), 35 (continuous)
Sideslope Angle (Maximum)	Deg	35	35	35
Turning Circle (Kerb to kerb)	mm(in)	12.0(39.0)	12.0(39.0)	12.0(39.0)
Wading Depth (Maximum)	mm(in)	700(27.6)	700(27.6)	700(27.6)

Range Rover - The Anniversary Guide

Specification Sheets

	UNITS	5.0-Litre V8 Petrol	5.0-Litre V8 Supercharged Automatic	3.6-Litre Diesel Automatic
PERFORMANCE				
Maximum Speed	kp/h(mph)	209(130)	225(140)	200(124)
Acceleration 0 - 100 kp/h	secs	7.6	6.2	9.2
Acceleration 0 - 60 mph	secs	7.2	5.9	8.6
FUEL CONSUMPTION				
Urban Cycle (EC)	l/100km (mpg)	20.8(13.6)	22.6(12.5)	14.4(19.6)
Extra Urban (EC)	l/100km (mpg)	10.0(28.3)	10.4(27.2)	9.2(31.2)
Combined (EC)	l/100km (mpg)	14.0(20.2)	14.9(19.)	11.1(25.4)
CO_2 Emissions (EC)	g/km	326	348	299
City (EPA)	mpg(US)	12	12	N/A
Highway (EPA)	mpg(US)	18	18	N/A
ENGINE				
Type		V8	V8	V8
Fuel		Petrol (Gasoline)	Petrol (Gasoline)	Diesel
Number of Cylinders		8	8	8
Number of Camshafts		4	4	4
Valves per Cylinder		4	4	4
Valve System		Twin overhead variable camshafts	Twin overhead variable camshafts	Twin overhead camshafts
Bore	mm(in)	92.5(3.64)	92.5(3.64)	81.0(3.19)
Stroke	mm(in)	93.0(3.66)	93.0(3.66)	88.0(3.47)
Capacity	cc(cu in)	5000(305)	5000(305)	3630(222)
Compression Ratio	:1	12	10	18
Cylinder Head Material		Aluminium alloy	Aluminium alloy	Aluminium alloy
Cylinder Block Material		Aluminium alloy	Aluminium alloy	Cast iron
Lubrication System		Frame mounted oil pump in sump, chain driven	Frame mounted oil pump in sump, chain driven	Oil pump driven by crankshaft nose
Fuel System		Direct injection. Variable inlet tract. Denso PAN PAG EMS Generation 1		Siemens pcr2.4
Ignition System		Distributorless via ECU. Electronic throttle. Drag torque control		N/A
Boost System		None	Twin vortex Eaton supercharger	Twin turbochargers
Cold Start System		Automatic via ECU	Automatic via ECU	Automatic with heater plugs
Air Cleaning System		Paper element	Paper element	Paper element
Cooling System		Cross flow with aluminium radiator	Cross flow with aluminium radiator	Cross flow with aluminium radiator
Battery Capacity	Amp/hr	90	90	90
Max Power	kW(bhp)	275(370)	375(503)	200(268)
At	rpm	6500	6500	4000
Max Torque	Nm(lb/ft)	510(376)	625(460)	640(472)
At	rpm	3500	2500	2000

Range Rover - The Anniversary Guide

Range Rover Third Generation — Phase Four — Technical Data

Specification Sheets

	UNITS	5.0-Litre V8 Petrol	5.0-Litre V8 Supercharged Automatic	3.6-Litre Diesel Automatic
CAPACITIES				
Engine Oil Sump and Filter	l(Imp Gall) [US Gall]	8.0(1.76)[2.11]	10.9(2.4)[2.88]	9.9(2.18)[2.62]
Cooling Circuit	l(Imp Gall) [US Gall]	15.0(3.30)[3.96]	16.0(3.52)[4.23]	14.0(3.08)[3.70]
Fuel Tank (Maximum Usable)	l(Imp Gall) [US Gall]	104.5(23)[27.6]	104.5(23)[27.6]	104.5(23)[27.6]
TRANSMISSION				
Type		ZF6HP28 6-Speed	ZF6HP28 6-Speed	ZF6HP28 6-Speed
Flywheel		Fluid torque converter with lock up	Fluid torque converter with lock up	Fluid torque converter with lock up
Gearbox Type		Automatic with 'Command Shift'	Automatic with 'Command Shift'	Automatic with 'Command Shift'
Number of Forward Gears		6	6	6
Selection Mechanism		Remote lever with 'sport' setting and 'Command Shift' manual override		
Transfer Box Type		Chain drive, permanent four wheel drive		
Number of Ratios		2	2	2
Selection Mechanism		Motor driven operated by console mounted switch		
Slip Control System		Electronically-controlled variable differential		
Front Prop Shaft Type		Open with rubber coupling at rear, shrouded spline connection to front differential		
Rear Prop Shaft Type		Open split shafts with centre rubber bush bearing. CV joint connections to transfer box and rear differential		
Front Axle Type		Single reduction mounted onto engine sump, open drive shafts		
Rear Axle Type		Single reduction, open drive shafts	Single reduction, open drive shafts	Single reduction, open drive shafts
Wheel Type		Cast alloy, J-type rim.	Cast alloy, J-type rim.	Cast alloy, J-type rim.
Wheel Size - Standard	in	18 x 7.5	20 x 8.5	18 x 7.5
Wheel Size - Options	in	18 x 8, 19 x 8, 20 x 8.5 (Accessory)	N/A	19 x 8
Tyre Size - Standard		255/60R18	255/50R20	255/60R18
Tyre Size - Options		255/55R19, 255/55R19, 255/50R20 (Acc)	N/A	255/55R19
RATIOS				
1st Gear Ratio	:1	4.171	4.171	4.171
2nd Gear Ratio	:1	2.340	2.340	2.340
3rd Gear Ratio	:1	1.521	1.521	1.521
4th Gear Ratio	:1	1.143	1.143	1.143
5th Gear Ratio	:1	0.867	0.867	0.867
6th Gear Ratio	:1	0.691	0.691	0.691
Reverse Gear	:1	3.403	3.403	3.540
High Range Ratio	:1	1.000	1.000	1.000
Low Range Ratio	:1	2.930	2.930	2.930
Front Axle Ratio	:1	3.540	3.540	3.730
Rear Axle Ratio	:1	3.540	3.540	3.730
1st Gear Ratio Overall High Range	:1	14.765	14.765	15.558

Specification Sheets

	UNITS	5.0-Litre V8 Petrol	5.0-Litre V8 Supercharged Automatic	3.6-Litre Diesel Automatic
2nd Gear Ratio Overall High Range	:1	8.283	8.283	8.728
3rd Gear Ratio Overall High Range	:1	5.384	5.384	5.673
4th Gear Ratio Overall High Range	:1	4.046	4.046	4.263
5th Gear Ratio Overall High Range	:1	3.069	3.069	3.234
6th Gear Ratio Overall High Range	:1	2.446	2.446	2.577
Reverse Gear Overall High Range	:1	12.047	12.047	13.204
1st Gear Ratio Overall Low Range	:1	43.262	43.262	45.584
2nd Gear Ratio Overall Low Range	:1	24.271	24.271	25.574
3rd Gear Ratio Overall Low Range	:1	15.776	15.776	16.623
4th Gear Ratio Overall Low Range	:1	11.855	11.855	12.492
5th Gear Ratio Overall Low Range	:1	8.993	8.993	9.475
6th Gear Ratio Overall Low Range	:1	7.167	7.167	7.552
Reverse Gear Overall Low Range	:1	35.297	35.297	35.297
SUSPENSION				
Front Suspension Type		MacPherson strut with air springs and hydraulic dampers. Negative ground level offset. Anti roll bar		
Rear Suspension Type		Double wishbone with air springs and hydraulic dampers.		
Front Springs		Interlinked, electonically-controlled variable-rate air springs		
Rear Springs		Interlinked, electonically-controlled variable-rate air springs		
Front Dampers		Telescopic, Adaptive Dynamics with DampTronic Valve damper units		
Rear Dampers		Telescopic, Adaptive Dynamics with DampTronic Valve damper units		
Anti Roll Bar Diameter Front	mm(in)	30(1.18)	30(1.18)	30(1.18)
Anti Roll Bar Diameter Rear	mm(in)	N/A	N/A	N/A
STEERING				
Type		ZF speed proportional power assisted rack and pinion		
Assistance		Belt driven pump	Belt driven pump	Belt driven pump
Number of Turns Lock to Lock		3.46	3.46	3.46
BRAKES				
Type		Hydraulic with power assistance and ABS. Self adjusting discs all-round.		
Front Disc Type		Cast iron, ventilated		
Front Disc Diameter	mm(in)	360(14.17)	380(14.96)	360(14.17)
Rear Disc Type		Cast iron, ventilated	Cast iron, ventilated	Cast iron, ventilated
Rear Disc Diameter	mm(in)	350(13.78)	365(14.37)	350(13.78)
Park Brake Type		Mechanically operated drum integral with rear discs		
TECHNOLOGIES				
Dual Line Braking System		Yes	Yes	Yes
Anti Lock Braking System (ABS)		Bosch DSC8	Bosch DSC8	Bosch DSC8
Electronic Traction Control (ETC)		Four-wheel system integrated with ABS		

Range Rover - The Anniversary Guide

Range Rover Third Generation — Phase Four — Technical Data

Specification Sheets

	UNITS	5.0-Litre V8 Petrol	5.0-Litre V8 Supercharged Automatic	3.6-Litre Diesel Automatic
Electronic Brakeforce Distribution (EBD)		Yes	Yes	Yes
Emergency Brake Assist (EBA)		Yes	Yes	Yes
Dynamic Stability Control (DSC)		Yes	Yes	Yes
Hill Descent Control (HDC)		Yes	Yes	Yes
Terrain Response™		Yes	Yes	Yes
Adaptive Dynamics		Yes	Yes	Yes

NOTES

Data acquired from the best available sources but the publisher is not liable for any mistakes or omissions. Readers are advised to consult other sources e.g. manufacturer's workshop manuals before working on vehicles. The publication of performance and capability figures does not imply that this will be achieved in practice. Caution must be exercised in all driving activities especially off-road.
Units are expressed in the relevant international standard (SI). Where appropriate recognised conversion factors have been applied.

CHASSIS and ENGINE NUMBERS

RANGE ROVER THIRD GENERATION PHASE 4

VEHICLE	PERIOD	MANUFACTURER	MODEL	TRIM CLASS	BODY STYLE	ENGINE CODE		TRANSMISSION CODE		MODEL YEAR		BUILD LOCATION	
Range Rover L30/L322	2002 on	SAL	Land Rover LM	Range Rover	A Standard	M 4-Door	D	5.0-litre V8 petrol NA	3	RHD Auto	9	2009	A Solihull
						E	5.0-litre V8 petrol supercharged	4	LHD Auto				
						2	3.6-litre V8 diesel						
						7	3.6-litre V8 diesel with DPF						

The Range Rover (L30/L322) is identified using the 17-digit Vehicle Indentification Number (VIN) system. This consists of a combination of letters and digits defining the vehicle type, engine fitted, transmission, model year and build location according to the table above. This is followed by a six-digit number unique to a particular vehicle. The VIN was stamped on a plate riveted inside the engine bay and on another plate visible through a gap in the lower windscreen masking on the left hand side ('Visible VIN').

Range Rover - The Anniversary Guide

Specification Sheets

Range Rover - The Anniversary Guide 213

| Range Rover Third Generation | Phase Four | Advertising |

Advertising & Brochures

THE RANGE ROVER

2010 MODEL YEAR

Even for Range Rover customers, it was difficult to obtain the new brochure for the 2010 model year – most were kept under lock and key in the sales manager's desk. The price list had reverted to a simple print out. Most information was expected to be gleaned from the Land Rover website such was the impact of the virtual world

216　　　　　　　　　　　　　　　　　　　　　　Range Rover - The Anniversary Guide

Advertising & Brochures

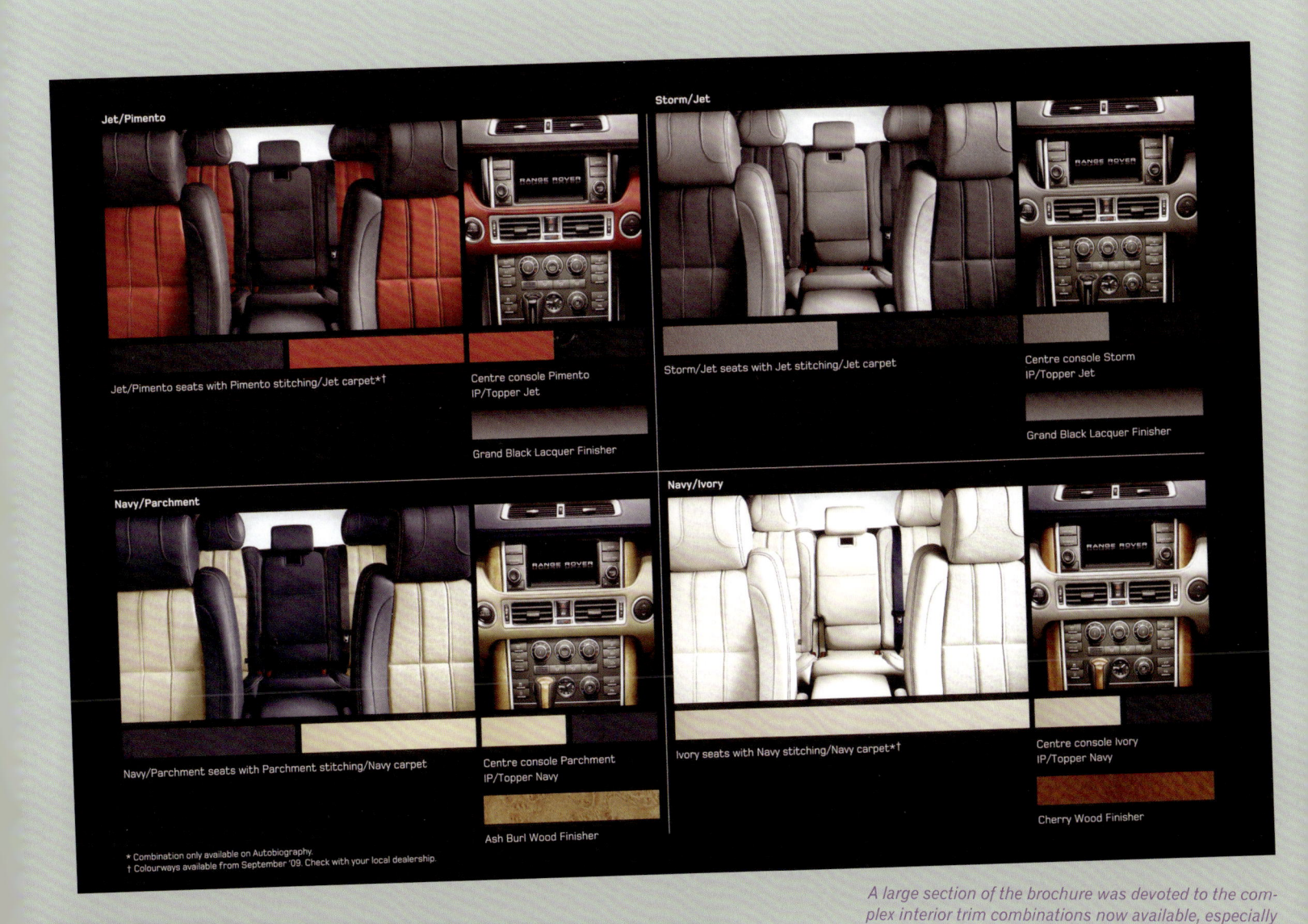

Jet/Pimento
Jet/Pimento seats with Pimento stitching/Jet carpet*†
Centre console Pimento IP/Topper Jet
Grand Black Lacquer Finisher

Storm/Jet
Storm/Jet seats with Jet stitching/Jet carpet
Centre console Storm IP/Topper Jet
Grand Black Lacquer Finisher

Navy/Parchment
Navy/Parchment seats with Parchment stitching/Navy carpet
Centre console Parchment IP/Topper Navy
Ash Burl Wood Finisher

Navy/Ivory
Ivory seats with Navy stitching/Navy carpet*†
Centre console Ivory IP/Topper Navy
Cherry Wood Finisher

* Combination only available on Autobiography.
† Colourways available from September '09. Check with your local dealership.

A large section of the brochure was devoted to the complex interior trim combinations now available, especially as the Autobiography had been integrated into the range

Twin images illustrated the benefits of the dual-view display

Craftsmen at work underlined the hand-built nature of some of the new features such as the leather headlining

Range Rover - The Anniversary Guide   217

Range Rover Third Generation | Phase Four | Advertising

Advertising & Brochures

The Range Rover was definitely for the man or woman at the top while the technological advance of the 'virtual' instrument pack was shown as an inset gallery

218 Range Rover - The Anniversary Guide

The new 'signature' LED lights in the front lamp cluster were featured strongly in the imagery for the 2010 model year

Range Rover - The Anniversary Guide

Technical Description

BODY AND CHASSIS

An Exterior Design Pack option was introduced in a choice of eight colours. The Pack consisted of a revised front bumper with fog lamp surrounds, front grille and side vents in 'Titan' finish combined with revised side sills, rear bumper and stainless steel exhaust finishers.

Optional illuminated treadplates with the 'Range Rover' name backlit by LED lights were introduced from summer 2011.

Two new exterior colours – Fuji White (replacing Alaska White) and Baltic Blue (replacing Buckingham Blue) were added to the range.

ENGINE

The 3.6-litre TDV8 engine was replaced by an all-new 4.4-litre unit. Comprising elements of the earlier TDV8 and the 3.0-litre TDV6 of the Discovery 4, the 4.4-litre V8 diesel featured a Parallel Sequential turbocharger system to boost the engine's efficiency enabling it to deliver 230kW (309bhp) of power and 700Nm (515lb/ft) of torque while returning nearly 20% better fuel economy and producing 14% less CO_2. The new engine met the full requirements of the EU5 emission standard.

The cylinder block, cast in Compacted Graphite Iron, was based on the previous component but was taller to accommodate the extra stroke

The Autobiography Black was a limited edition to celebrate 40 years of the Range Rover. Finished in unique Barolo Black, it also featured 20-inch diamond turned wheels and was distinguished by a mesh grille with bright surround and a special treatment to the side vents. Inside, there was a choice of unique colour combinations with the Autobiography logo appearing embossed into the leather and on the Grand Black veneers

Technical Description

of the pistons and longer to make room for the duplex timing chains.

Although larger, the complete engine assembly weighed no more than the earlier unit thanks to optimisation of the new design. The oil filter, engine oil cooler and Exhaust Gas Recirculation (EGR) valve were also configured as one unit, sitting in the 'vee' of the engine to facilitate installation in the vehicle. The oil system was designed so that old oil could be extracted from above, rather than being drained from below, negating the need for a ramp.

The third-generation common rail fuel injection system was derived from that of the 3.0-litre TDV6 and operated at pressures of up to 2000 bar (29,000 psi) using eight-hole piezo injectors. New ceramic glow plugs that operate at higher temperatures with improved durability were fitted, enabling them to be run for a longer period after start-up to improve engine efficiency and reduce emissions.

TRANSMISSION

TDV8 engine variants were fitted with the ZF 8HP70 eight-speed automatic gearbox. This gearbox used a new gear set with only two elements being open in each gear to reduce drag losses and improve efficiency. The gearbox, while weighing less than the six-speed 6HP28, was capable of handling torque of up to 700Nm. The transmission could accomplish gear changes in 200 milliseconds as well as multi ratio shifts – from eighth to second, for example.

Combined with adaptive shift programming technologies, this improved the driving experience as well as providing significant improvements in fuel consumption and in CO_2 emissions. Another innovative feature was Transmission Idle Control which disengaged 70% of the drive when the vehicle was stationary. The transmission was also programmed to run the engine at the best speed to either heat up or cool down the cabin, depending on ambient temperature.

The CommandShift gear lever was

The 2011 model year Range Rover introduced a new, 4.4-litre V8 diesel engine featuring sequential turbochargers. While delivering a significant power and torque increase, it was also more efficient and less polluting. The 4.4-litre TDV8 was mated to a ZF eight-speed automatic gearbox which, thanks to its new design, also offered significant efficiency improvements. Gear selection was by a new 'Drive Select' knob supplemented by wheel-mounted paddle shifters

Range Rover - The Anniversary Guide

Technical Description

While the 40th Anniversary limited edition, the Autobiography Black, retained the 'three finger' design theme and LED signature lights of the earlier model, it was distinguished by a new mesh grille with a bright surround

replaced by a rotary 'Drive Select' knob. Rising from the centre console when the ignition is switched on, the knob provides a choice of Park, Reverse, Neutral, Drive or Sport modes with further control being offered by steering wheel-mounted paddle shifters. To avoid confusion, the previous Terrain Response® knob was replaced by a Terrain Response® Optimisation Switch.

The 5.0-litre supercharged V8 petrol engine continued to be mated with the ZF 6HP28 gearbox.

The Terrain Response® programmes were enhanced by the addition of Hill Start Assist and Gradient Acceleration Control algorithms. Hill Start Assist held brake pressure long enough for engine torque to build up to prevent roll back on hill starts while Gradient Acceleration Control used brake pressure to control descents on steep grades even if Hill Descent Control was not engaged.

WHEELS AND TYRES

A new 19-inch wheel style was introduced.

Autobiography was once the name of the Range Rover's personalisation programme but was adopted to identify the brand's most prestigious vehicles. The Autobiography Black carried this distinctive badging to supplement its other unique features

Technical Description

Forty years of heritage is evident in this image which clearly shows how the Range Rover design has evolved over four decades while retaining the essential cues that make it such a distinctive vehicle. As new models evolve, these will be taken into a new era of lightweight structures and hybrid transmissions but they will still be every inch a Range Rover

Range Rover Third Generation — Phase Five — Technical Data

Specification Sheets

	UNITS	5.0-Litre V8 Petrol	5.0-Litre V8 Supercharged Automatic	4.4-Litre Diesel Automatic
TECHNOLOGIES				
Dual Line Braking System		Yes	Yes	Yes
Anti Lock Braking System (ABS)		Bosch DSC8	Bosch DSC8	Bosch DSC8
Electronic Traction Control (ETC)		Four-wheel system integrated with ABS		
Electronic Brakeforce Distribution (EBD)		Yes	Yes	Yes
Emergency Brake Assist (EBA)		Yes	Yes	Yes
Dynamic Stability Control (DSC)		Yes	Yes	Yes
Hill Descent Control (HDC)		Yes	Yes	Yes
Terrain Response™		Yes	Yes	Yes
Adaptive Dynamics		Yes	Yes	Yes
NOTES				

Data acquired from the best available sources but the publisher is not liable for any mistakes or omissions. Readers are advised to consult other sources e.g. manufacturer's workshop manuals before working on vehicles. The publication of performance and capability figures does not imply that this will be achieved in practice. Caution must be exercised in all driving activities especially off-road.
Units are expressed in the relevant international standard (SI). Where appropriate recognised conversion factors have been applied.

Specification Sheets

| Range Rover Third Generation | Phase Five |

Range Rover - The Anniversary Guide

Limited Editions

FIRST GENERATION 1970 – 1995

'IN VOGUE'

While British Leyland may have let the Range Rover lie largely fallow during the 1970s, several specialist coachbuilders, notably Wood & Pickett, were quick to upgrade the vehicles to meet the requirements of customers - particularly from the Middle East - who loved the Range Rover but weren't fond of its rather utilitarian interior.

Vogue, the upmarket fashion magazine, would occasionally assemble a selection of complementary top-line products for an 'advertorial' feature. The Range Rover was chosen (along with Jaeger clothing and Lancôme cosmetics) for an eight-page promotion in the March 1981 edition, with a photo shoot taking place in Biarritz.

Land Rover, by now an autonomous division of BL, decided to use this opportunity to create a special edition which would provide a sales boost to the two-door vehicle ahead of the planned introduction of a four-door variant. A number of suppliers, including Wood & Pickett, provided ideas and components for this vehicle. The *Vogue* magazine feature formed the core of the brochure for the Range Rover 'In Vogue' and a vehicle was squeezed through the doors of Jaeger's Regent Street store, featuring in a window display for several weeks.

Land Rover produced three versions of the 'In Vogue' limited edition covering two and four door models and featuring the newly-introduced automatic gearbox. The 'In Vogue' vehicles were the company's first attempt to seriously develop the luxury side of the Range Rover's character, hitherto the province of specialist coachbuilders

Land Rover also decided to fit the Vogue vehicle with the three-spoke alloy wheels, then about to be offered as an option. This prototype installation used special nuts that provided inadequate retention for the wheel, an issue that caused problems for the photo shoot being organised in Biarritz by Range Rover Marketing Manager, Kevin Beadle, and Lancôme's Managing

Range Rover - The Anniversary Guide

Limited Editions

While the photo shoot for the first 'In Vogue' was in Biarritz, this later version used the Gleneagles Hotel as a location. Clothing and other accessories were by up-market clothier, DAKS at Simpson of Piccadilly

Director. Having lost some of the wheel nuts on the journey through France, those remaining had to be repositioned during the photo shoot to ensure a full complement was visible.

While the production 'In Vogue' special edition of 1981 used steel wheels as engineers developed a solution to the problem of retaining the alloy wheels, it did feature the high compression engine specification and revised gearing for smoother cruising. Other features included polished burr walnut door cappings – sourced from a local cabinet maker, a stowage box between the front seats and map pockets behind the front seats.

The 'In Vogue' was distinguished by a metallic paint finish – the first on a Land Rover product. Vogue Blue was actually a variant of British Leyland Denim Blue and its application proved to be quite a challenge to Land Rover's paint shop. It also had a double grey coachline applied from a proprietary roll of decal material. It was equipped with a special hamper, stowed in the rear loadspace area, starting the fashion for Range Rover 'tailgate picnics'. Supply was initially to the home market only although a version was exported to the Middle East.

The first 'In Vogue' was followed, in 1982, by a four door version to showcase the newly-installed Chrysler three-speed automatic gearbox. The brochure featured an equally impressive *Vogue* photo shoot, using the Gleneagles Hotel as a location. The vehicle was available in either Sierra Silver or Nevada Gold metallic paintwork with a more discrete coachline decal. With the alloy wheel problem solved, these were now specified and featured a grey finish to the nave area. Marking its way forward as a luxury vehicle, the 'In Vogue' Range Rover automatic had stylish inlay wood cappings, front and rear armrests and an upgraded radio/cassette player – this featured a four-speaker system with the rear speakers mounted in the headlining above the tailgate. Air conditioning was an option. Gone, however, was the picnic hamper, replaced by a cool box.

The third evolution of the 'In Vogue', launched in 1983, was available in either five-speed manual or three-speed automatic versions. Photographed against the backdrop of New England, it introduced another metallic colour, Derwent Blue, as well as having the convenience of central locking. This third generation 'In Vogue' Range Rover re-introduced the picnic hamper as well as retaining the cool box – complete

Range Rover - The Anniversary Guide

Limited Editions

The CSK celebrated the 'father' of the Range Rover, Charles Spencer 'Spen' King, recalling the designer to Solihull so that his signature could be copied for the vehicle's badging

with 'Range Rover' identity on its lid.

There would be no more 'In Vogue' limited editions but 'Vogue' would later be used to identify high specification Range Rover variants – a practice which continues to this day, although the latest Vogue models have ceded their place at the top of the range to the Autobiography.

CSK

With the 20th anniversary of the Range Rover looming, Land Rover turned its thoughts to how to celebrate the occasion. One of our sources asserts that the idea for a limited edition themed on the designer of the original vehicle, Charles Spencer 'Spen' King, originated in Range Rover of North America and that Solihull turned the idea down flat, only to resurrect it later.

The idea of a sporty version of the Range Rover based on the two-door was not new. Two concept cars, one codenamed 'Parrot' and the other 'Olympic' (after Birmingham's bid to stage the 1992 games), were shown at various motor shows in the 1980s. The advent of more powerful, fuel injected versions of the V8 engine made it more realistic, but it was the development of front and rear anti-roll bars that made the package viable.

With the Discovery sharing the same chassis and suspension as the Range Rover and selling in a different market segment, the issue of body roll had made itself felt. While the vehicle remained stable, the amount of lean could be alarming to new drivers. Though anti-roll bars were an obvious solution, their use was an anathema to Land Rover designers steeped in the lore that articulation was the key to traction and off-road ability. It took a lot of work to develop an installation that placed minimum restriction on the supple nature of the Range Rover's suspension. Even so, it was an irony that they were first fitted to a vehicle bearing the name of the man who first conceived the benefits of long travel coil springs in an off-road environment.

Although by 1990 most Range Rovers were four-door variants, it seemed appropriate to make the 20th anniversary limited edition a two-door to celebrate the first production vehicles. The body was finished in Clear Over Base (COB) Beluga Black paint and bore the initials of its creator, 'Spen' King who visited Solihull specially to ensure the authenticity of his signature. The external appearance was completed with a coach line, chrome bumpers, driving lamps, front spoiler, fog lamps and special five-spoke black-edged alloy wheels. The interior featured leather trim with perforated seat facings enhanced by American walnut trim on the doors and fascia.

The driveline comprised the 3.9-litre fuel-injected V8 petrol engine developing 138 kW (185 bhp) coupled to a five-speed manual gearbox with (surprisingly for a vehicle with sporting pretensions) an automatic option. An ABS braking system was specified as were sports hydraulic dampers to complement the anti-roll bars – the combination increasing roll stiffness by 25%. At the time, Land Rover claimed it to be the fastest production Range Rover.

The CSK was limited to 200 examples, all right hand drive, and each vehicle had a numbered plaque. Every example came with a special owner's pack containing the original sales brochure, the plaque and a certificate of authenticity bearing 'Spen' King's signature. The cost in 1990 was £28,995 for the manual version and £30,319 for the automatic.

Sadly, the CSK seemed unusually prone to corrosion problems and the Range Rover Register estimates that less than half of those built survive

Limited Editions

The Brooklands Green Range Rover limited edition featured a new body kit as well as the eponymous paintwork

after 20 years and the condition of extant vehicles varies widely. A good example, complete with plaque and owner's pack, and with good provenance, remains a collector's item.

There was also a CSK limited edition of 400 sold in Australia but this version used a standard four-door vehicle with only special decal treatment to distinguish it.

BROOKLANDS

The 'Range Rover in Brooklands Green' appeared in 1992 and showcased a new body kit comprising a plastic front bumper and spoiler, plastic rear bumper and moulded side sills, all colour-keyed to the Brooklands Green paintwork. The interior was virtually standard but featured Winchester Grey cloth trim rather than leather.

The 'Range Rover in Brooklands Green' was only available with automatic transmission but also had the anti-roll bars from the CSK. Power came from the standard fuel-injected 3.9-litre V8 petrol engine. Although Land Rover claimed that its wheels were new, they were actually from the CSK, albeit in a different grey colour with bright finished rims.

Only 150 were made, each costing £31,500.

25th ANNIVERSARY

Although the Second Generation Range Rover was launched in 1994, the earlier model continued in production long enough to celebrate its 25th anniversary in 1995. To round off its long run, Land Rover produced a limited edition of only 25 vehicles.

Priced at an impressive £40,000, the Range Rover 25th Anniversary was finished in Oxford Blue paint and featured chrome bumpers. The body kit of the Brooklands, having given so much trouble mating it to the Range Rover's wide tolerance levels, was quickly abandoned. A special '25th Edition' badge adorned its flanks with a special commemorative addition to the Land Rover 'jewel' badge on the tailgate.

The interior, based on the new 'soft dash' air bag-equipped fascia, was in Light Stone leather. The headrests were embossed with the 25th Anniversary logo and each vehicle had a numbered plaque attached to the centre console.

The vehicle had a standard

Range Rover - The Anniversary Guide

Limited Editions

sills and mirror heads. Wheels were of the five-spoke design with red detailing along the spokes. It had Light Stone leather seats with contrasting red piping and carpet mats. Price in the UK was £38,995 for both the 2.5-litre diesel and 4.0-litre V8 petrol engine variants.

Westminster

The Westminster was available in Java Black, Bonnatti Grey or Blenheim Silver and came with 18-inch 'Gun Smoke' Hurricane alloy wheels. The interior featured Poplar Anthracite wood veneer trim while the specification included satellite navigation complete with the Trafficmaster™ jam warning and avoidance system. The in-car entertainment included a fascia-mounted centre fill speaker. Price in the UK was £46,950 for both the 2.5-litre diesel and 4.0-litre V8 petrol engine variants.

Vogue SE

The Vogue SE was available in Oslo Blue, Alveston Red, Epsom Green or Java Black complete with body-coloured bumpers, sills and mirror heads. Eighteen-inch 'Comet' alloy wheels were specified. The leather seats came with a choice of coloured piping, matching the carpet colour and the wood and leather steering wheel, which was also trimmed in Maple veneer. The vehicle featured an upgraded in-car entertainment system with 17 speakers, satellite navigation with Trafficmaster™ while a TV with DVD player and wide screen displays for rear seat passengers was optional. Power came from the 4.6-litre V8 petrol engine and its price in the UK was £53,995 or £57,995 when equipped with the DVD system.

The Westminster included a satellite navigation system in its specification along with distinctive Hurricane wheels

LAND ROVER OF NORTH AMERICA LIMITED EDITIONS

As with the First Generation Range Rover, Land Rover of North America introduced limited or 'special' editions to boost sales.

Kensington - Introduced for the 1997 model year, the Kensington featured additional walnut veneer trim with Light Stone leather interior and an upgraded in-car entertainment system. The edition was of 650 vehicles in either Black or British Racing Green.

Vitesse - Again introduced for 1997, the Vitesse was based on the 4.6 HSE and came in either Monza Red (200 examples) or AA Yellow (150 vehicles).

TRěK - A small edition of only 16 vehicles to celebrate the TRěK inter-dealer outdoor competition, they were produced in AA Yellow only with TRěK decals, safari rack and ladder, brush bar and additional lights.

50th Anniversary - Land Rover of North America developed its own limited edition to celebrate its parent company's 50th anniversary. Featuring Woodcote Green paintwork with commemorative badging and complete with body colour spoiler and side mirrors, it had a special interior in Walnut leather with contrasting Light Stone piping. Eighteen-inch 'Proline' wheels were specified. The edition ran to 275 examples for the United States and 50 for Canada.

Calloway - Not strictly a limited edition, but offered as a model line derivative, the Calloway featured a 240 bhp version of the 4.6-litre V8 petrol engine together with other modifications. Technically only available in Niagara Grey, a few were produced in Epsom Green and Rioja Red. The Calloway production run numbered

Limited Editions

220 examples in the 1999 model year.

Rhino - The Rhino limited edition for the 2000 model year featured Grey 'Rhino Hide' leather seat trim with grey wood veneer. Exterior colour was Granite Grey.

Holland & Holland - Similar to the UK version, it first appeared on the American market for the 2000 model year with 126 vehicles, a further 75 appearing in 2001.

30th Anniversary - Produced to mark the 30th anniversary of the Range Rover, these vehicles featured an Oxford leather interior.

Rhino – 2002 Model - Similar to the version first seen in 2000, this later model had a slightly different interior and an updated navigation system. Only 125 examples were produced.

Westminster - Although bearing the same name as its UK counterpart, the American version was very different featuring Java Black paintwork with black leather interior and black veneer trim. The edition ran to 250 examples selling for $74,000.

Borrego - This striking limited edition featured special yellow paintwork with black Oxford leather interior trim with contrasting yellow piping. Mounted on 18-inch 'Kryton' wheels, it ran to 100 vehicles selling for $72,000.

Linley - One of these exclusive models was sold in the US in 2002.

THIRD GENERATION 2001 ON

Autobiography Black

The Autobiography Black was introduced in 2010 as a limited edition of 700 vehicles to celebrate the Range Rover's 40th anniversary. In many ways, this version echoed the themes of the Range Rover Linley.

As the name suggests, the finish was in a new unique colour – 'Barolo

The Vogue SE limited edition not only featured satellite navigation but also offered the option of a TV and DVD system for the rear passengers

Black' - with three choices for the interior: Jet, Jet and Ivory or Jet and Pimento. The exterior featured 20-inch diamond-turned wheels and a mesh grille in 'Titan' finish complemented with a bright chrome trim and black grille surround. The grille finish was echoed in the side vents, also in mesh with bright chrome bars and black vent surround. The door handles were in body colour and the vehicle was distinguished by its tailgate 'Autobiography Black' badge.

The interior featured the Autobiography logo embossed on the rear seat armrest and on the Grand Black veneer panels. The front door tread plates were illuminated with the Range Rover name backlit by LED lights. The wood and leather steering wheel featured Grand Black veneer while petrol engine models had a veneered gear lever knob.

Range Rover - The Anniversary Guide

Range Rover Concepts | Range Stormer

Range Stormer

Concept vehicles from Land Rover are few and far between. In fact, the only one worthy of the name had been the Defender SVX of 1999. But the value of concept vehicles is immense, both in terms of public relations and as a way of assessing consumer reaction to new designs.

The ownership of Land Rover by Ford had brought a new dynamism to the company as well as a well-funded new model programme. With the third generation of the Range Rover developed under BMW ownership, the first fruit of Ford's investment was the T5 vehicle platform which would eventually form the basis for two models – the Discovery 3 and the Range Rover Sport.

Both of these models had grown out of designs developed under BMW ownership and were known by the codenames L20 and L25. Both mid-range Sport Utility Vehicles (SUVs), one was to be a seven-seat direct replacement for the Discovery Series II, the other a sportier five-seat vehicle. During the transition to Ford ownership, this vehicle was re-invented as the 'Baby Range Rover', the name 'Range Rover Sport' first appearing on a sketch by its designer, Mike Sampson. While initially Land Rover was happy to accept this bold extension of the Range Rover brand, doubts began to emerge – especially in the marketing area – as to whether this would affect sales of the model they had just launched.

Land Rover was also in need of a PR boost – especially for its premium brand. It had been several years since the Range Rover's launch and, although the company was girding its loins for the release of the new models waiting in the wings, they needed to keep up the momentum of publicity and 'seed' the media for some of the dramatic revelations to come.

So the Range Stormer was conceived. Design of the vehicle actually began after the style of the production derivative, the Range Rover Sport, had been finalised but before it had been launched. It was also built on the chassis and floor pan of the Second Generation P38A Range Rover, rather than on the new platform. While the design and clay model was done at Land Rover's Gaydon design studio, the actual vehicle was constructed by Stola in Italy.

The design team was led by Richard Woolley, who had been involved more with Rover cars including the Rover 600 and the Rover 75, but found himself at Land Rover after the sale of the Rover Group. Other members of the team were Mark Butler, Sean Henstridge, Paul Hanstock – who had worked with Mike Sampson on a joint submission for the L30 design – and Ayline Koning, who was mainly responsible for the interior.

With Land Rover an American-owned company, the Range Stormer's début took place at the Detroit Auto Show in January 2004, with its first European outing being at Geneva a few weeks later.

Land Rover was very open about the Range Stormer being a preview of a new vehicle platform that would feature some of the new technologies shown on the concept. These included Terrain Response™, described as offering, "The best possible on- and off-road composure and control by optimising the entire vehicle set-up, including suspension, powertrain, throttle response and traction control". As

The Range Stormer theme included the Range Rover's 'floating roof' with its blacked out roof pillars as well as the strong horizontal lines seen in the original vehicle

Range Rover - The Anniversary Guide

243

Range Rover Concepts | Range Stormer

Range Stormer

displayed on the Range Stormer, the system featured six settings, including a 'Dynamic' programme which would not be seen on a production vehicle for five years.

Underlining the Range Stormer's sporting potential was its power unit – said to be a Jaguar V8 supercharged petrol engine. This was, in fact, part of the Range Rover Sport programme but was not actually fitted to the concept vehicle.

It also featured variable height air springs – nothing new to Range Rover but this time the suspension was tuned to support the Range Stormer's obvious on-road bias, again something Land Rover was anxious to get a reaction to, as this would be a key part of the Range Rover Sport marketing platform.

Introducing the vehicle, Design Director Geoff Upex, was anxious to point out its Land Rover design cues although in truth, the clamshell bonnet with its castellations, straight waistline and floating roof, were pure Range Rover. The design featured a two-door arrangement, something not seen on a Range Rover for years, although it had been considered for the Range Rover Sport. On the Range Stormer the top half of the electrically-operated units opened upwards with the bottom half extending outwards to provide an entry step. The whole sleek body with its overt vented 'power bulge' on the bonnet and side vents, was finished in a dramatic metallic orange paint scheme.

The interior was no less dramatic featuring seats covered in saddle leather and based on the Möbius strip. Natural materials predominated and the whole was lit by a full-length piece of glass forming the roof.

The Range Stormer achieved all its objectives, being received enthusiastically by the press, employees and customers alike. Crucially this reception helped Land Rover make up its mind about the naming of the Range Rover Sport. Its job on the show circuit over, the Range Stormer can now be seen at the Heritage Motor Centre, near to the studio where it took shape.

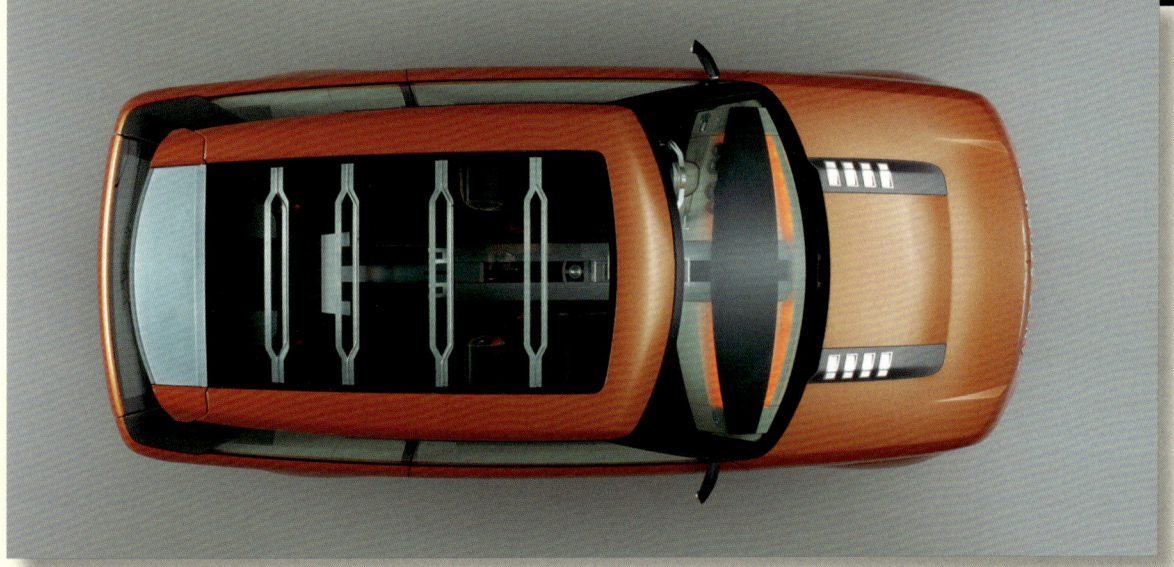

(Top and Above) The Range Stormer featured 'crushed ice' texturing inside the front and rear lamp units and also introduced the 'two finger' theme which became part of the design for the 2010 model year Range Rover Sport

The full-length glass roof made the interior light and airy and would make its production début in a modified form in the Discovery 3

Range Rover - The Anniversary Guide

Range Stormer

The Range Stormer had noticeable Range Rover themes but the full-height, rather than a split, tailgate was new to Land Rover

The doors were massive units that swung up out of the way and would hardly have been practical in low car parks, although the bottom half opened to help getting in and out of the vehicle

The interior introduced sweeping lines that would later feature in the Range Rover Sport and the Range Stormer débuted Land Rover's new technological innovation, Terrain Response™

Range Rover - The Anniversary Guide

| Range Rover Concepts | LRX |

LRX

In 2009 Land Rover announced that a production version of the LRX concept vehicle would be sold as a Range Rover and manufactured at its Halewood plant on Merseyside. It was also announced that a two-wheel drive version would be produced with reduced levels of CO_2 output

246 Range Rover - The Anniversary Guide

LRX

"Great design is the gateway to desirability." So said Gerry McGovern, Land Rover Design Director, when he introduced the LRX concept vehicle. If he – and those who believed that this would be very similar to a new production Range Rover Cross Coupé – is right, then Land Rover is going to be working overtime to meet the demand.

The year 2008 marked the 60th anniversary of Land Rover and the celebratory year was begun in spectacular fashion with the début of the LRX at the Detroit Auto Show in January. It was a bold move. The world was on the brink of a major recession with Land Rover's parent company in severe financial difficulties. The previous year, Ford had sold Land Rover's sister company, Aston Martin, and then announced that the rump of what had once been the Premier Automotive Group, the now-combined Jaguar and Land Rover were up for sale as well, with Tata Motors as the preferred bidder.

With this background, the LRX was a dramatic assertion, both of Land Rover's heritage and its confidence in the future.

The team under Gerry McGovern included young designers such as Jeremy Waterman and Sandy Boyes as well as Mark Butler, who had worked on previous Range Rover projects. Julian Thomson worked on the advanced aspects of the concept, alongside Craig Carter of engineering design. Joanne Keatley was responsible for colour and material selection.

While the LRX was not initially declared to be part of the Range Rover family, it was pretty clear from the familiar design cues like the clamshell bonnet and floating roof that it was intended to be. Land Rover confirmed this the following year with the announcement that a vehicle based on the LRX would go into production at its factory at Halewood on Merseyside in 2010, with a sales launch in 2011.

The LRX was a very different Land Rover. At only 4.35 metres (173in) long and just over 2.0 metres (82in) wide, it was smaller than other vehicles in the luxury SUV class, and smaller than the Freelander 2. This was to save weight, as was the use of polycarbonate materials for the roof and side glass, and the extensive use of aluminium in the structure. The design itself had dramatically sloping lines with the floating roof evolving to echo the style of wrap-around sun glasses and visors, something complemented by the pure white paintwork of the vehicle unveiled in Detroit. By its European début at Geneva, the original LRX had been joined by a black and silver example.

The interior reflected all the luxury of the Range Rover but used new materials, such as suede made from recycled plastic bottles, while any leather avoided the use of chromium-based tanning agents in favour of vegetable materials. The fascia introduced the 'virtual' instrument pack using a Thin Film Transistor (TFT) screen that would later appear on the 2010 model year Range Rover. Another feature was the interior's 'mood' lighting that changed colour according to driving style – green, for economy driving, being preferred.

The interior also had a variety of stowage positions appropriate to the 21st century, including an iPhone™ dock while older pastimes were catered for by cup holders built into the tailgate for the traditional picnic.

The LRX was powered by a 2.0-litre version of the four-cylinder diesel used in the Freelander 2 but connected to Land Rover's version of the hybrid concept. Here, the engine is coupled to the Electric Rear Axle Drive (ERAD) which features an electric motor in the rear transaxle. In a modification of the Haldex transmission used in the Freelander 2, this can feed electric power to all four wheels for emission-free traction in urban environments or to supplement diesel power off road. Power came from a lithium-ion battery pack, taking up no more space and weighing no more than a conventional spare wheel. The Terrain Response™ system was revised to give an 'Eco' setting to maximise the driveline's energy-saving potential. Using ERAD, the LRX was quoted as having the potential for up to 60 miles per gallon (4.7 litres per 100 km) with CO_2 emissions of only 129 g per km.

As with other concepts, the LRX had a job to do. The reaction from press and public alike was overwhelmingly positive and convinced Land Rover that a production vehicle along the same lines was a more than viable proposition. The revelation of the innovative ERAD drive system showed that Land Rover was serious about the environment but, perhaps most important of all, the quality of the design and technology it showcased was instrumental in persuading finance houses to bankroll Land Rover's operations to ensure the company's survival through the turbulent times ahead.

Range Rover - The Anniversary Guide

Range Rover Concepts — LRX

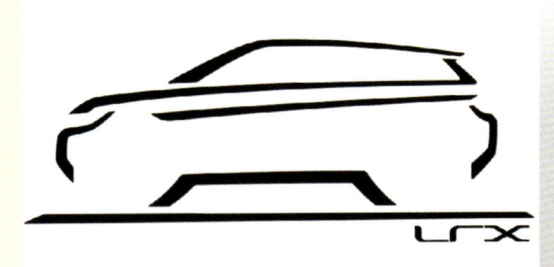

The LRX design was formed around very simple but dramatic lines

Conceived for a new, more environmentally-conscious age, the LRX employed new construction techniques and was smaller than other vehicles in the Land Rover range

In keeping with the ecological theme the interior, while luxurious, made use of re-cycled materials and avoided the use of harmful dying processes. Open structures for the seats also saved weight

The instruments and the interior ambient lighting were colour-coded to reflect the owner's driving style. Green meant the driver was making full use of new Land Rover technologies such as the ERAD hybrid drive system

248   Range Rover - The Anniversary Guide

LRX

Phil Popham, Land Rover's Managing Director, launched the LRX at the 2008 Detroit Auto Show where it shared the stage with HUE 166, the first production Land-Rover, to mark the 60th anniversary of the brand

The Land Rover oval branding continued to evolve, now appearing in a more high-tech silver and black style

By Geneva, the original pristine white LRX had been joined with another in black – albeit with a white roof. Appropriately for a Swiss show, it sported roof bars suitable for the attachment of a ski rack

Range Rover - The Anniversary Guide

249

Range Rover Sport

The launch of the Discovery in 1989 had been a huge success for Land Rover and, when it was later introduced into the American market, began to exploit new sectors. In the mid-1990s, the company began a study to examine the future of the Discovery. As Land Rover saw this vehicle at the centre of its brand identity, the study was called 'Heartland'.

It was clear that good on-road performance was as important to its new Discovery customers as its off-road supremacy and this led to the appearance of Active Cornering Enhancement (ACE) on the Discovery Series II which was, in many other ways, a compromise product. This was largely due to the necessity to extend the vehicle length to accommodate a forward-facing arrangement for all seven seats. To save money, the vehicle retained the 100-inch wheelbase of the original vehicle and so had a large rear overhang which, in turn, predicated air suspension to keep the vehicle level. Again because of cost, this was specified for the rear only leading to some odd handling characteristics.

With the experience of the Discovery Series II, Land Rover determined that the mid-range sector should be addressed with not one, but two vehicles – one to meet the demand of the family-orientated sub-sector that required a full seven-seat package, the other for a more sporting audience that only needed five seats but demanded more performance. Coming off the same platform to keep investment costs low, they were, under the BMW naming system, called the L20 (Discovery) and L25.

Studies were still under way when the Ford Motor Company acquired Land Rover in 2000. While the design of the L20 (now the L319 under Ford programme numbering) had proceeded well, the styling studio was struggling with the L25 (now L320) concept. That was until someone called it a 'Baby Range Rover' – an event that designer, Mike Sampson, recalls as being like, "A light turned on". Sampson penned the name 'Range Rover Sport' on one of his sketches and the name stuck.

Under Ford direction, Land Rover had now developed the 'T5' platform for L319/L320. To be built at a new facility at Solihull, T5 reverted to a conventional body - albeit a very stiff monocoque - mounted on a conventional chassis frame, again made extremely strong by the use of the latest manufacturing techniques. It also featured independent suspension all round with air springs and the cross-linking system first used on the Third Generation Range Rover.

The design of the L320 rapidly evolved using the styling cues of the Range Rover – clamshell bonnet, floating roof, and strong horizontal lines. To extend the roof line backwards, designer Mike Sampson added a peak to the tailgate, prompting Ford's Premier Automotive Group chief, Wolfgang Reitzle, to

Range Rover Sport

While obviously focussed on the primarily on-road 'Sports Activity Vehicle' market dominated by vehicles such as the BMW X5, the Range Rover Sport was a fully-capable off-roader too thanks to its two-speed transfer box, variable-height air suspension and Terrain Response™

comment that it had the character of a teenager with his cap on back to front. The rear end design eschewed the trademark Range Rover double tailgate in favour of a full-height opening hatch, although it had an upper section that could be opened independently to load small items and shopping.

The interior, although using many components of the L319 – the two products had over 60° commonality – was much more Gran Tourer orientated with a high centre console, higher waistline and a virtually 2 + 2 configuration.

While the L319 had a wheelbase of 114 inches to better package the sixth and seventh seats and to improve access to them through the rear side doors, the L320 eventually settled at 108 inches – the same as the Second Generation Range Rover. Now, having virtually the same dimensions as the earlier Range Rover and also evolving into a stunning design, Land Rover marketing began to think that, with a Range Rover nameplate, it would impact on the sales of the 'true' Range Rover whose very size was being perceived as an obstacle in some markets.

While Ford's vice-president of design, J Mays, remarked, "Of course it's a Range Rover," Sampson was forced to re-style the bonnet to remove the original 'castellations', deleting an obvious bit of Range Rover DNA. Thankfully, the reaction to the Range Stormer concept vehicle convinced the company

The interior featured the sweeping lines of the Range Stormer concept vehicle although it had considerable commonality with its sibling, the Discovery 3. For more of a cockpit feel, the centre console was raised with the gear lever mounted on the driver's side

Range Rover - The Anniversary Guide

Range Rover Sport

that the Range Rover Sport and the Range Rover could live side by side.

The L319 was launched as the Discovery 3 in 2004, with the L320 emerging as the Range Rover Sport the following year. The Sport entered a market sector dominated by the BMW X5 and the Porsche Cayenne but it had all of its competitors' sporting attributes plus the off-road capability of a Land Rover.

The Range Rover Sport was launched with a choice of power units – two Jaguar-derived V8 engines in 4.2-litre supercharged and 4.4-litre naturally-aspirated versions as fitted to the Range Rover and a 2.7-litre V6 diesel from the Discovery 3. The only transmission offered was a six-speed automatic gearbox with Command Shift™ manual override. For the V8 supercharged variant, this was programmed to give a throttle 'blip' when down-shifting to mimic the 'heel and toe' technique used by sports car drivers. The rest of the transmission included a two-speed transfer box to ensure full off-road capability, with an electronically-controlled rear differential being offered as an option.

The handling was developed by Jaguar's Mike Cross and included revisions to the T5 suspension to raise the roll centre, reducing the roll couple to improve on-road performance without affecting off-road capability. A new system, Dynamic Response, was an evolution of the ACE system used on the Discovery Series II and further improved handling.

The Range Rover Sport was a massive success. It soon became Land Rover's best-selling vehicle. Sharing a platform and the manufacturing facility with the Discovery 3, it had much the same cost base but, with its Range Rover badge, commanded a much higher price. Its sales performance and profitability made no small contribution to Ford's finances in a time of deep crisis for Land Rover's owners.

With the arrival of the TDV8 diesel engine, this too became an option for the Range Rover Sport but it was not until 2009, and the 2010 model year, that the vehicle received a facelift. Its external appearance was altered with a new front bumper, grille, light cluster and front wings to give a smoother appearance. New light units were designed for the rear but the distinctive rear peak was retained. While the TDV8 power unit was unchanged, for 2010 the Range Rover Sport was available with the new 5.0-litre supercharged V8 petrol engine

Designer Mike Sampson's sketches revealed how much of the original theme was carried through to production. Following an attack of nervousness as to whether it should carry the Range Rover brand, the lines of the bonnet were changed to smooth out the characteristic 'castellations'

While the Range Rover Sport shared the Terrain Response™ system with the Discovery 3, the control knob was retractable so as not to interfere with the actions of a more engaged driving style

Range Rover - The Anniversary Guide

Range Rover Sport

For 2010 model year, the bumper lines were smoothed out with much more emphasis being placed on the front lower intake area. LED 'signature' lights were also introduced alongside the 'two finger' theme in the light clusters and air intakes – a style seen on the Range Stormer concept vehicle

The 2010 model year Range Rover Sport saw a dramatic re-design of the interior with a more integrated look to the fascia and console interface. With more control via the touch screen display, there was less clutter and the quality of the materials was significantly upgraded

Range Rover Sport

The Range Rover Sport-based 'range_e' was created to develop future hybrid technologies. It featured a TDV6 diesel engine coupled to a ZF eight-speed gearbox together with an electric motor to achieve low emissions while maintaining an impressive performance

and a derivative of the earlier V6 diesel with increased capacity to 3.0 litres and twin sequential turbochargers.

For 2010 the Discovery 4 had acquired the suspension modifications applied to the Range Rover Sport but, to maintain its handling edge, the Range Rover Sport was now available with Adaptive Dynamics which used electronically-controlled predictive active damping working in conjunction with the Dynamic Response system. Other changes were made to the transmission, suspension and brakes to match the power available from the 5.0-litre supercharged engine.

In line with the Discovery 4, the 2010 Range Rover Sport had a restyled and upgraded interior with a new fascia, centre console, door casings and instrument pack. The specification of the materials used was significantly altered to improve the tactility of the 'driver interface'.

The Range Rover Sport was the product of a typical Land Rover process - well thought out project definition, an enthusiastic and skilled design team, sound and innovative engineering and skilful marketing. Coupled with the reputation built up by the company over more than 60 years, it was a formidable combination leading to what history will probably see as Land Rover's most successful product.

Once Land Rover's bespoke customisation programme for the Range Rover, the Range Rover Sport Autobiography was launched in 2009. It was distinguished externally by a mesh grille and unique wheels

Range Rover Sport

The LED signature lights provide the Range Rover Sport with a distinctive look reminiscent of the Range Stormer concept vehicle

The Range Rover Sport Autobiography was available with a range of interior colour ways. The Autobiography logo was embossed on the head rests to further distinguish the model

Range Rover - The Anniversary Guide

Range Rover Specials

With its long-travel coil spring suspension, the First Generation Range Rover was the ideal basis for an ambulance conversion, offering rapid response and a comfortable ride for the patient. Like all conversions, ambulances, like those offered by companies such as *Herbert Lomas* and *Pilcher Greene*, had to be approved by the Special Projects section of the Land Rover Engineering department at Solihull who produced coachbuilders' drawings of the chassis and offered advice to converters

The Lomas ambulance featured a 254mm (10 in) extension to the basic Range Rover chassis and had a double skin fibre glass body with metal framing between the skins. Several different combinations of patient and attendant accommodation were offered and the vehicle was also available for export

The Pilcher Greene Range Rover ambulance also featured a chassis extension to enable a recumbent patient to be carried in the rear. Pilcher Greene offered two versions – one with aluminium panelling for the rear body, the other in fibre glass over an aluminium frame. In the days before the Range Rover was available with air conditioning, fibre glass wool insulation was provided to keep out the extremes of climate

Range Rover Specials

RANGE ROVER AMBULANCE

Range Rover ambulances had a long life often passing to volunteer organisations such as the St John Ambulance and the Red Cross when disposed of by their original owners

With a growing threat from terrorists and kidnappers, companies such as MacNeillie and Hotspur began to offer discreetly-armoured conversions of the Range Rover. It was an ideal vehicle for the task providing the comfort expected by diplomats, politicians and businessmen but having the capability to carry the weight of armour plate and glass. Such vehicles were designed to be virtually indistinguishable from a normal Range Rover but were able to resist attacks by small arms and grenades. They could also be fitted with run flat tyres to enable an escape to be made from an attack. Fuel tanks were filled with fire suppressant material and other equipment could include public address systems and gas masks. The vehicles were fitted with Land Rover 110 rear axles and modified springs to increase the gross vehicle weight for the armour

Armoured Range Rovers were also used to escort nuclear weapons convoys and armouring is still offered on the latest Range Rover models

Range Rover - The Anniversary Guide

Range Rover Specials

The Autobiography programme began with the First Generation Range Rover but reached its height during the Second Generation – the name plate being used for Range Rover's top models. Administered by Land Rover Special Vehicles, it offered an exclusive range of colour and trim although the vehicles could be customised to any choice of colour

Range Rover Specials

Autobiography vehicles were produced in black on the production line before going to a coachbuilder for a multi-coat paint finish to the highest standards. Seats were built on standard frames by a specialist company and were trimmed completely in leather using special patterns. Veneers were hand-selected and matched, and applied to the standard components before receiving a multiple lacquer coat. Autobiography Range Rovers often saw the début of new technologies such as satellite navigation and TV and DVD systems. Some features such as body-coloured bumpers and wing mirror surrounds found their way onto Second Generation limited editions

The Carawagon firm produced a number of motor caravan conversions on Land Rover vehicles including the Range Rover. The elevating roof gave some measure of headroom although, being built on the standard chassis, accommodation was cramped. Nevertheless, Carawagon managed to squeeze in cooking and washing facilities ... and even a refrigerator

Range Rover - The Anniversary Guide

259

Range Rover Specials

From the start, Range Rovers were used in competitions and expeditions, including the British Trans Americas Expedition with its famous crossing of the formidable jungles of the Darien Gap. A Range Rover, driven by René Metge and Bernard Giroux won the Paris-Dakar Rally in 1981. While Land Rover did not generally support motor sport or expeditions, they played an active part in preparing the VSD Range Rovers for the Paris-Dakar and produced a brochure on rally preparation based on their experiences

Range Rover - The Anniversary Guide

Range Rover Specials

Range Rover Turbo Diesel vehicles took part in the 1987 Camel Trophy held in Madagascar while Land Rover also prepared Third Generation Range Rovers for their own G4 Challenge. However, the winner of the first G4 Challenge in 2003, Belgian fighter pilot Rudi Thoelen, declined his prize of a new Range Rover in favour of two Defenders

Left. One of the estimated four hundred occasions on which the ladders were used.
Below. An artist's impression of the Range Rovers used in the Trans-Americas Expedition, showing many of the special fittings and equipment.

1 Front mounted capstan winch 3,000 lb capacity
2 Reinforced bumper/cow catcher guard
3 Petrol tank undershield
4 Raised exhaust extension
5 Four Quartz-Iodine spot and fog lights
6 Two swivel spot lights
7 Split charge two battery system
8 Heavy duty alternator
9 Radiator muff
10 Four extra towing eyes
11 Sirens and air horns
12 Swamp tyres
13 Removable wing panels
14 Roll-bar
15 Roof mounted spare wheels
16 Special low-temperature shock absorbers
17 Insulated body panels
18 Roof rack
19 Steps on tailgate
20 Power point in rear of vehicle for cooker etc.
21 Heated rear screen
22 Wiper/washer equipment for rear screen
23 Extra instruments – tachometer, oil pressure and temperature gauges, ammeter for split charge system
24 Map reading and interior lights
25 Two-way vehicle radio
26 Stereo-tape player and radio
27 Reclining seat with full safety harness and headrest
28 Built-in safe
29 Water keg
30 Partitioned stowage lockers
31 Inspection light, 26ft lead
32 Fully comprehensive tool kit
33 Medical supplies
34 Extra equipment, hand winches, ground anchors, cable, tow ropes etc
35 Coffee maker

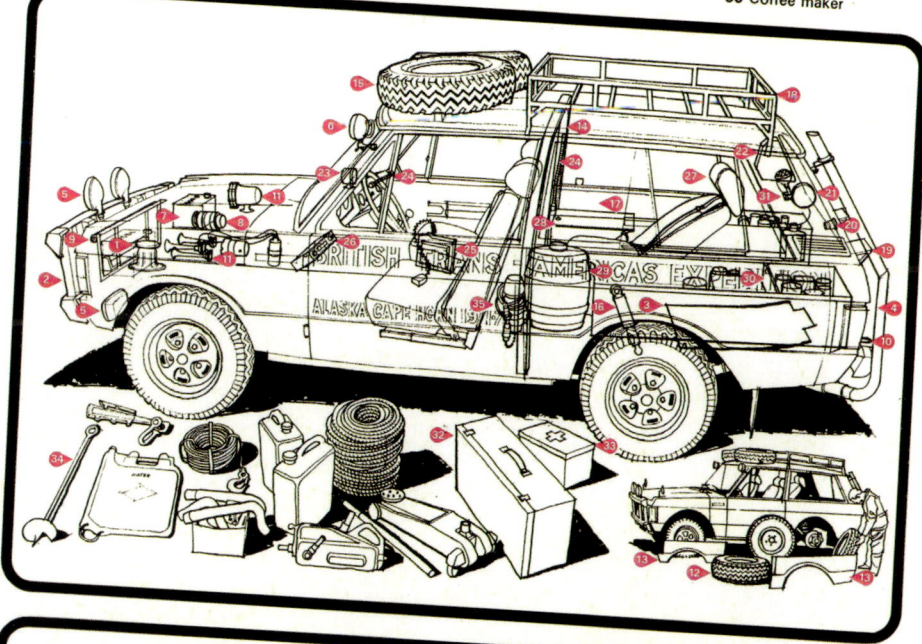

ROVER
BRITISH LEYLAND U.K. LIMITED
SOLIHULL · WARWICKSHIRE · ENGLAND

Printed in England by Jolly & Barber Ltd., Rugby.

844/9.72

Range Rover - The Anniversary Guide

261

Range Rover Specials

It was quickly realised that the two-door configuration of the Range Rover was handicapping its potential as a luxury vehicle. Very soon, conversions appeared including those by FLM Panelcraft and Monteverdi. The Monteverdi offering was clearly of better quality and more pleasing design, thanks to the arrangement of its roof pillars, and was eventually chosen by Land Rover to be the basis of their own four-door version

Range Rover Specials

THE · GLENFROME · WESTBURY

Other companies, such as Wood & Pickett and Glenfrome used the Range Rover as the basis for luxury vehicles, mainly intended for the lucrative Middle East market. Some examples included lengthy chassis extensions and well-equipped interiors complete with televisions and bars. Other more extensive conversions included specialised hunting vehicles with rifle racks and hawk stands. They were not afraid to try improving on the original design with different headlamp arrangements, new front grilles, special paint finishes and vinyl roofs. Some still exist as highly-prized collector's items such as this Wood & Pickett Range Rover owned by Richard Beddall

Range Rover - The Anniversary Guide   263

Range Rover Specials

Police and emergency services soon realised the potential of the Range Rover and a police specification was rapidly developed, seeing service with many forces, usually as a motorway patrol vehicle. In this role, it was able to recover broken-down heavy vehicles as well as being able to carry a good load of emergency equipment. Many vehicles were fitted with a telescopic light mount that could illuminate the scene of an accident. Range Rovers were also popular overseas such as this restored German emergency vehicle, resplendent in its Day-Glo paintwork seen at the Heritage Motor Centre's event to celebrate the Range Rover's 40th anniversary in May 2010

Range Rover Specials

While Land Rover offered the Range Rover as a military communications and command vehicle, few were used in this role with officers sticking with front-line Land Rovers or normal staff cars. A notable exception was the Range Rovers used by the British Commander-in-Chief's Mission to the Soviet Forces in Germany (BRIXMIS). The Mission was virtually free to travel anywhere in the Soviet sector and their intelligence gathering activities led to some hair-raising escapes when the Range Rover's capabilities were tested to the full. Other secret organisations, mainly in the Middle East, were also believed to use Range Rovers

Range Rover - The Anniversary Guide

Range Rover Specials

The high stance and peerless prestige of the Range Rover, coupled with its ability to be driven in low range, made it ideal as a review vehicle for heads of state. One of the most famous was the Popemobile, used on the visit of Pope John Paul II when he visited the UK in 1982. Following the earlier assassination attempt, the vehicle was fitted with armoured glass so that he could be safely seen by the crowds

Her Majesty The Queen's review Range Rover is, on the other hand, completely open. Versions have been made on all three generations of the Range Rover but the general layout has remained the same, although the air suspension with its lower access facility has been a benefit on later models. The interior is fully padded for comfort and generously supplied with steadying hand rails. Other features include holders for umbrellas and a hook for the royal handbag

Range Rover - The Anniversary Guide

Range Rover Specials

Drivers were specially trained by Land Rover and some were Land Rover company chauffeurs who had received special briefings from the Royal Protection Squad

Range Rover - The Anniversary Guide

Range Rover Specials

With the original Range Rover transmission originating in the military 101-Inch 1 tonne Forward Control, it was soon pretty clear that an automatic version was needed. Before Land Rover produced their own version, a conversion was offered by Schuler Presses. Not only did Schuler fit an automatic gearbox, using the same three-speed Chrysler 727 that Land Rover would later adopt, but they linked it to a transfer box giving a 40/60 front-to-rear torque split controlled by an automatic viscous coupling. Ferguson Formula (FF) anti-lock brakes were also offered, both systems pre-dating the factory installation by several years. Schuler also offered an engine upgrade with a larger capacity and revised carburettors, boosting power to 149 kW(200 bhp), taking the Range Rover to 96 kp/h (60 mph) in 10.5 seconds

The six-wheel version of the Range Rover was developed by Carmichael of Worcester to meet a requirement for an Rapid Intervention Vehicle (RIV) for the Royal Air Force. A vital part of the specification was for the vehicle to be able to reach a downed aircraft quickly. It also had to carry enough kit – including fire suppressant foam – to be able to extinguish any fires and to rescue the crew

Range Rover Specials

CARMICHAEL COMMANDO

RAPID INTERVENTION VEHICLE
A new and modern dimension in fire fighting ability

The Range Rover with its V8 engine had enough power to meet the requirement but needed a major conversion to be able to carry the payload required. This was achieved by extending the chassis to accommodate a third trailing axle, the wheelbase between the front and intermediate axle remaining standard. This gave a 6 x 4 configuration, with the third axle retaining the coil spring suspension with a link arrangement to ensure that the load was equally distributed

Carmichael also marketed the six-wheel conversion in civilian form, enabling it to provide the elusive four doors, albeit on a massive vehicle. The Commando Custom featured air conditioning, power steering and alloy wheels. Other features included chrome bumpers, electric windows and a stereo radio/cassette player

Range Rover Specials

Several different versions were produced, including one with bodywork by Gloster Saro, in a variety of configurations to meet evolving requirements. Most featured a massive brush guard to facilitate access through gates, fences and hedges when required to reach a wrecked aircraft. Other versions featured fire pumps, ladders and foam dispensers

Range Rover Specials

Today, the six-wheel Range Rover warrants its own club, the Six Appeal Wheel Group, whose members attend events all over the UK. Many of the ex-RAF vehicles are kept in full working order and supply fire cover at outdoor occasions

Range Rover - The Anniversary Guide

Range Rover Production — Timeline

1970 - After years of development, the Range Rover is launched. It has a price of less than £2000 but is an automotive sensation with supercar features like a V8 engine, permanent four-wheel drive and disc brakes all round. Form follows function in its simple design revealing its Land-Rover heritage.

1976 - The utilitarian interior is softened with the addition of carpet trim and brushed nylon seat trim.

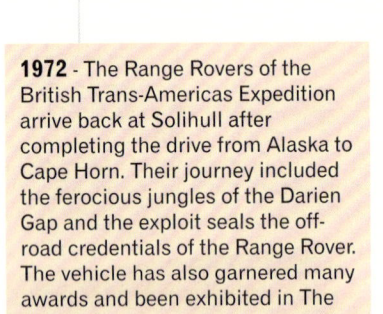

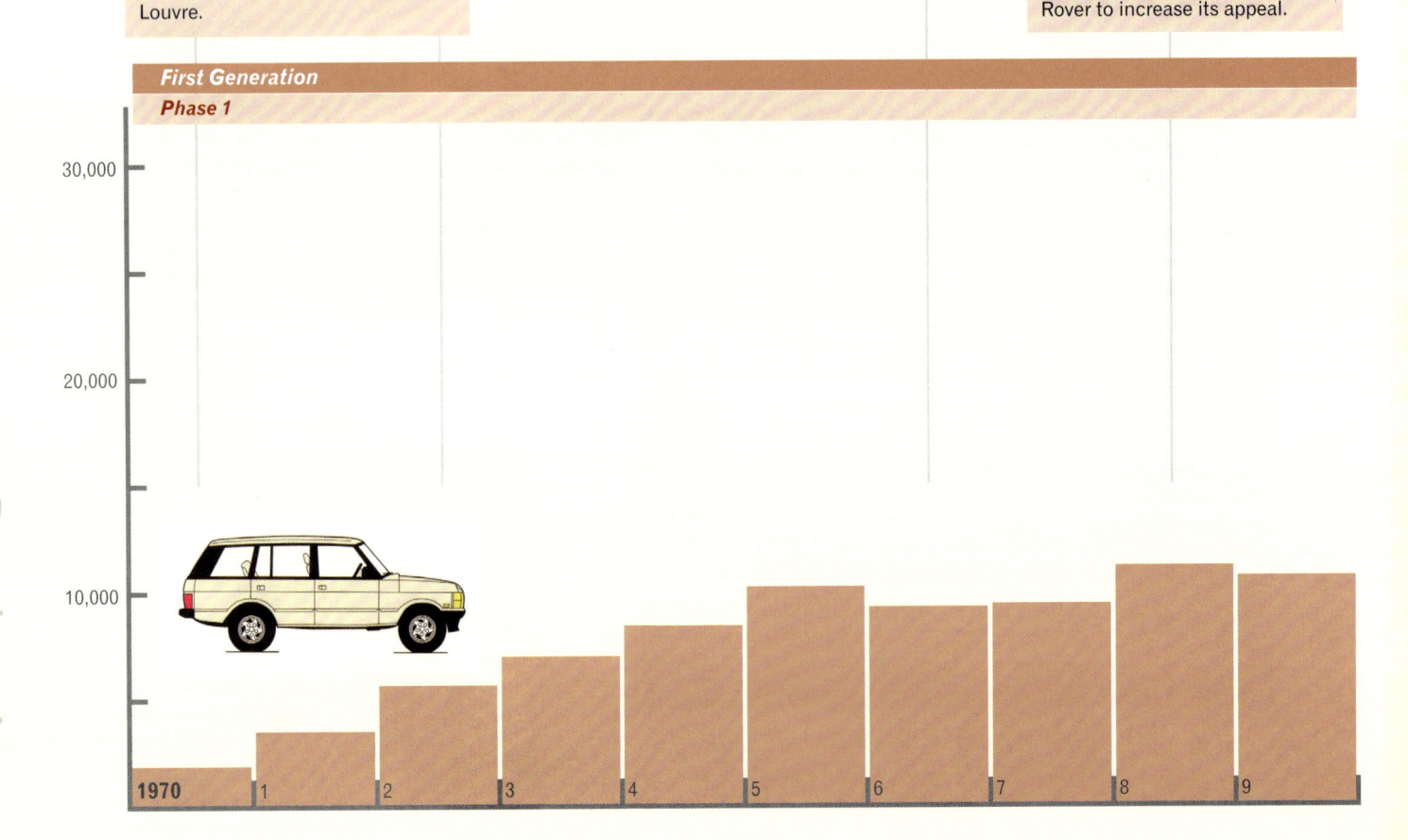

1972 - The Range Rovers of the British Trans-Americas Expedition arrive back at Solihull after completing the drive from Alaska to Cape Horn. Their journey included the ferocious jungles of the Darien Gap and the exploit seals the off-road credentials of the Range Rover. The vehicle has also garnered many awards and been exhibited in The Louvre.

1978 - Land Rover Limited is formed as a separate company within British Leyland with promises of investment to expand its productive capacity and introduce new models. Work begins to enhance the Range Rover to increase its appeal.

First Generation
Phase 1

Range Rover - The Anniversary Guide

Timeline

1981-3 - The four-door version of the Range Rover is launched. Based on a design by Monteverdi of Switzerland, its extra doors are accommodated on the same chassis and wheelbase. Following a photo shoot in *Vogue* magazine featuring an upgraded Range Rover, the 'In Vogue' limited edition is introduced with metallic paint and an improved interior, full carpeting and wood detailing. An automatic variant appears using a Chrysler three-speed gearbox while the old manual gearbox is replaced by a five-speed unit.

1988 - The gear-driven transfer box with manual locking centre differential is replaced by a Borg-Warner chain driven unit featuring an automatic viscous coupling to control the differential.

1987 - The US specification Range Rover débuts at the Los Angeles auto show. The comprehensive specification includes air conditioning as standard along with power seats and an upgraded interior. A full three-year, 36,000-mile warranty is offered with parts support coming from the Caterpillar organisation. The Range Rover benefits from work being done on 'Project Jay', which will be launched as the Discovery and which shares a common structure with the Range Rover. Improvements include a new pressed floor, a welded sub-structure and a revised fuel system.

1985-6 - The 3.5-litre V8 engine receives a new fuel injection system replacing its Zenith Stromberg carburettors. The Range Rover's automatic option is upgraded by the introduction of a more refined ZF 4-speed gearbox. To tackle the important European market a diesel-powered version of the Range Rover is launched with a 2.4-litre turbo-charged VM engine. The benefits of the new engine are underlined when a diesel Range Rover breaks 27 speed and endurance records.

1989 The Range Rover's engine has its capacity enlarged to 3.9 litres, giving the vehicle a useful power boost. Detail design changes give it a sleeker profile with concealed front door hinges. The vehicle also benefits from a much improved interior.

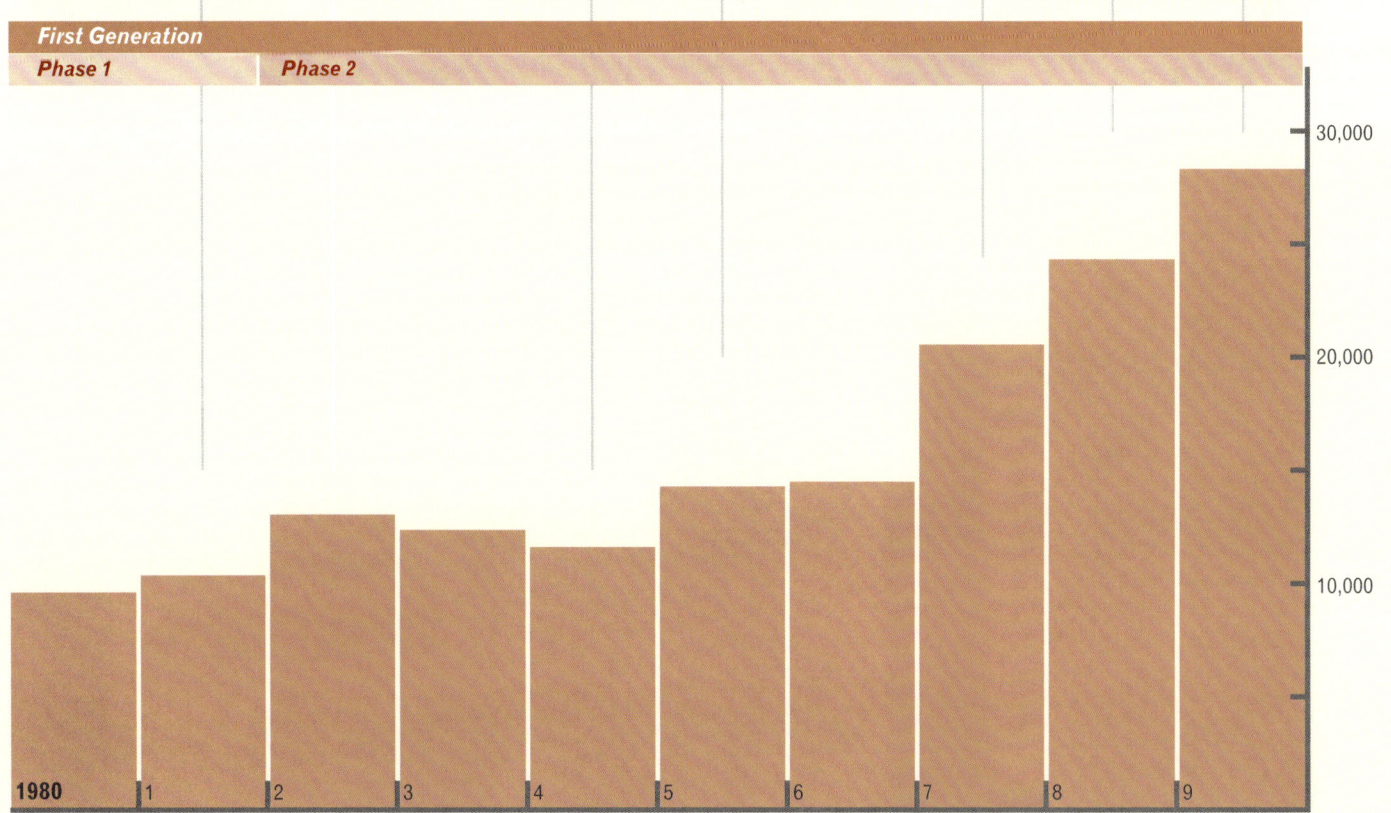

First Generation
Phase 1 | Phase 2

Production

Range Rover - The Anniversary Guide

Range Rover Production — Timeline

1990 - The 20th anniversary of the Range Rover is celebrated by the introduction of a four-wheel, four channel ABS braking system, the first in the world designed for optimum performance off- as well as on-road. The anniversary is also marked by the 'CSK' limited edition named after Charles Spencer King, the 'father' of the Range Rover. The black two-door has special interior trim and anti-roll bars to take advantage of the extra power of the 3.9-litre engine.

1994 - The New Range Rover is launched. The all-new vehicle has a long wheelbase chassis and an electronically-controlled air suspension system with a semi-monocoque body for rigidity. Power comes from developments of the V8 petrol engine with a BMW six-cylinder diesel alternative. Both manual and automatic transmissions are offered with a two-speed transfer box and viscous coupled centre differential. Additional off-road capability is offered by an improved electronic traction control system. The old model receives a new airbag fascia and continues in production as the 'Classic'.

1992 - The Range Rover LSE is launched to the press and dealers in Morocco. The vehicle - known as the 'County LWB' in America - showcases a number of 'firsts' for an off-road vehicle including variable height air suspension and electronic traction control. The LSE also features a 4.2-litre version of the V8 petrol engine. The VM diesel engine was replaced by the home-grown 200 Tdi that débuted in the Discovery.

1995 - The First Generation Range Rover bows out after a quarter of a century in production with a special 25th Anniversary limited edition.

1998-9 - The Range Rover's V8 engines are upgraded and it receives a subtle facelift. Special editions such as the Holland & Holland and the £100,000 Range Rover Linley appear.

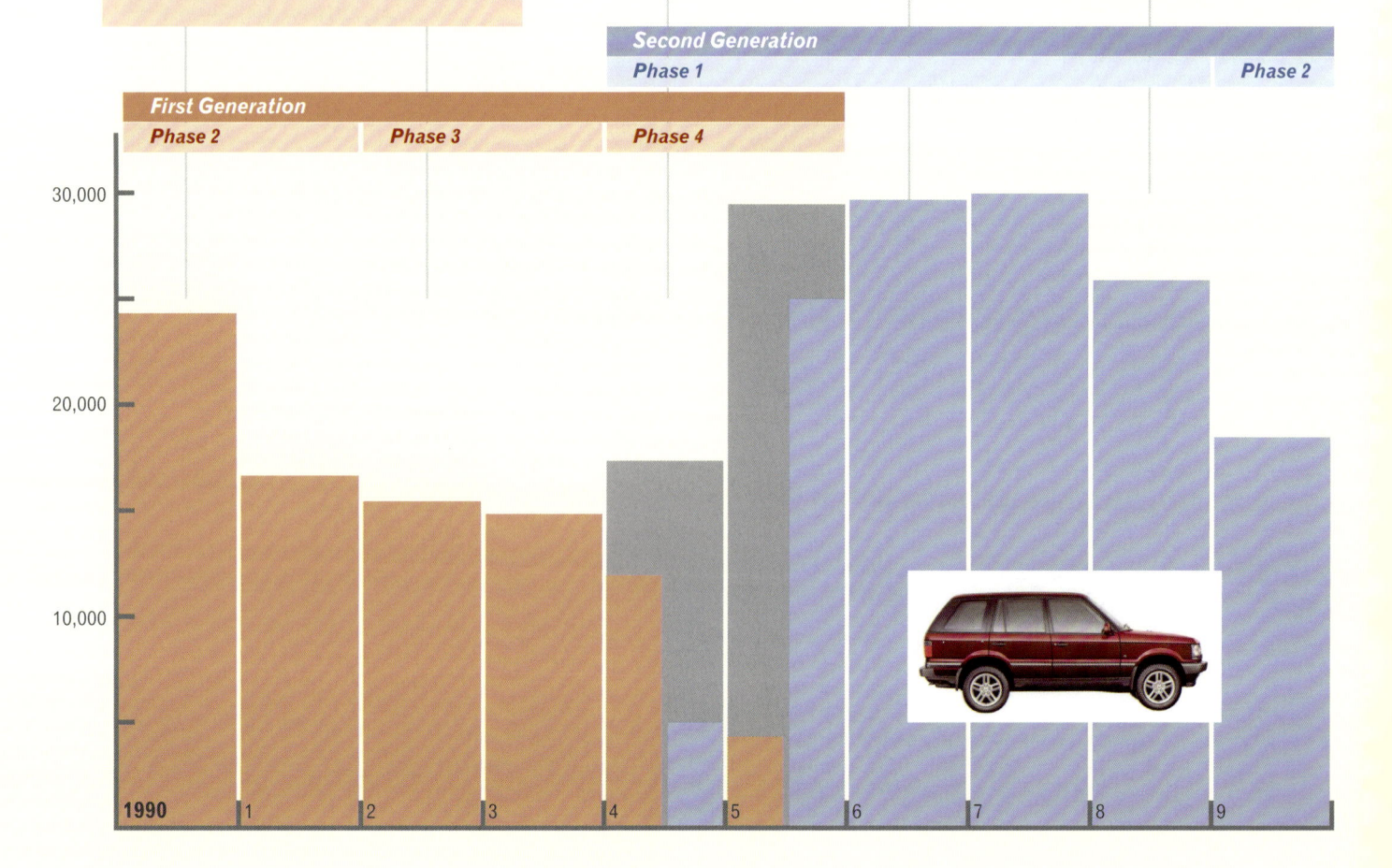

Second Generation — Phase 1 … Phase 2

First Generation — Phase 2 | Phase 3 | Phase 4

Production (years 1990–9, axis marks 10,000 / 20,000 / 30,000)

276 Range Rover - The Anniversary Guide

Timeline

2001-2 - The new Range Rover is launched. Its investment cost of £1 billion makes it the biggest project carried out by the British motor industry. The new vehicle is very different from its predecessor. It is larger and of monocoque construction, making much use of aluminium in the structure to save weight. The suspension uses air springs but is independent all round with an innovative linked system to replicate the action of a beam axle to maximise off-road articulation. The vehicle is powered by two BMW engines – a 3.0-litre six-cylinder diesel and a 4.4-litre V8 petrol. Only a five-speed automatic transmission is offered with a two-speed transfer box incorporating a Torsen™ centre differential. The dramatic external styling, inspired by power boat design and the stylish interior epitomise presence and luxury.

2004 - The Range Stormer concept vehicle, heralding a new Land Rover design direction, is revealed at the Detroit Motor Show.

2005 - The Range Rover gets an all-new V8 petrol engine line-up of a 4.4-litre naturally aspirated and a 4.2-litre supercharged power unit based on a Jaguar-developed engine. Petrol variants are now fitted with a new transfer box featuring an electronically-controlled centre differential. Minor styling changes accompany the new power units. Following the success of the Range Stormer concept vehicle, the Range Rover Sport is introduced as the first extension of the Range Rover brand.

2006 - The Range Rover 2007 model year vehicle introduces a new V8 diesel engine. The 3.6-litre TDV8 is based on the technology used in the smaller V6 but uses twin turbochargers to provide virtually the same performance as the petrol engine versions but with vastly improved fuel consumption. Along with the new engine, the transfer box is replaced with the unit previously fitted to the petrol engine variants. The Range Rover is now equipped with the Terrain Response™ system which, at the turn of a knob, optimises the vehicle's engine, transmission, and traction control to a variety of on- and off-road conditions.

2009 - The 2010 model year Range Rover is launched featuring a new, 5.0-litre supercharged V8 petrol engine. There's also a new front bumper, grille and front light unit, featuring LED 'signature lights'. The interior is upgraded with a new Thin Film Transistor instrument display with 'virtual' dials. A world first is a dual-view centre screen which enables a passenger to watch TV or video programmes, simultaneously allowing the driver to concentrate on the satellite navigation. The top of the range model is dubbed 'Autobiography' – a name previously associated with the Range Rover's customisation programme.

2010 - The 2011 model year Range Rover is announced with a 4.4-litre version of the TDV8 engine mated to a new ZF eight-speed automatic gearbox. To celebrate four decades in production, a 40th Anniversary limited edition, the 'Autobiography Black' is announced. The third vehicle in the Range Rover brand is announced. Based on the LRX concept car, it will be available from 2011. For the first time in a Range Rover, it will feature two wheel-drive.

Second Generation — Phase 2

Third Generation — Phase 1 | Phase 2 | Phase 3 | Phase 4

Range Rover - The Anniversary Guide

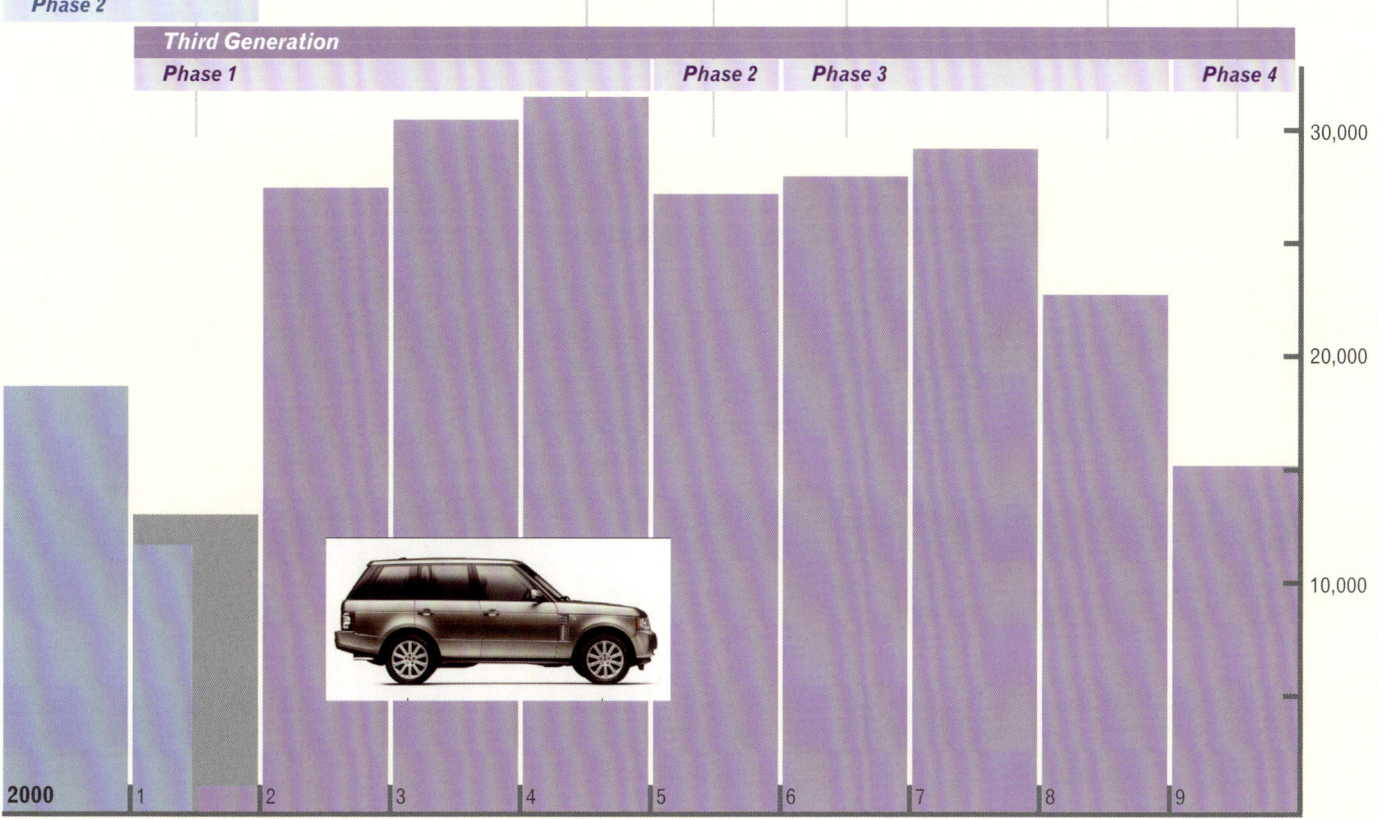

A selection of the books published by Porter Press

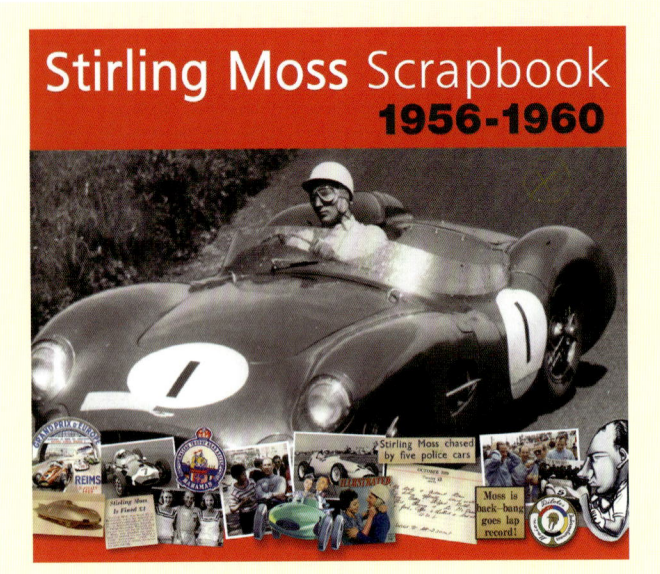

Stirling Moss Scrapbooks

Large format very different books, The Stirling Moss Scrapbooks were the inspiration for the Original Scrapbook series which has been enjoyed around the world. A very personal insight, they are packed with memorabilia from Moss's own scrapbooks. Written by Sir Stirling Moss and Philip Porter. Four books cover 1929-54, 1955, 1956-60 and 1961.

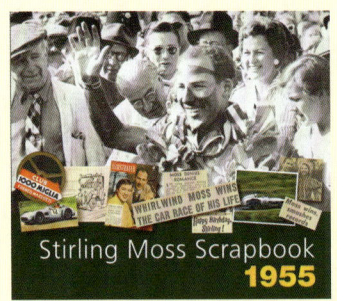

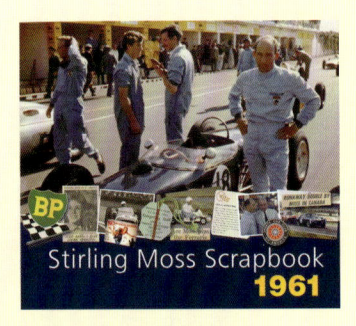

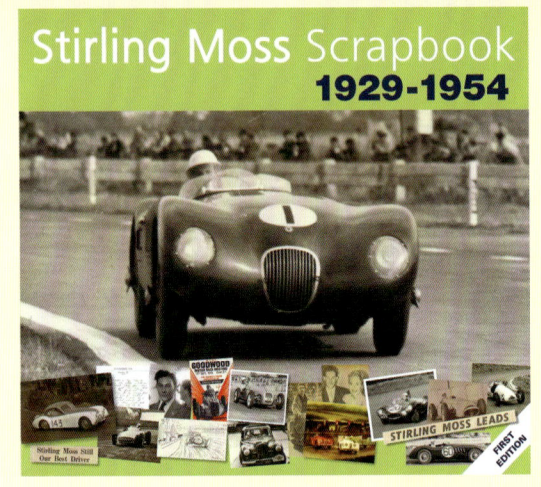

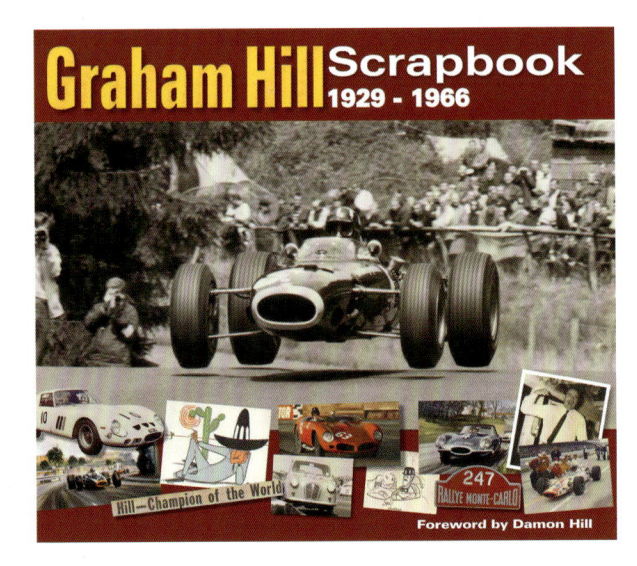

Graham Hill Scrapbook

Based on double World Champion Graham Hill's personal scrapbooks, this book is a moving and light-hearted tribute to the greatest character motor racing has ever known. Written by Philip Porter. Foreword by Damon Hill.

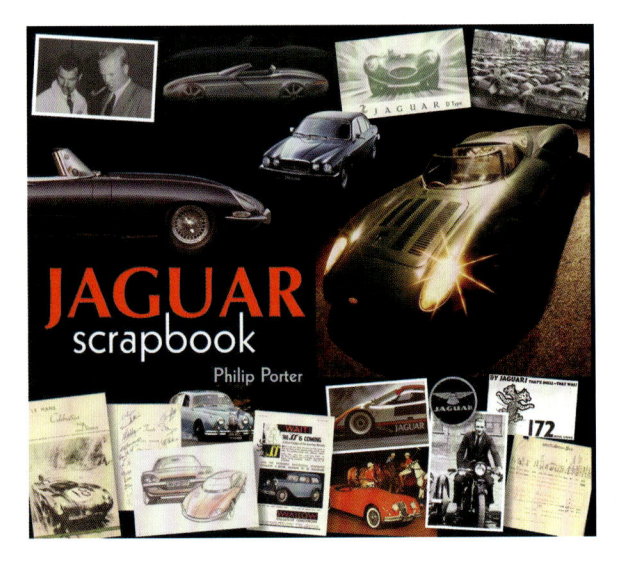

Jaguar Scrapbook

Compiled by Philip Porter, author of 15 Jaguar books, this one draws heavily on his extensive archives and many interviews over the last 25 years. Like all the Scrapbooks, it is copiously illustrated and beautifully presented.

www.porterpress.co.uk

A selection of the books published by Porter Press

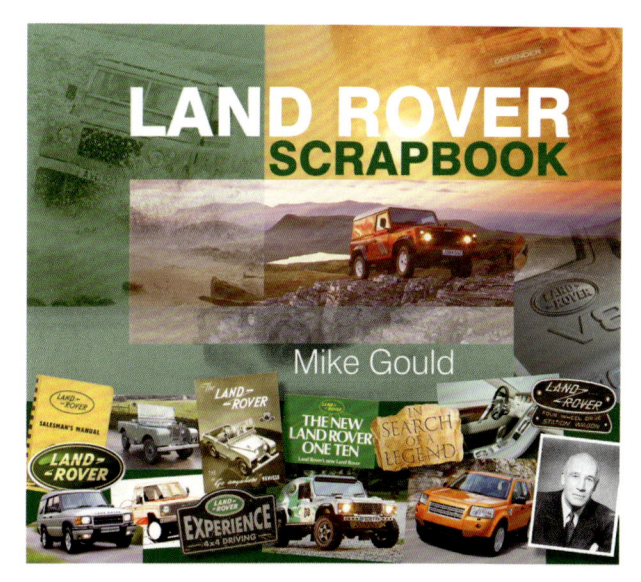

Land Rover Scrapbook

Written by Mike Gould who worked for Land Rover for over 30 years, this book is a very readable and rather different account of the great Land Rover story. Liberally illustrated with photographs and other material from the Land Rover archives.

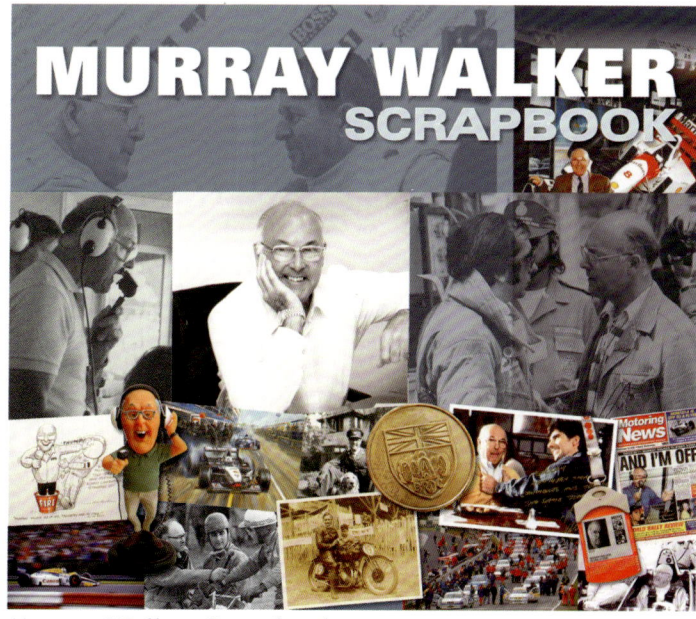

Murray Walker Scrapbook

A bestseller, this book features the most popular sporting commentator of all time. Packed with humour, comments and insights from people like Jenson Button, Lewis Hamilton, Sir Jackie Stewart, Martin Brundle and many others, this is a fascinating book spiced with material from Murray's own archives. Compiled by Murray Walker and Philip Porter.

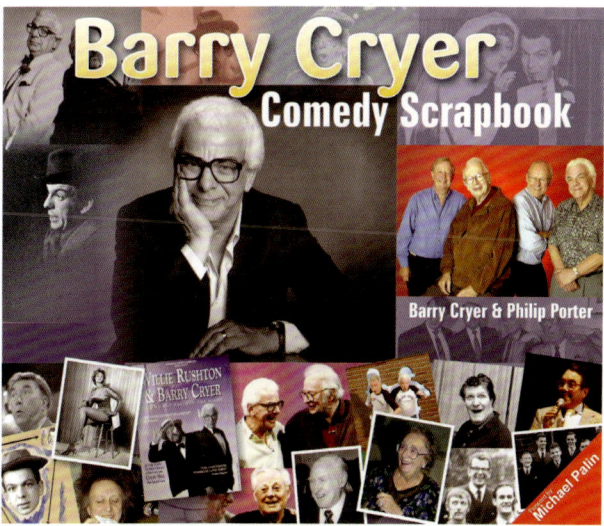

Barry Cryer Scrapbook

Barry's own story, in the popular and very different scrapbook format, this book features contributions from John Cleese, Alan Bennett, Ronnie Corbett, Graeme Garden, Bernard Cribbins and others. Illustrated by material from Cryer's personal archives, Barry talks incisively and fascinatingly about all the comedy greats he has known. Written by Barry Cryer and Philip Porter.

Future titles include: Ultimate E-type (the definitive history of the 12 Lightweight Es), The Italian Job Cars and the E-type Scrapbook.

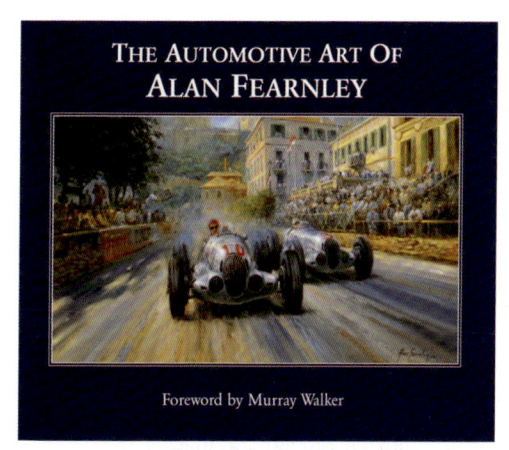

The Automotive Art of Alan Fearnley

Over 70 wonderful paintings, plus many pencil sketches, from one of the world's leading and most respected motoring artists. Subjects range from all decades of motor racing to vintage and classic cars, including E-types, but all reek of atmosphere. Foreword by Murray Walker.

+44 (0)1584 781 588   info@porterpress.co.uk